Paul has been living in Florida with his wife for about the last ten years. While this book, his first, is non-fiction, he spends his time writing mostly crime fiction and light fantasy. Paul has never tried to have any of his other works published; however, he has won 'The People's Choice Award' for two best short stories at public reading events.

Dedication

To Mia Kalafor 2004–2019, who sat with me through most of the writing of this book. Sadly she passed away the day the writing of this book was finished. She was a great comfort to me for the time that I knew her. She will be greatly missed.

And to my beautiful wife, who has stood by me no matter what life has thrown at us for the past thirty years. She is my muse and inspiration in all things.

Paul Woodis

The Odd Life of No One in Particular

AUSTIN MACAULEY PUBLISHERS™

LONDON · CAMBRIDGE · NEW YORK · SHARJAH

A CIP catalogue record for this title is available from the British Library.

ISBN 9781528988964 (Paperback)
ISBN 9781528988971 (ePub e-book)

www.austinmacauley.com

First Published (2020)
Austin Macauley Publishers Ltd
25 Canada Square
Canary Wharf
London
E14 5LQ

Acknowledgements

Thank you to Susanne Whelan, without whose help and support this book would not have been finished.

To MARY
Thank you
Paul Woodis

This is the story of a man named Shawn Williams. It is the story of how, as a child growing up in a small New England town controlled by two 'very well connected brothers', he suffered serious physical, emotional, and psychological abuse at home. During the time that he grew up, in the 50s and early 60s, everyone knew that sort of thing went on behind closed doors but it wasn't something that ever got talked about. The story will take you through his early childhood years, including the brutal assault and subsequent loss of his best friend, Sarah. You will read about the physical abuse Shawn suffered in the early years of school, and the extremely humiliating sexual assault he was forced to endure, for the same reason Sarah had been assaulted. Shawn talks about the sexual assaults he and some of his school mates endured at, what he believed to be the hands of two very evil twin sisters. As you continue to read, you will also find some bright spots of triumph, giving him some small bits of hope. And, after suffering through that very troubled childhood, Shawn would enter into a first and second marriage with much of the same emotional, and psychological abuse. You will then see how, with the help of his third wife, Shawn was able to overcome not just his very troubled past, but some very difficult health issues still to come in his life. This is sixty-five years of real life history. All of the names of the people in the story have been changed. Some of the locations and dates may also have been altered. By telling his story, Shawn has no intention of harming any real person(s) living or dead.

Much of the early information in this book was given to Shawn by his mother and oldest brother, before they each passed away. Because of the strokes, migraine induced strokes, and many near stroke episodes, his beautiful wife helped to fill in the holes in his memory from 2009 to present time. And because he is still dealing with some of the cognitive issues that remain with him, much of this book had to be spoken into his cell phone, and then copied into my computer. Having me write this book with him has been a great therapeutic undertaking for him. Shawn's hope is that his story will be an inspiration to others that have suffered in much the same way he did, and help them deal with their troubled past.

Table of Contents

Chapter One
In the Beginning

I was born in 1953, the third son of a lower middle-class blue-collar family. We lived in a small second floor apartment, in a small New England town, along the Massachusetts and Connecticut border. My father worked in a local factory while my mother stayed home to take care of the kids. I obviously have no recall of any of it, but my feeling is that it was a very stressful time for my parents. They were both heavy drinkers, and had a tendency toward violence. When I was about one-month-old, my grandfather, on my mother's side, gave them enough money for a down payment on a small but adequate three-bedroom, one bath mill house, which was one town over. My father was able to get a better paying job in a factory in the same town where we now lived. I think my grandfather may have had something to do with that, too.

When I was about one-year-old, my eldest brother, Kevin, was sent to live with my grandparents, on my mother's side. My other brother, David, and I were sent to an orphanage in a city about twenty miles from home. We lived there for about two years before being reunited with my parents and older brother. The reason for the separation was never really known, but Kevin, about five at the time of the separation, seemed to remember my parents having very frequent and violent fights, and my father leaving the house for almost two years. This must have made things very difficult for my mother. I believe it became impossible for her to care for us, leading to the separation.

The memory of my childhood really begins when I was between four and five-years-old. The house we lived in was in a nice neighborhood. The street was a hill that, if you stood in the front yard, ran top to bottom, from left to right. All of the houses were on the same side of the street, and the other side was forest land. There was a fire access road that went into the forest, directly across from my house. If you followed the road in far enough, it turned to the right, with foot paths coming into it at the corner from different directions. There were a few other children living on the street that were about my age. Down at the bottom of the hill were Tommy and Jill. We became fast and good friends. A few houses up the street was Sarah. She was one year younger than me and we became very good friends. She and I did everything and went everywhere together. I even went on a family vacation with her. Sarah's mother and my mother also became close friends. As neither one of them worked, they had plenty of time to spend together, drinking, smoking, and gossiping.

It was a different time back then, in the late 1950s and early 60s. Doors were never locked; kids were allowed to play outside unattended, and people had a more laid back and trusting approach to life. Daily drinking and chain smoking, for both men and women, seemed to be much more tolerated back then as well. As a result of that, the air in my house was almost always a light blue haze, with a very smoky quality to it. The drinking I think, may have played some small part in the fact that child discipline was also very different then. If you did something wrong while Dad was at work, you would always get some small measure of slapping, beating, or spanking from Mom and then you would hear the dreaded, "You just wait until your father gets home." This meant Mom was not satisfied with her part in the beating and he would be the real bad guy when he came home. Oh great, another fun and loving family evening to look forward to! Beatings from my father were generally swift and harsh. They could involve slapping, punching, beating with a rolled newspaper, or whipping with a leather belt.

Despite the living conditions and income being better, my parents apparently had a very difficult relationship. They fought physically and violently, sometimes as much as twice a week. These fights often included lots of flying pots and pans, broken dishes and glass, and always lots of very loud screaming and yelling from both of them. On occasion, these fights would spill over to include two of the kids. Kevin, the eldest, would always get the worst of the beatings in these battles, with me the youngest coming in a close second. My middle brother, David, never seemed to get dragged into the family evening 'quality time'. Now, if you were to go outside our house and pick up a rock, you could literally throw it and hit the local police chief's house. Since most of these battles happened at night, during the week, this seemed to be an open invitation to Mr. Police Chief to come to our house for a visit. He was a frequent visitor! Sometimes, when he came, he had the good forethought to bring along the local town doctor. I think he could tell from the sounds coming from our house if the Doc was going to be needed or not.

Apparently, my father knew about how long one of these battles could go on before being interrupted by the police. He would use this time to the best of his ability and then leave the house, sometimes for weeks at a time. He was almost always gone before the police showed up, but my mother was generally going to need some degree of medical attention. Her injuries were, for the most part, minor in nature, a cut here a bruise there, and were dealt with quickly. On one occasion, I can remember going into the kitchen, after a particularly nasty battle, and finding my mother lying on the floor with a knife sticking out of her belly. She was awake and somewhat coherent and I remember thinking that she didn't seem to be in too much pain. I thought, at the time, that maybe it was because it was just a table knife. No charges were filed; no charges were ever filed. I think Sarah's father, a close friend of my father's, may have had something to do with that. You will learn about Sarah's father, and his 'connections' later. My mother went to the hospital and we were left home with my father, who had not had time to flee the scene before the police arrived. My mother was home in a couple of days, and our life went back to 'normal' once again.

The house right next to ours, on the up-hill side, belonged to an elderly couple. The husband was a retired mounted police officer, from a nearby city. When he retired, his horse was also retired and lived in a shed at his house. The horse was very large, but also very gentle. The man would often give the kids in the neighborhood rides on the horse. The rides were lots of fun. He would take us into the forest and ride up and down some of the trails. When the riding was done, he would show us how to take care of the horse before putting him away. The man passed away in the spring when I was still very young. His wife was too old to take care of the horse, so one day, the horse just disappeared. It was a sad day for many of the kids in the area.

During the summer when I was five, almost six, and Sarah was four, our mothers were busy doing what they did. This left Sarah and me to roam the street, play in the woods, or go down to visit Tommy and Jill. Sometimes the four of us would get together and go up the foot path, from the corner of the fire road, to a group of large rock formations. There were three separate formations. The first two were separated by large jagged rocks. Each of these two formations had several caves and tunnels in them, and were great for climbing, exploring, and crawling around. The jagged rocks made great rock-climbing walls. Some of them were close enough together so that you could wedge yourself between them and work your way to the top. At the end of the second formation was a large flat open area, with no trees or rocks. It was lined in sort of a semi-circle, on the outside edge, by a thick growth of trees. This made it seem almost like a courtyard, or meeting area of some kind. If you walked straight back from the second formation, you walked up a slight hill. When you got to the top of this hill, you were standing at the top of a cliff. Looking straight down, this cliff was maybe 16 to 18 feet high. At the bottom of the cliff was a large, very flat rock. The rock was about three feet high, 25 to 30 feet long and about 20 feet wide. We called these formations our 'Bedrock Playland'. Sarah, Jill, Tommy, and I would later find that the flat rock would be the site of many parties, and as you will see, they were very sexual in nature.

While doing some unrelated research, I came across documents that suggested that this area may have been used as a temporary village by some of King Phillip's group of followers during his savage march through Massachusetts, New York, and on up into Canada in the mid-1670s. Sarah, Tommy, Jill, and I spent many hours climbing the rocks and exploring the caves as young children. Sometimes kids from other parts of town would come and play, and spend lots of time climbing and exploring the rocks, too. Occasionally some of the school yard bullies would show up and chase away the rest of the kids. More about the bullies later. As you will also learn later, our 'Bedrock Playland' would become the cause of the loss of my best friend Sarah, and the site of my first encounter with sexual abuse. The loss of Sarah was something that I have never really been able to fully deal with, and the sexual abuse, well, there's more to come.

The street we lived on was called Summer Street. As a four or five-year-old child, I thought this was a fine name for a street, and thought it meant that it was going to be like Summer all year. Oh boy, was I mistaken! At the bottom of the hill, Summer Street formed a 'T' intersection with Dixon Avenue. Tommy and Jill lived in neighboring houses on the corner of the two streets, and shared a large yard between them. Sarah and I would sometimes go to their houses to play in the yard. They had a nice, big, flat yard with a few really good climbing trees. If you grew up in the country, you know what I mean by that. The trees were easy to climb, with large heavy branches that went off in every direction, and were close to the ground. You could climb up and go off onto one of these branches and find a nice comfortable crook between branches to lay in, quite nicely. Tommy's father had a large shed in the back yard. He told us we were never to go into this shed. Well, you know if you tell children not to do something, they do it. Both of Tommy's parents worked so they were not home during the day. This gave us lots of time to go into the forbidden shed. In it, there were lots of tools of every kind, lots of interesting little things here and there. Tommy's father apparently liked to do small woodworking projects. The projects he would be working on never seemed to get any further along, no matter how long it had been since the last time we were in there. He even had an old car motor from one of the family's past cars. I'm not sure if he was taking it apart or putting it back together; it too never seemed to change.

On the other side of Dixon Avenue were the railroad tracks. Back in those early days of the late 50s and early 60s, the tracks were very busy. There were at least two large freight trains going in each direction every day, and a couple of passenger trains a week. When a train was coming through, they would always blow the whistle to let us know they were coming. We always knew, anyway, by the rattling and shaking of everything in the house. I don't know how Tommy's family could stand it, being right across the street from the tracks, with all that loud racket and rumbling. Sometimes the four of us would go to the tracks and walk about a quarter mile to the west. The old railroad station was there. It was no longer being used and was in very bad disrepair. We would go inside and play around the front desk and office areas, pretending that we were managing the passengers and freight. If any of our parents found out we were in there, we would be in for trouble. Yup... just one more reason for a good old fashion beating at my house.

We never really talked about it, the four of us, but I think we all knew what went on behind closed doors at each of our houses. Sarah, we knew, got the least of the physical abuse. Even though she had sisters, she was most definitely Daddy's little girl. Tommy's parents were not close friends with anybody on the street. Without saying anything, we all knew which ones had a bad time at home the previous night. If Sarah and I got together with Tommy and Jill, and we could tell one or more of us had a bad night, we would go to the Bedrock Playland and just hang out. Sometimes just sitting on the edge of one of the rocks and letting our feet dangle was somehow very soothing. Sometimes we would go to the second formation. It had a cave that passed all the way through, from one end to the other. There were other small openings on the side of this cave that let in enough light to see. We would go in there and just sit and talk. I don't remember what we talked about, kid stuff I suppose, or maybe the fact that we would be heading to school soon. We hoped we would all be in the same class. Sarah of course was one year younger, so she would not be with us in school.

Chapter Two
The Early School Years

Well, summer was over, and Tommy, Jill, and I headed for the first grade while Sarah went into kindergarten. I was very small for my age, and a bit shy. As a result of that, by about the middle of the first year, I became known as "Wee Willy Shawn" and the preferred target of the school yard bullies (yes people… bullying is not new; it has been around forever). Let me tell you what school yard bullying was like back in the late 50s and early 60s. Three or four larger kids would seek out a smaller one, circle the target, and throw him around between them as hard as they could. Then the target kid was punched, kicked, thrown to the ground and would almost always have a torn shirt or, at the very least, some missing buttons. By the time you had to return to class, you generally looked like you just came from working at the farm or were out digging ditches somewhere. My mother was always getting mad at me about coming home with my clothes like that. I don't think she believed that I was beaten up to varying degrees almost every day; with no help from friends, other students, or even family members. Teachers never got involved with what went on in the school yard, and nobody ever got punished for what went on out there. However, if you did something your teacher didn't like, in the classroom, you got your knuckles whacked with a wooden ruler, up in front of the class. (Go ahead, try whacking your knuckles with a wooden ruler! I'll wait. You'll find that it hurts, a lot!)

While we're on the subject of teacher-student discipline, let's take a brief look at some of the methods of discipline used back when I was in school. I'm not sure 'discipline' is the right word here; punishment might be a better fit. I remember a student, in one of my classes, getting caught chewing gum. The student, a bit of a 'bad guy' type, refused several demands by the teacher to get rid of it. After apparently being done making demands, the teacher who was a very tall and muscular man, picked the student up out of his seat. While holding the student by the front of the shirt, he took the time to tell the rest of the class that we were done with the information on the black board. He then erased the information, using the back of the student's shirt, with the student still in it. Another favorite discipline, for gum chewing in class, was to be made to place the gum on your nose and stand in the middle of the hall during class change while loudly announcing, "I was chewing gum in class. I've been very bad and won't do it again." The high school football team's coach was my history teacher. History, that's a funny subject. Apparently, United States and world history was very different back then. For some reason, the way we seem to remember the events of the past have changed quite a bit. But, anyway, back to the subject. If you did something in that teacher's class, that upset him, he would place you in front of the class in a sitting position with your back against the wall. He would however always forget to put the chair under you. If you have never done that, go ahead, try it. Place yourself in a perfect sitting position, with your back against the wall. Count how many seconds you can stay there. I'll give you a hint. It won't be long, and your calves are going to be very upset with you for a while.

The bullying continued until, about, the middle of the fifth grade. One day, while getting my, almost daily beating by a lone bully, the biggest, toughest kid in the schoolyard, I decided I had had enough. I turned to face him, and as I did, I let a left hook fly with every ounce of strength and weight I could muster behind it. Yup, a southpaw. (He didn't see that coming). I connected with the side of his face, his legs turned to Jello and he went down. As I stood there, looking at him lying on the ground, holding the side of his face and head, crying, I felt wonderful! I was the new king of the school yard. When the bell rang for us to return to class, I noticed he was not going back to his class. He was being helped to the school nurse's office, by one of his bully friends. The bullying stopped after that, but it was too late for me. I had come to hate going to school. Hating school, I think, generally leads to getting bad grades. At least that was the case with me. I was a 'C- /D' student, through the first six years of school.

During the summer, when I was nine, while Sarah, Jill, Tommy and I were playing at the Bedrock Playland, we heard sounds coming from beyond the third rock. Sounds of several people having lots of fun. We all went to the top of the cliff and looked down to see about 18 to 20 people. NAKED PEOPLE! They were all older than us. The youngest, we recognized to be, a relative of one of the kids in our little group. He was fourteen years old at the time. More of their relatives were there. They were all older. There were blankets and towels spread out over the big flat rock, at the base of the cliff. All of these people, some we recognized and many we didn't, were having sex together. Every kind of sex you can imagine. We laid down and just peeked over the top of the cliff. We didn't want to be seen. We laid there and watched in complete and utter fascination. It was a real, live orgy. At ages eight and nine, we didn't know people could do a lot of the things we were seeing: boys doing things with boys, girls with other girls, girls with boys, and sometimes more than one at a time. There was lots of beer drinking and they were smoking something that smelled kind of funny. Thanks to my brother, David, I would later find that to be marijuana. One of the girls, I recognized in the group, I would meet again several years later in a professional capacity. I think, as the realization of the last time we saw each other set in, it made for a bit of an awkward meeting.

After a while, things started to slow down, people started getting dressed and leaving. Some of them just laid on the rocks, still naked; sleeping, I guess. We all left and went about our playing. About two weeks later, just before school was to start, we heard the same noises coming from the flat rock again. Of course we had to peek over the top of the cliff and watch again. And watch we did. A couple of days later, I could not find Sarah anywhere. After looking in all of the usual places, I decided to go down to visit Tommy and Jill. Maybe Sarah had gone down there. She wasn't there, but I stayed and played with them in the yard. The following morning, Sarah's mother was at my house talking to my mother in very hushed tones. I was told to go to my room and stay there. And again, if you tell a child to stay, he moves. I went to the top of the stairs where I could hear most of the conversation. Sarah's mom told mine that Sarah had been gone all day, the day before, and when she came home she was having trouble walking and had been badly beaten. Sarah was crying inconsolably and was obviously in a lot of pain. Her mother said she took her to the town doctor and, after Sarah was examined, he told her that she may have been sexually assaulted. She was only eight years old! Sarah was not talking. This became a very big problem for me. It was assumed that I may have had something to do with it. How could anybody think I would do such a thing to my best friend? I loved her. I felt so bad for her, trying to imagine what she must have gone through. Then the true reality of her not talking set in, and I got the beating of my life that night. Not with just the leather belt, but closed fisted punches, slaps and just being thrown around the room in general. I tried to tell them that I had nothing to do with what happened to her, but my parents wouldn't listen.

Our frequent visitor, Mr. Police Chief had a new reason to come to the house. The chief came to me and asked if there were going to be any odd or distinguishing marks, or features, on or around my private area that Sarah was going to know about? This seemed like an odd question to me. I didn't know why he would ask me such a thing. I told him flat out that no there were not. The chief asked me if I knew how Sarah got hurt? I told him that I only knew what my parents had told me. He then asked me where I was or who I was with when Sarah got hurt? I said that I had been playing with Tommy and Jill in their yard, and if he would like to check with them, I was sure they would tell him about it. He said he would. I don't think he ever did, at least they never mentioned it to me.

After a few days, Sarah told her mother who did it, and exactly what was done. It was those relatives that we had recognized on the rock! She said they told her, "Now that [she] had gotten [hers], I was going to get mine." They said it was because they saw us watching the 'sex parties' on the flat rock. Sarah's mother came to my house and told my mother all about it (that's okay Mom and Dad, no apology needed for the excessive beating). Sarah's father and uncle were members of the Laborer's Union. They were also, apparently, somewhat important members of some other organization. There seemed to be a lot of big, shiny cars in their yards from time to time; with men in suits standing around, always looking up and down the street and into the woods across the street. The local police chief was apparently told that this was a 'family matter' and he was not to bother himself with it. Sarah's father seemed to have a lot of control over the police, in town. I don't know what happened to those relatives, but I don't remember seeing them around for a while. But they would return, and they would find me! From that day on, Sarah would have nothing to do with me. I don't know the real reason but I can only speculate that she placed some of the blame on me. If she hadn't been up on that cliff, watching with us, none of that would have happened to her (I am so very sorry, Sarah, for what you must have gone through. But I don't think it was fair not to talk to me about it). I was so hurt. It broke my heart then, and it still does to this day. After that, Sarah surrounded herself with her girlfriends. She even took Jill away from me.

At the end of the sixth grade, I had to go to summer school and get a passing grade there if I wanted to go on to the seventh grade. Going to the seventh grade was a scary thought. The elementary school was small, and only served our little town. And it was in walking distance from my house. Going to the seventh grade meant riding on a school bus, to a much larger school, about six miles away. This larger school was a regional school; serving grades seven through twelve, and five towns, and having about 1,000 students. I figured this meant a much higher chance of getting bullied, and by much larger kids. I was not looking forward to that. My time in elementary school was not a happy one, at school or home, but at least the school part was over. I did move on to the seventh grade. I was never bullied at the new school. I started to like school, and started to get better grades.

Chapter Three
Summers and Baseball

When I was twelve years old, and getting ready to go into the eighth grade, I was walking down the street to go visit my friend, Tommy. As I went past a small remote area at the edge of the forest, a man came out. I had never seen him before but he seemed to be a nice guy. He was, maybe, in his late teens or maybe even twenty. He said that he had heard of some rock formations, with really good caves to explore, in the area but had been unable to find them. He asked if I could tell him how to get to them? Since Tommy didn't know I was coming to his house, I decided to take him on a shortcut that I knew would get him there quicker. I took him to a foot path that came out at the large clearing, at the end of the second formation. From there you could enter the cave that went all the way through that rock and came out on the other side. He asked if I had ever been in there. I had. The cave is long and it curves to the right a bit. This was the cave that had the smaller openings on the side that let in light. These smaller caves were only big enough for a very small person, like me, to crawl through but they let enough light into the larger cave so you could see. As we were standing in the cave, the man suddenly put his hand on my chest, and pushed me against the side of the cave. He grabbed the front of my shorts, always elastic waist, always hand me downs, and always a little too big. As he pulled the front of my shorts toward him, he asked, "What have you got hiding in there?" Still holding me against the wall, he then put his hand down my shorts, grabbed my penis and began to massage it. I was paralyzed with shock and fear. But wait! As my mind was yelling, "This is wrong, this is wrong", this didn't feel half bad. Then, all of the sudden, I felt like I had to pee really badly. Well, I exploded in my shorts, and it wasn't pee! The man wiped his hand off in my shorts, and on my T-shirt, and then smiled at me and left. And that was my first sexual abuse encounter (more to come). Maybe I was lucky he didn't kill me afterward. I don't think I have ever seen him again.

Each summer, since I was eight or nine until maybe about fourteen, my maternal grandfather and his two sisters rented a cottage. They rented the same cottage every year, except for the last year. The cottage was at a beach along the southern shores of Rhode Island. It had three bedrooms, a small kitchen, living room and a bathroom. There was a small shower in the bathroom, but there were also two enclosed outside shower stalls. The cottage was about two blocks from the beach and the tourist trap center, with all of its shops filled with souvenirs and necessities that visitors may have forgotten or ran out of. While the cottage was rented for two weeks, my family would go and stay for one week each summer. My grandfather, his second wife, his two sisters and four of his children, would be there for the two weeks. When my family was there, there were thirteen people staying in that three-bedroom cottage.

Despite the cottage being very cramped, I looked forward to those weeks. I missed it the year I had to go to summer school. My father stayed home with me that week. He worked during the day and I was on my best behavior in the evenings. We had fun in the weeks we were there. One year my brother, David, bought a box kite and one ball of 250 feet of heavy string. He got the kite up easily and ran it out to the end of the ball of string. He sent me to the store for another ball. We tied the ends together and he ran the kite out to the end of the second ball. Now, just being able to see the kite, he wanted a third ball of string. Attaching the ends of the second and third balls together, he ran the kite out to about one half of the third ball; and then the string went limp. We couldn't really see the kite so we weren't sure where it went. We tried following the string but lost it in a very dense pack of thickets. We never were able to find the kite. Sometimes just for fun, my grandfather's kids, plus my two brothers and I, would go to some of the tourist trap stores. While some of the kids kept the shop keepers busy, the rest of us would take things from the shelves and put them on other shelves, where they didn't belong. None of us ever took anything without paying, at least not that I know of.

Across the street from the cottage, on the inland side, there was a very large blueberry patch. The bushes were maybe as tall as six feet. My grandfather called them 'highboy' plants. I don't know if that's an actual type of blueberry plant or not. Each year, we would go into the bushes and collect bucket loads of berries. The berries were the largest blueberries I have ever seen, some about the size of grapes. After picking all those berries, all of the kids would set about cooking everything blueberry. We made blueberry muffins, cake, pies, pancakes and waffles. For some reason, one year, an argument broke out between two of my grandfather's kids. Their argument quickly escalated to an all-out blueberry batter fight; with batter balls, about the size of tennis balls, flying in every direction around the kitchen. The fight only lasted about a couple of minutes before being brought under control by the grownups. However, in those couple of minutes we managed to get blueberry batter on the floor, ceiling and all of the walls. After each of us cleaned ourselves up, in the outside shower stalls, we were made to clean up the mess we made in the kitchen. The mess that took only a couple of minutes to make, took several hours to clean up. We were never allowed to pick blueberries again.

The days that my family was there, all of the kids would get up early, eat breakfast and head to the beach. Some days when we got there, we would only see a few other people on the beach. We liked getting there early. Before a lot of people started to go into the water, we could find lots of jelly fish close to shore. They were small, the biggest being maybe about six inches in diameter. They were not the kind that would sting you if you touched them, at least none of us ever got stung by one. We would also go out on the breakwaters to try to grab baby sand sharks by the tail, as they chased crabs into the breakwater. A breakwater, for those of you who don't know, is a very large stone wall, five or six feet across, extending from the beach out into the ocean for maybe 50 or 60 feet. The breakwaters were placed about 100 to 150 feet apart, all along the beach. Their purpose was to break up the dangerous rip tides, caused by the ever-present heavy surf. We would go most of the way out on them and get down to where the stones went into the water. If you sat there long enough, you would see small sand sharks, maybe up to 18 or 20 inches long, chasing crabs into the rocks. If you were fast enough, you might be able to grab one of these little sharks by the tail, on its way by. Fortunately, none of us were ever fast enough.

The last year, my grandfather rented a cottage at the beach, he couldn't get the same one. He ended up getting a cottage at a beach about four or five miles east of the one we had been going to. The owner of that cottage lived in a nearby house and kept checking on us. One day, he came to the cottage while almost all of us were there. He spoke very broken English, with a very heavy Spanish accent. We were all out in the yard, playing a game; I don't remember what it was. He went to the eldest of my aunts and uncles; my aunt, from my grandfather's second marriage, was nineteen at the time. Her boyfriend had come with her that year, so that made fourteen people staying in the cottage. He began to yell at her about the number of people living there. She sent him to talk to one of my grandfather's sisters. My grandfather's sister was the only adult at the cottage, at the time. She had been sitting in the yard, drinking beer and sunning herself; something she did often in the summer. With the homeowner standing in front of her yelling angrily, she got out of her chair and started making very loud, angry and scrambled grunting noises at him. And then her arms began flailing about wildly. The owner was either so shocked or frightened by her, that he turned and ran from the yard yelling something in Spanish. We didn't see him the rest of the time we were there. This sister of my grandfather's was left unable to hear or speak from a childhood disease, and was a little tipsy at the time. My aunt sent him to talk to her because she thought it would be interesting to see what would happen between the two of them.

I played Little League baseball, for a couple of years. When I was thirteen, I joined the town's Babe Ruth League team. I was a catcher in Little League, and thought that's what I would do again. The coach had other ideas. As it turned out, I was an excellent center fielder. One day, during practice, I was playing pass with another player and the coach came and asked if I would try out as a pitcher. As it happened, my father played baseball in the army; he was a catcher. He learned all the really good pitches and how to throw them. To my shock and surprise, he took the time and interest to teach some of these pitches to me. I had a slider, a 'not so fast' fast ball, but as it approached the batter, it would suddenly rise up about six to eight inches. That made it a little more difficult to hit. I also had a sinker, a very good curve ball, more effective against right-handed than left-handed batters. I had something that would start to sink about halfway to the plate and then rise maybe as much as a foot; then as it approached the batter, would fall again almost to the dirt. We didn't have a name for that one. Lots of batters would swing at it; nobody ever hit it.

The night of our first game, we were playing against another team with a very good pitcher. He was one of the high school team's star pitchers. I was all set to go stand in center field, but the coach had other ideas. I was going to be the starting pitcher. I was very nervous; I didn't want our first game to be a loss. I struck out the first batter. Okay, maybe this wasn't going to be too bad. When the second batter came to the plate, a very good hitter I was told, my catcher called for a curve ball. Since the batter was right-handed, I decided to go with it. As the ball headed for the batter, he hit the dirt. I think he thought I was going to hit him in the head. However, as the ball approached the plate, it fell in to be a perfect strike. The umpire took the ball from the catcher, walked to the mound and said, "Did you mean to throw that ball like that?"

I said, "It was a curve ball. It was a strike. Wasn't it?"

"Oh yes", he said, "it was a strike. And probably the best curve ball I have ever seen as an umpire." I struck out fifteen batters and walked only one. I did hit one, oops! I gave up only one hit and we won the game, one to nothing. I played in the League for three years.

At the start of the second season, a new team from another town was added. The team, though not very good as a team, had a monster pitcher. This kid was about six feet tall, maybe six foot one, and must have weighed between 250 and 300 pounds. The baseball looked like a tennis ball in his hand. The only good thing about him was that all he had was a fast ball, nothing else to throw at us. He did have pretty good control, so you always had a good idea where the pitch was going to be. The first time I stepped up to the plate against him, he was left-handed, so I was batting from the right side; he threw three pitches. I swung at all of them, and missed. All of them! It seemed as if he was just winding up, and the catcher was already throwing the ball back to him. The second time I came to bat against him, I swung and missed the first pitch. I decided I would swing at the next one, even if I felt like it was too early to swing. I heard the crack of the ball hit the bat and felt the weight of that, perhaps, 200 mph projectile hit my wooden stick. I stood at home plate and watched. To my great surprise, the ball sailed high down the first base line, maybe five or six feet, to the fair side of the foul line. As I watched the ball make its way to the home run fence, I started to jog to first base. Taking my eye off the ball to make sure I stepped squarely on the first base bag, I made the turn and headed for second base. As I looked back at the ball, I saw it sail over the home run fence, a three-and-a-half-foot tall snow fence, and into the glove of the right fielder's outstretched arm. That bastard! He caught the ball! My home run was not a home run, it was an out. As I walked back to my team's bench, on the third base side of the field, I walked past the pitcher and heard him chuckle a little and say, "I bet you thought you had that one."

Without looking up at him I simply said, "Yep!" And, I kept on walking. I never got a hit off that pitcher.

With five or six games left in my second season, at the age of fourteen, I was pitching another game. All of the players on the team that we were playing against were much bigger than all of our players. Some of them even had moustaches! Keep in mind, Babe Ruth Baseball is for thirteen through fifteen year olds. Our coach had checked with the league and been assured that all of the players from that town met the age requirements. At one point, with a runner on first base, the batter hit a very high pop up, about halfway down the first base line. My first baseman had to hold the runner on first; the ball should have been taken by my catcher, but he wasn't moving. The batter stayed at home plate for a few seconds, and I went over to the first base line to catch the pop up. As I was standing on the first base line, with both arms up above my head, ready to catch the ball, the batter came down the base line and ran his shoulder into me; just below the ribs on my left side. He apparently flipped me up and over his back, with me landing on my back. The first thing I remember after that was sitting on the bench; in so much pain that I passed out and fell on the ground. The next thing I remember was being in a hospital room.

I remained in the hospital for about five days. The batter was kicked out of the league. I had two cracked ribs and a very badly damaged spleen; I was peeing blood for days. My parents were in New Jersey with Sarah's parents, and did not return until the day before I was released from the hospital. I had not taken my final exams at the end of the ninth grade yet, and I did not return to school until the start of the tenth grade. The school allowed me to pass without taking any of the required final exams based on my grade performance throughout the ninth grade.

At some point during my last year in the league, we had a Thursday night game which I pitched. Another win! We then had a Saturday morning game, and I was all set to go stand in center field when the coach had other ideas. I was going to pitch this one, too. I told him my arm was still sore from the previous game but he insisted. As it turned out, there were two college scouts in town and the coach had arranged for them to come and check me out. This was the worst game of my life. I pitched three innings, gave up four runs, struck out nobody and walked three. We lost that game miserably. I can only wonder about what might have been, if I had been pitching with a fresh arm that Saturday morning. My parents never came to see me play.

Chapter Four
High School and Sex

I was fortunate enough to go to a high school that offered college prep, standard high school and trade prep courses. While never wanting to be an Architect, I did have a great interest in designing and building houses. This school had a very comprehensive residential design course along with a program that had the students go out and actually build one house each year, for some lucky homeowner. This not only gave the students the design knowledge needed, but also taught us how the design was put to use in the field. Practical knowledge, of both how a plan is developed and how it is interpreted by a builder, can give you an enormous advantage as a designer.

Now you may be thinking, sure, take a trade course; the easy way out. Well, my ninth-grade residential design course started with 26 students. While my graduating class had a total of 162 students, the residential design course, had just four students left. All the other students either flunked out or changed courses for something easier. The fact was, in the eleventh and twelfth grades, the residential design course took you through college level calculus, trigonometry, building anatomy and building science. Obviously not many students survived it. From what I saw of some of the college prep students, I know they wouldn't either. I enjoyed the design classes very much, and gave up any study periods I had to take extra designing. I finished the residential design course in three years. In the twelfth grade I took a beginner's course in steel and concrete design; very boring!

At the beginning of my sophomore year, I became a member of the National Honor Society. I know, it was a little early, but two of us went in as tenth grade students that year. I went to most of the meetings, but never really got involved. I didn't have much for close friends in high school. Tommy had taken a standard high school course. That was in a different section of the school and I rarely got to see him during the day. We would still get together sometimes after school in the early days of high school. But then, Tommy dropped out and went to work. I didn't get to see him much after that. Tommy had lied about his age to get the job. Sarah and Jill were in the same school with me now. Both had taken college prep courses. While I did spend some time in the end, at the school they were in, they still stayed away from me and wanted nothing to do with me. Back in those days, we all had to take the same bus to school. Unlike now, the bus didn't stop at every house on the street. We all had to walk to the center of town, to a central location, to get the bus. Even there, all the girls would stand in one area and the boys in another. It was very awkward.

Sometimes, in the early years of high school, I found it very peaceful to walk home after school. It was about six miles, but a pleasant walk. One day, in the very late spring, when I was fourteen, as I was walking home, a car came by and stopped just up the road from me. An arm came out the window and someone in the car yelled, "Come on, we'll give you a ride." I didn't recognize the car, but thought these may be some of David's, my brother's, friends. When I got up to the car, a man jumped out and, before I could move, grabbed me and threw me into the back seat of the car. These were not friends, I realized. They were the missing relatives!

Yup, they had returned, and they had found me. They drove to the other end of the fire road, which goes into the forest in front of my house. That end came out on a seldom-used road, maybe about one and a half or two miles from my house. They drove in a short distance, stopped, and everybody got out of the car. I was brought around to the front of the car, standing with my back to the car. The now men, the youngest being nineteen, formed a semi-circle around me. They all had some sort of pocketknife. Some just your standard three or four inch 'jack' knife, to one approximately six-inch switch blade. This one scared me a bit more than the others. As my assailants closed in around me, knives drawn, I was ordered to remove my clothes. All of them! Not having much choice, I slowly removed all of my clothes. Now, standing there in front of the four of them, naked, all sorts of nasty and probably painful things going through my head; they began to laugh at me and taunt me, jabbing at me with their knives. I was then told that I was getting my punishment for watching the 'sex parties' on the rock all those years ago. They ordered me to get on my knees, and the first of the assailants stepped in front of me. The six-inch knife blade was placed on the top of my shoulder, between my collar bones. I was told if I didn't behave myself, the knife would be pushed in, to its full depth, and turned ninety degrees, moved around a bit and then pulled out. This sounded very painful. They would then cut my penis off, put it in my mouth and make me chew and swallow it. If I spit it out or threw it up, I would be made to pick it up and eat it again until it stayed in. I decided I would behave myself.

(As Shawn is telling me this part of the story, I can tell he still has trouble with it.)

I was ordered to open the first man's pants, take his penis out and perform oral sex on him, until he made his deposit in my mouth. I was made to swallow it. Two more of the men followed in the same manner. The fourth man told me I was to hold his deposit in my mouth. When he was done, he told me to stand, and spit it into my hand; I was then told to rub it all over my own penis. The laughing, taunting and name calling had been going on the entire time. It had been a very humiliating part, of the whole experience, but this was almost unbearable. Now, standing there crying, thoroughly humiliated, they pushed me to the ground, off to the side of the car; they got in the car and left me there. I laid there, on the ground, crying for a little while. Then I stood up and gathered my clothes. I cleaned myself off with my t-shirt, as best I could, got dressed and

28

put my school shirt on; without the t-shirt, which I left lying on the ground. As I was still crying, I walked down the fire road to my house. I never told anybody about what had happened, until forty-eight years later.

School continued! I was fifteen now, still with no real close friends, just good classmates. Occasionally, I would get invited to a dance party at someone's house. We weren't allowed to have parties like that at our house, so I would go to most of the ones I got invited to. They were fun, and usually only had about ten or 12 kids there. If there was a party going on at one kid's house, the parents of that kid would always get together with some of the parents of the other kids; at one of their houses. This left us to play music, dance and have fun without being bothered by the grown-ups.

On one occasion, it also left us open to an attack, by four older men and one older woman. By older, I mean and I'm guessing here, maybe early twenties. These people were armed with knives, the apparent weapon of choice back in the late 60s. They also came with a bottle, a beer bottle I think. They made all of us sit in a circle, in the middle of the room. Meanwhile, one of the men and the woman, had gone into another room. The remaining men, knives openly displayed, put the bottle on the floor in the middle of the circle. The bottle was then spun, the person it pointed to when it stopped was told to stand, remove all of their clothes and go into the room with the man and woman. Each person that went into the room was apparently ordered to perform some sort of sexual act with either the man or woman. I'm not sure if the sex of the person going into the room had any bearing on whom the act was to be performed. When the person came back out of the room, he or she was told to stand in the spot they had been sitting, with their hands down by their sides. They had to stand there, until each of us had gone into the room. I felt fortunate that I was almost the last one to go in. Just two girls were left after me. That meant that I wasn't going to be standing naked, in front of the other kids, for very long.

When the bottle pointed to me, I was told to remove my clothes and go into the room. As I entered the room, the man and woman were standing beside each other. I was told to sit on the floor, in front of the woman. The man then went behind me, grabbed the hair on the back of my head, and forced me to lean back on my hands. He then pulled my head back, so I was looking at the ceiling. The woman then straddled me and dragged her vagina across my face, from my chin to my forehead. She then moved back and placed herself directly over my face and said to me, "Now tongue fuck me!" Not being exactly sure what to do, I stuck my tongue out and it went right inside her. What felt like a river of fluids ran into my mouth. Some of the fluids, I recognized as coming from boys. I didn't know what to expect, and the taste of the fluid began to change a bit. I was having some trouble breathing and had to keep pulling my mouth away from her, to catch my breath. This whole thing was very humiliating for me. After a very short time, she moved slightly and came to rest on my nose. She began to move around a bit, and started to make little moaning sounds. She began to press harder on my nose, I thought she was going to break it. After a short time, the moving got faster and the moaning got louder. Then, she made a noise that sounded like a stifled scream, and then backed away from me. She told me she was done with me and to go back to the other room.

I was sitting on the floor, with my knees drawn up, feet together on the floor. The man had let go of my head at this point and was standing behind me. I asked her if I could wait a couple of minutes before getting up. The man then grabbed me, in a kind of bear hug, and picked me up to a standing position. At that point, they knew why I didn't want to go to the other room just yet. I had developed an erection! This development was humiliating enough, just standing in front of the two of them. Going out and standing in front of all the other kids like that, would have been more than I could bear. The real problem was that I now had this woman all over my face, in my nose, and in my mouth. The problem wasn't going away any time soon, at least not by itself. The two of them were talking. I couldn't hear what they were saying. The woman then came over to me, the man beside her, and she said, "Well, as long as you've got it, you might as well use it." She then turned around, got on her hands and knees in front of me, and spread her legs.

I had never had sex before; I wasn't sure exactly what to do. I got on my knees, centered myself with her, and just moved up to her. Apparently, the rest of it comes naturally. As I slid into her, the thing I remember most, was the feeling of being inside her. It was so much more than I could have ever imagined. I didn't seem to have any trouble doing what needed to be done. When I was finished, it didn't take very long, neither one of us moved for a bit. Then she pulled away from me, and the man put his hand on the back of my head again, and while pushing my face down said, "Now give my wife a kiss where you just fucked her. And thank her for helping you with your little problem." I did as I was told and then, as slowly as possible, got to my feet and went to the other room where I took my place in the circle. I stood there with my penis, and probably my face, still wet from the activity in the other room. But I don't remember feeling terribly humiliated, standing there naked with my hands to my sides. I think I was more focused on the fact that I just had sex, for the very first time in my life. And did I just do that with some man's wife, while he stood there watching me, or was that just something he said? I will never know.

The other two girls in the circle were made to strip, and go into the room together. After what seemed to be a long time, they both came out together. With everyone having gone into the room and come back out, the raid was done and the older people left. We all quickly got dressed. Those that needed rides called for them, and those of us that could walk home did so. Nobody ever said a word to me about that night, and I didn't tell anyone about it for forty-eight years. There were no more dance parties for a while, at least none that I know of.

After a few months, the parties started again. I went to three or four parties, all without incident, and then it happened again. Older men, I'm not sure if they were all the same ones, and one older woman. The woman I know, was not the same one that came to the previous party. The same routine was followed. This time I was not so lucky with the bottle. I was the third or fourth one picked. This meant standing naked, with my hands at my side, in front of the other kids for a very long time. When I went into the room with the man and woman, the woman was on her back with her knees drawn up and legs spread. She was positioned so that as you walk in, you were looking directly at her vagina. I was told to, "Just get on her and fuck her." With her in that position, I wasn't going to be able to see what to do. I started to panic a little, how was I going to see how to line things up? I got down, and crawled on top of her, and as I slid into position, I slid right into her. Again it must be something that just comes naturally. I did what I was told; it didn't take long, and I went out to take my place in the circle. I found this experience to be just as humiliating as everything I had gone though at the first party. I never told anyone about this one either, until forty-eight years later. And I never went to another dance party, at anyone's house again. So with that, comes the end of the saga of my sexual abuse. Sarah and Jill never went to any of the parties that I know of.

During the summer, before the school year in which these dance parties took place, a new family moved to a house at the top of Summer Street. They had twin daughters. I'm not sure how old the girls were. I never saw them in school, or on the school bus, so I don't know what grade they were in. They were very pretty, kind of tall and thin with long straight hair. But they were nasty, just mean and nasty to everyone. I saw them around town a few times, with two of the men that I remembered from the first party raid. It made me wonder if they may have had something to do with the raids, as punishment or retaliation for not being invited to any of the parties, even the ones in the neighborhood. I never saw any of the school kids with them, so I don't think they had any friends from school. I also did not mention this idea to anyone. It brings visions of a mob of angry teenage kids attacking their house in the middle of the night, with torches and pitch forks.

After forty-eight years, I told my first mental health therapist about all of the sexual abuse. It still bothered me to tell someone about it; I was embarrassed and still found it to be humiliating. When I finished telling her about it, her only reply was, "You should write a book. You're a very good storyteller." I don't know if it was that she didn't believe me, or that she just thought it would make a good book. I stopped seeing her shortly after that.

Chapter Five
The Rest of High School, and Beyond

In the summer between the eleventh and twelfth grades, I built the first of many houses on my own. It was just a summer cottage, but a house none the less. It had a kitchen, one bathroom, a large family room, and a small loft above the family room that served as a bedroom. I worked six days a week on it that summer, and weekends until just before Thanksgiving that fall, to finish it. The cottage was built on a hill; overlooking a small, secluded lake in Connecticut, about thirty-five minutes from my house.

In the spring of my twelfth grade, I was approached by a contractor and offered a job when I finished school. His company built subsidized low-income housing, all over Western Massachusetts. Since I had no intention of going to college, I agreed to take the job. At least, I thought, I would have something solid and positive waiting for me after graduation. A couple of months before graduation, the Honor Society members were offered a chance to take a prequalifying entry test to the organization called Mensa. Somehow I passed the test (I think it may have been a fluke). I never took it any further than that, and didn't join their little club. I was a straight 'A' student all through high school, with the exception of one 'A-'. I graduated at the top of my class and in the top five percent, of the three other schools, in the district. Life at home got a little better; I guess my parents were mellowing a bit with age. The fights weren't as violent or as frequent. We didn't see Mr. Police Chief very often, anymore. In the later years, my parents actually became somewhat entertaining, as you will see. About two weeks before graduation, I was told that as Valedictorian I would have to give a six-minute speech. I promptly declined, sighting the fact that I had never had any public speaking courses and knew nothing about giving speeches.

Okay, so not being able to get out of my assigned speaking engagement, I sat on the stage looking out at approximately seven hundred people. I was trying to figure out how I was going to get through this. When my time came, to give my speech, I got up from my chair and walked to the podium. I looked out at all those people, and two microphones from two local radio stations, and I knew I could not do this! But, in that moment, I somehow convinced myself that I was some random actor and this was just another scene in some random movie. I began to speak, a little shaky at first, but by a couple of minutes in, I was going along as if I did this every day.

On a Saturday afternoon, in the summer after graduation, a friend called to see if I would be interested in playing in a pick-up baseball game being organized at the ball field, in the school yard. I said I would be right there, grabbed my glove and favorite bat, and headed out. I decided to take one of the foot paths through the forest that I had taken many times before. It was only about a quarter mile to the ball field, going that way. The path left from the north end of the second rock formation of our Bedrock Playland, and as you followed it you came to a fork. If you went to the right side, you would go down a small embankment to a lower level of the forest floor. At the lower level, you would be walking about five or six feet out from a rock wall, on your left that was maybe eight or ten feet high. If you went to the left side of the fork, you would be walking along the top of the rock wall. After about 20 or 25 yards, the left path came down to meet with the right side at the lower level. I took the right side of the fork. As I made my way past the rock wall, maybe halfway along its length, I heard a distinctive rustling sound. I glanced to my left, just in time to see two brownish projectiles, each about six inches long, launching from a small ledge in the wall. They were both headed right at my face. I managed to bend back, just fast enough, and just far enough, to watch two baby snakes sail past my face. I also saw a much larger, brown snake with dark brown markings on it; maneuvering into what I took to be a strike position. I wasn't going to hang around to find out. I started to backpedal as fast as I could. After eight or ten feet, I turned around and ran as fast as I could, back to the fork in the path. Once there, I took the left side of the fork, and ran all the way to the ball field.

I didn't know there were rattlesnakes in the area. At the first chance I got, I went to the library. Some of you will remember that we used to go to the library to read and do research, with real books. I looked it up and sure enough, Timber Rattlesnakes were very common in the entire area. They were, in fact, very common all over Southern New England. The really odd part, I found, was that they say there are no venomous snakes in Maine. The State must have a pact with all of the bad snakes in the rest of New England. It made me wonder what would have happened if, while crawling through one of those tight little caves at the Bedrock Playland, one of us ran into a snake. In all that time, and all the kids that played, crawled and climbed around there, nobody ever saw or heard a rattlesnake. It was the only encounter I ever had with one in that area.

Chapter Six
Meet the Family

If you have done the math correctly, you now know that I graduated high school in 1971, at the age of seventeen. So as long as we're talking about me, let's take some time to get to know a little about my family. My name is Shawn Williams, 'Willy' to most people in my life. I have been tested to show above average intelligence. I never went to college, never had any desire to. Over the years I have, however, taken the odd college course or two, mostly in connection with my work. Despite the fun and seemingly loving childhood, you just in part read about, my (third) therapist seems to think I am reasonably well adjusted, having gone through what I did. My training in high school gave me all the tools I needed for a solid, productive life. I have enjoyed many fine crafts, skills, and hobbies throughout my adult life. Some of them, you will read about in this book.

My middle brother, David, is about one-and-a-half years older than me. He too is very intelligent. He is the quietest, gentlest and laid back of the three of us. He spent many years in different colleges, taking a variety of studies. Dave, now retired, spent the last twenty-six years working in a government job, in Washington DC. He is a voracious reader and book collector. He once rented a mid-sized U HAUL truck, loaded it with books, and drove about 400 miles back to the area we grew up in and donated them all to two local libraries. Having his house free of the clutter of all those books, he started collecting all over again. His wife is not happy about that. Like me, David is a wine lover. If you ever have the chance to tour some of Virginia's wineries, don't pass that up. They have some excellent wines there. David no longer lives in Virginia.

My oldest brother, Kevin, passed away in 2015 at the age of sixty-six. He was about four-and-a-half years older than me. Also very intelligent, he was a gifted artist. He never went to college, although he too took some college courses over the years, all work related. He was offered a high-level position in the graphic arts department of a large, national company, right out of high school. Kevin was not a happy person, through most of his life. He leaned heavily on the rough childhood we all had, as the root cause of all that went wrong in his life. He married young, and I think he realized his mistake very early on. There did, however, seem to be two hobbies that made him happy. The first, drinking as much whiskey as possible, and the second, was having an ongoing affair with his secretary. These two hobbies would lead to the end of his job, and his marriage. Kevin had two children. After five or six years, his marriage would start to fall apart. It was not a surprise, to many people, and they ended it with a divorce. His wife later moved, with the children, somewhere down South. He didn't have much contact with the kids after that.

I don't know if any of the 'fun' things that happened to me as a teenager happened to either of my brothers. I never told them about what I was going through, and they never said anything to me about ever having the same kind of trouble. They were, however, both Catholic altar boys and went away with the priest, every summer, for a few days (Not trying to say anything here, just wondering).

My parents you have already sort of met, but I will introduce them to you. My father, Michael, was born in 1926 to English/Scottish parents. He grew up on a dairy farm owned, at that time, by his father and uncle. As a child, he would get up very early every morning to go with his uncle and deliver fresh milk to customers in town. After the milk run was finished, he was then allowed to go to school. I don't think my father had a very easy time with school and even less interest in it. When the United States entered World War II, he waited until he turned sixteen, lied about his age and joined the Army. He fought in Europe for two years and then came home. I believe it was about that time that he met my mother. She lived in another town, close by, and they began to see a lot of each other. Not wanting to stay on the farm, and with an older brother in the Navy, my father decided to join the Navy. I'm thinking the thought was, he would serve with, or at least close to, his brother. Before shipping out, my father proposed to my mother; she accepted. This did not sit well with either family. You see, my father was English and my mother, 100%, Irish. Unfortunately, while my uncle served as a Navy pilot on an aircraft carrier, somewhere in the Atlantic Ocean, my father ended up on a ship somewhere off Japan.

After the war ended, my father remained in Japan until 1947, before returning to the United States. I'm not sure if he was still in the Navy during that time. When he came home, he returned to work on the farm, but life was different. His family was still very upset about his engagement, to my mother. It apparently became clear, that life on the farm wasn't going to get any better. So my mother and father set a date to be married and rented a small apartment in the center of town. My father left the farm and took a job in a local factory. When they got married, I have been told that, most of my father's family did not attend. Despite my mother's family being upset with her choice of husband, they did attend, and her father did walk her down the aisle.

When we were very young children, I was maybe between six and nine-years-old, I remember my father taking my brothers and I to the farm, where he grew up. It was still being run as a moderate-sized dairy farm, by his father and uncle. My father's uncle had four or five kids, all much older than us, and they all worked at the farm. Even though the farm had an automatic milking machine, for some reason, my father felt that we should know how to milk a cow the old fashion way. The way he had to do it when he was young and working there. Growing up to milk cows was not something I would have looked forward to, I did not enjoy it. The milk was then taken from the cows to a collection tank in the barn and then pumped to the milk house across the street from the barn. The milk house had three large holding tanks, for the milk. Every day, a large tanker truck would come and empty the holding tanks. When the tanks were emptied they had to be cleaned, thoroughly. Someone would get into a tank, with what looked like a power washer. The machine was actually a steam gun and that's how they cleaned the tanks. While we were there, we would visit with my grandfather. My grandmother had died in 1938. We went to the farm maybe three or four times, over a period of a couple of years. My mother never came with us. After that, I don't remember having any more contact with my father's side of the family.

My mother, Caitlyn, 'Lynn' to most of her friends, was born in 1930, in the upper Ohio River Valley. Both her father and mother were born in Ireland and came to this country at a young age. Although very intelligent, my mother did not go to college. She was the only one of four siblings, and four half siblings, not to attend. Her mother died giving birth to her fourth child. Now a single parent, my mother's father needed someone to look after the other children. That someone was my mother. After some years had passed, her father got married again and had four more children. As a result of that, I have an uncle that is younger than I am. I refuse to call him 'uncle'.

My mother had some, well let's call them little quirks, about how Christmas was to be handled in my house. First came the tree, always real. Even after the fake ones started to come out. The tree was shopped for and purchased about one week before Christmas. It was placed on a stand, in the corner of the living room. Once a day, every day until the afternoon of Christmas Eve, the tree was examined and turned until the best side was facing out into the room. Then, on Christmas Eve, we would start to decorate it; all of us except my father. His job was to drink, dig the decorations out of storage, maybe drink a little more and watch us do the work. In the end, it was always up to him to place the lighted star topper, on top of the tree. Before we could get to that point, the first thing to go onto the tree were the lights; the big ones, the kind that got so hot, if you touched one, it would take all of the skin off whatever part you touched it with. And there had to be lots of lights; many, many strings. After the lights came the glass balls and ornaments. Some of the glass balls were from my mother's childhood. Break one of those and see just how merry Christmas was going to be. It seemed like hundreds of balls and ornaments were placed on that tree.

Then came the garland; big, unruly, long strings of fuzzy, multi-colored cellophane rope. That always had to be placed on the tree, starting at the top, wrapping around the tree to the bottom. Now, depending on how long the decorating to that point had taken, my mother may have had to take two or three smoke breaks and had at least one or two beverages. After the garland came the icicles. I don't know if they still sell them, but icicles were bright silver colored cellophane strands; very thin and about 1/8 of an inch wide and, maybe, eighteen inches long. Most of them were salvaged from my mother's childhood, and were twisted, wrinkled, and had lost most of their luster. According to my mother, each icicle strand was to be placed on the tree, one at a time, and carefully arranged. Apparently that process did not have to be completed on Christmas Eve. My mother would continue to add icicles, and any other decoration she felt the tree was lacking, well after Christmas.

Even if we had not been to church more than a couple of times a year, Midnight Mass on Christmas Eve was not to be missed. Getting cleaned up and dressed for church would often interrupt the tree decorating. After Midnight Mass, my grandparents, on my mother's side, would usually come to our house with their kids, for Christmas Eve dinner. All of the grown-ups would sit at the dining room table and the kids all sat at the kitchen table. The dinners would not take long. Santa was coming and the grandparents had to get their kids home, and we had to go to bed so he didn't skip our house. My parents were generally pretty generous with their gift giving to us. However, whether a gift came from Santa or my parents, if it was wrapped, the paper had to be very carefully removed, folded and saved for reuse the next year. If there was a bow involved, that too had to be saved for future use. Don't even think about ripping the paper or ruining a bow, which would cause an instant mood change, not for the better, for most of the rest of the day.

After Christmas, the tree stood in the corner of the room. My mother would sometimes add some little extra decoration to it, as she passed by. On the day after New Year's Day, the tree had to come down even if she was still putting stuff on it. Now, to un-decorate the tree was a major ordeal. First all of the icicles had to be removed, one at a time, and placed in their original package. That process alone would take several hours, but it had to be done that way. My mother was not going to go out each year and spend 55 cents, or whatever little amount they cost, for new ones. All of the garlands then had to be removed and, somehow, stored so as not to ruin the fuzziness of them. The glass balls and ornaments were carefully placed in the original boxes, saved from my mother's childhood. Most of them were falling apart and had been taped together so many times that there was just no helping them anymore. The lights were then removed, wound in some sort of circle, stuffed in the storage box with the rest of the stuff and put away until next year. The tree was always taken into the forest and left to return to the earth.

When my parents felt we were old enough to be left on our own after school, and all day in the summer, my mother went to work. Even though she had not gone to college, through her efforts, she got an entry level job at a large national insurance company. It didn't seem to take long for her to work her way up, to a very high position in the department where she worked. She later transferred to better positions in other departments. She did very well at that company and remained there until she retired. Even with my mother working, the tension between my mother and father continued. I wonder, if some of that was caused by their two families being at odds; which remained throughout my parent's entire lives. Or maybe it was just that English and Irish really don't mix.

Chapter Seven
The First Job and the Bank Job

Okay then, now that you have met the family, let's continue with the story they have to tell. Well the story I have to tell, but they are all going to contribute to it.

As you know, I graduated in 1971. After that, I did take the job with the construction company, building low income housing in all those towns so very far from my home. Now having all that traveling to do, I was going to need very reliable transportation. So, being young and well paid, I decided it had to be a new car. The natural choice then had to be a brand-new Mustang with a very large, very fast, motor. Of course, to make it go fast, you need to feed it, a lot. As it turned out, this was a very hungry horse. If I was careful, and didn't play with it too much, I could squeeze about eight mpg out of my new ride. With all of the work being so far from home, I would start out in the morning, with a full tank of premium gas; which was about 30 cents per gallon at the time. After arriving, and working all day, I then had to fill the gas tank to get back home. When I got home, I would have to fill the tank again, to be ready for the next day. I was getting paid well, but my horse was eating too much of my money.

I made a few friends in my time working for that company. One of the guys could have been Art Garfunkel's twin brother (I know, some of you are saying, "Who the hell is Art Garfunkel?" Google him). One of the better friends I made, Keith, lived sort of on the way to work. It was a short detour from my normal route, so I would sometimes go to his house and pick him up, or leave my car and ride with him. Keith told me that he was a member of a NASCAR Modified race car pit crew. The car he worked on, raced on Saturday nights, at a local one half mile paved oval track. I asked him if he had ever driven the car. His NASCAR license was for pit crew only, and did not allow him to drive. He was always trying to get me to go and watch the races. I asked how fast the cars can go on that track. He said because of the short length and very low banked turns, he thought the top speeds were around 115 mph. Maybe a little more with a really good handling car. I told him I might go if I could get into the pit area to see the car, and talk to the driver.

Keith was also fascinated with my new Mustang. I told him I had driven the car at speeds up to 125 mph. At 128 mph, the front of the car would start to come up off the ground. While the car was capable of a little more speed, flipping the car over was not worth the speed. While I did like the car very much, I found the aerodynamics lacking at high speeds. Keith said to me, while having a conversation about speed and racing, on the way home from work one day, "I don't believe this car can go that fast, and I think you're too much of a pussy to go that fast!" While I didn't really care if he believed the car could go that fast, he called me a 'pussy'. There was a section of road coming up in about three or four miles, which I knew had a gentle sweeping turn leading to a long straight section, ending in another gentle curve. As I approached the turn leading to the straight road, I slowed the car a bit and down shifted to third. I could see Keith look at me out of the corner of my eye. Now entering the middle of the turn, I down shifted into second gear and slammed the gas pedal to the floor. As the car bolted forward, I took a quick look at Keith, and then at the tach: time to shift to third. Another look at Keith, who had no color left in his face. Time to go to fourth gear. A quick look at the speedometer showed just above 115 mph. I told Keith to look at the speed, but he was frozen, mouth open, eyes bugging out of his face and still had no color. With the corner fast approaching, I let the speed come down some on its own. Just before entering the turn, I gently applied the brakes. I took the car through the turn, maybe just a little too fast, but just fast enough to push Keith into the side of the car. Keith never called me a 'pussy' when it came to speed or driving again. Off and on, I did go and watch Keith's friend race. It was okay, but I wanted to watch cars go faster.

After working for the company for about a year and a half, I left to take a job with a local contractor. Tobias, my new boss, built the occasional new house, but did more additions and renovation work. The main point here is, that all of the work was local. There was one other person working for Tobias. His name, I think, was Scott. We always called him Scott, but in a little while you will read about his name being called into question by a police officer. Before we get to that, there was a second person working for Tobias, but he would leave in a few weeks. His name was John. He was married, and his wife's name was Danny; Danielle, I suppose. John and Danny, like Tobias and Scott, were motorcycle people. Danny had lost the lower half of her right leg in a motorcycle accident. She had a prosthetic leg and seemed quite comfortable with it. They were moving to Tennessee or Kentucky, or somewhere in that area.

When moving day arrived, Tobias enlisted Scott and me to help with the moving of stuff and loading the truck. They lived in a second-floor apartment, in a large commercial block, in the center of their town. Danny and I were to stay at the truck, and do the loading, as the others brought stuff down to us. At one point, with the loading just about complete, all of us, except for John, were standing at the back of the truck. Suddenly we heard an unbelievable racket and rumbling coming from the second floor. As I tuned to look up the stairs, I saw John, on his motorcycle, riding down the stairs. I looked at Danny, and she said with almost no expression, "He had to get the bike ready for the trip. We don't have a garage, so the next best option, in John's mind, was the living room." The thought then came to mind, if he rode the bike down the stairs, he must have ridden it up the stairs first. I would have loved to have been there for that. After a quick check of the cargo, and some goodbyes, they left. John took the lead on his bike, and Danny followed in the truck. I don't know if they kept in touch with Tobias or Scott. Nobody ever mentioned them.

Working for that first contractor, and doing all that traveling, I never really had time for any kind of social life. I would quickly find that an added bonus of working locally, was that it gave me the time I needed to have some sort of social life. I met some local girls and started dating. I was still living at home, with my parents, at the time. I was the only one left there with them. Kevin was now married, and David was off to one college or another; he seemed to change schools frequently. I met a girl, about the same age as me, who seemed to be a good fit for me and my mother liked her very much. Even though she was well liked by my mother, and I think my father as well, my working and dating seemed to cause some added friction in the house. At the age of eighteen, headed for nineteen, my parents still wanted me home too early for a date to even get started. I did not date her for very long. It was also about that time when Sarah's family, along with her uncle and cousins, unexpectedly moved from the area. Her mother never said anything to mine about the move. One day they were all there, and the next they were all gone. My mother was upset, distraught, wondering what could have happened. She never heard from Sarah's mother again.

Early in 1973, I met the girl that would become my first wife. Yes, I said 'first' (Keep reading). Her name was Rachel. She was five-feet eight-inches tall, had jet black, very curly hair, brown eyes with a pretty face, and had a very well-proportioned body. She had a very clear and smooth, deep mocha complexion, and was about a year younger than me. She came from what seemed to be a very nice mixed-race family, from a small town in CT. We began dating and spending as much time together as possible. While dating Rachel, I continued to work with Tobias and Scott. Both of them were married and Scott's wife took an immediate liking to Rachel. She and I would spend a lot of time at Scott's house, on weekends and after work. Scott began spending less time there. In the late spring of 1973, Tobias took a job renovating a barn into an in-law apartment for a local bank manager. Scott asked Tobias if he could live in the barn while we worked on it. Tobias said no. Scott moved out of the house, I don't know where he was living, but he continued to work with us. He seemed to change, became a little distant and less pleasant to be around.

The barn we were renovating, was about 20 miles from my house. Sometimes I would take my car to the job and sometimes, because I had to go past Tobias's house, I would leave my car there and ride with him. In either case, Scott was almost always there when we got there. I think he was living somewhere very close by. Now, riding in Tobias's van was always a treat. The van, a retired mid-1960-something telephone line truck, was not in good shape. As was typical back then, the floor behind the rear wheels was rotted out, with holes in it. The motor was the standard fleet economy model and very tired. It had a three-speed shift on the column that occasionally hung up between gears. The rear doors would sometimes open if you hit a good bump. This was a fine machine indeed. He had boxes, along the side, for small tools so they would not fall out of a hole or the back doors.

When the weather was nice, Tobias, Scott, and I would pile into the mighty van and go to the center of the town, to sit and watch the people while we ate lunch. Now, to get to the center of the town, there was a very long, steep hill that we had to go down. That would, of course, mean that we also had to go back up that same hill to get back to work. Remember this is the mighty 'Tobias Van' we're talking about. The center of this town was small, but busy. There was a large church and, what I think was, a moderate sized all-boys school on one side of the street. That side had perpendicular parking all along it. The other side had a diner, bank, small hardware store, a laundry mat and a small bakery. After sitting in the van eating our lunches for a few days, Scott said something about the fact that we had parked in front of the bank every day. Maybe two or three minutes later, we could see the light bar on top of a police cruiser, cutting slowly across the back of the bank's parking lot. The cruiser came to a stop, still hidden behind other cars in the lot. Then to our shock and surprise, the light bar lit up and the car came through the parking lot, headed right at us. As that was happening, another cruiser came at us from down the street to the left of us and another one from the right. All three cruisers came to rest, blocking our escape. The parking lot cruiser had two police officers in it. We'll call them, Barney Fife numbers One and Two. Each of the other cruisers had one officer in them; we'll call them, Barney Three and Four. All of the Barney's got out and stood behind the doors of the cars. They all had their guns drawn, and pointed right at us. I still think their bullets were in their pockets. Even though Barney One was close enough to talk to us in a normal voice, he chose to key up the PA system in the car.

When Barney One ordered all of us out of the van, over the PA system, it was so loud that it echoed in the van. Tobias got out the driver's side door, hands held up and palms open. I stepped out the side cargo door, also with hands held up and palms open. Scott didn't move. Barney One, clearly a little anxious now, repeated his command. Tobias also yelled at Scott to get out. When Scott got out of the van, the Barneys all moved in a little closer, guns still pointed at us. Barney One asked for ID's from all of us, Tobias and I quickly gave up our driver's licenses, and then after more prodding Scott finally gave up his. While Barney One took our licenses back to his cruiser to check them, the other officers had us standing in front of the van, still with our hands up; guns still on us. I couldn't help noticing the people in the bank were all standing staring, and watching. After a while, Barney One came back to the van and handed Tobias and me our licenses. He then stood directly in front of 'Scott', just a little too close, and said, "Scott Allen Pierce, have you ever been arrested before?"

Scott took a few seconds before giving his answer. "No sir, not under that name."

He said. "How would you like to try Allen Pierce?" the officer shot back.

Scott, Allen, whoever he was, said, "Yup, that one works, but that was a long time ago." Barney One asked why the use of the name 'Scott' now? The reply was simply, "Because it is my real first name, always has been."

Barney One gave Scott/Allen his license back. After moving over to center himself with the three of us, Barney asked what we had been doing there for the past three days. Tobias decided to speak for all of us. He explained about the renovation job, up the giant hill, and gave the police the contact info for the homeowner. He then told them, that we were simply coming to the center of their beautiful, little town to watch the people as we ate our lunch. Barney One made note that we had been parked in front of the bank every day. Tobias countered with, "We take whatever parking space is open." The Barneys got together in a tight huddle, and after a few minutes, came back and told us to get in the van; go back to the job site, and don't let them see us in town again.

As the police cars moved out of the way, Tobias eased the van out on the road, and headed back to the job. The two police cars with one Barney each, left to go harass some other poor souls. Barneys One and Two, took up a position about three or four car lengths behind the van, and made it clear they would be following us. Normally, this would not have been an issue, but remember, this is the 'Tobias van' we're talking about. And we have a very long, very steep hill to climb ahead of us. The past couple of days Tobias would wind up the van, to maybe 45, or 50 mph as we approached the hill. The speed limit in the area was 35. By doing that, he was able to get the van over the top of the hill, in first gear, moving just enough to say it's moving. With the police right behind us, ten or 15 mph over the speed limit was not going to be an option.

The three of us, looking at each other, knowing the van was not going to make it over the hill, began to laugh, a little at first. But as the van entered the bottom of the hill, and began to slow, we all started to laugh a little harder. I looked out the back windows, and saw the police car had closed to about two to three car lengths behind us. Moving slower now, as the van made a gallant effort to ascend the mighty hill, she began to shudder and vibrate. Laughing very hard now, Tobias down shifted to second gear. The van surged forward for a few seconds, and then slowed right back down again. The van started to shudder and vibrate again. Now, with the three of us laughing so hard that Tobias can no longer control the van, small pieces and parts began falling out the holes in the floor. The police car dropped back a bit, and Tobias attempted to shift to first gear. As he was doing this, Tobias unfortunately ran the van into the curb at the side of the road. With a brief shudder, the van came to a complete stop and the back doors flew open. Both of them!

Through my tears of laughter, I saw both Barneys disappear below the dashboard of their car. The car was maybe three car lengths back. The light bar lit up again, and the siren made one sickly little burp. The Barneys again stepped out of the car, guns drawn, and stood behind the car doors. As the three of us are now all laughing like lunatics, the PA system of the police car again keyed up. "Everybody out of the van, NOW!" was the command from Barney One. This time, Scott and I got out. Tobias could not get out of the van. While Barney Two keeps Scott and I covered, One cautiously approached the side door to again order Tobias out of the van. Tobias, still laughing very hard, explained to the officer that if he got out of the van, the only thing keeping the van from rolling back down the hill would be the front of his police car. So far, these police officers had not been able to find any humor at all, in any of this (I don't understand it).

Scott and I were ordered to go and retrieve the pieces and parts that had fallen out of the van. After doing so, we were then told to store them securely in the van, close the rear doors and properly secure the doors. I was able to find a small piece of rope, and tied the door handles together to keep the doors from opening. Satisfied that everything was in order, the police told us to, "Get in the van, and get that piece of shit off this hill." Scott, as calmly as possible, explained that the only way that piece of shit was going over the top of the hill, was either being pushed or pulled. He suggested the police use their car to help us with this, since we didn't have money for a tow truck. No, that was not going to be a possibility, and again, no sense of humor. The next only option was going to be for Scott and me to push, as Tobias drove the van. The officers did not like this option either. Scott did a great job of convincing them that it was a good option, as we had used it before. With not much choice, the officers finally agreed, and got into their car and backed it off just a bit. Tobias let the van roll back from the curb into the street. Scott and I took up our places, one at each rear corner of the van, and with a pathetic moan the van began to move up the hill. Once over the top of the hill, Tobias stopped and Scott and I got in. With the police car still following us, we headed for the job site.

When we arrived at the barn, Tobias pulled the van up close to the front door. The police car was sitting on the side of the road, maybe 50 feet from the barn. We all stayed in the van for two or three minutes, and then threw the doors open and ran into the barn. The police car did not move. Tobias found a piece of cardboard about two by three feet, and with a large maker, and in very bold print, wrote 'The hide out' on it. He opened the front door just enough to slide the sign out, and let it lean against the front of the barn. With that, the car with the two humorless police officers in it, closed to within a few feet of the front of the barn. With guns in hand, an officer pounded on the door and ordered us to let them in. Once inside, as we were again held at gun point, one of the officers made a sweep of the building. I'm not sure what he thought he was going to find, but announced that the building was secure. Tobias tried to explain the humor of the situation. The policemen still couldn't find it. After giving us a very stern warning, about the perils of 'playing' with the police, they left. The next day the homeowner was waiting for us at the barn. While he did admit to seeing some humor in the situation, he too said, "Don't do anything like that again."

That night I replayed the incident to Rachel. Her only reply was, "So did you get arrested or not?" I should have known she was going to be trouble, right at that moment. We finished the job without further incident. After finishing the job, Scott stopped working for Tobias. I don't know where he went from there. Scott's wife moved to another state and I never heard from either of them again.

Chapter Eight
The First Wife, and Isabell

Tobias and I continued to work together, doing renovations and small additions. Still living at home with my parents, they seemed to slip back to their old habits a little. I don't think either one of them really approved of my new girlfriend. Things were uncomfortable at home, and so feeling a little trapped, and in a rush to get out of there, Rachel and I got engaged and set a date for the wedding. The news of that sent my parents into a downward spiral, and the wedding date couldn't come fast enough for me. Shortly before the wedding date, June of 1974, we rented an apartment in the same town John and Danny had lived. I was twenty, and Rachel had just turned nineteen. Was I making the same mistake my brother, Kevin, had made? Rachel moved into the apartment at the time we rented it, and I stayed with my parents until the wedding. When I met Rachel, I also met her best friend, Isabell. The two of them seemed to spend a lot of time together, more than I thought was normal. Isabell's family owned and operated a hardware store a couple of towns over, and she worked for them. She apparently had very flexible hours because she seemed to always be at the apartment.

I liked Isabell. She was a bit of a wild child, but very smart, funny and lots of fun to be around. She was also very easy to look at! She was about five feet tall, maybe a little less, with long, red hair and a very pretty face. She had bright green, sexy eyes; the sort of eyes that, when you looked at them, they sucked you right in. She also had a very athletic but not skinny body. Because she always wore loose, unflattering clothes, it was hard to get very detailed about her body (There will, however, be a time when I can, and maybe I will get a little more detailed). Isabell's parents came from some Eastern European country, maybe even Russia. I never asked. They had heavy accents and were sometimes hard to understand. While 'Izzy', as she preferred to be called, was born in the United States, she too had an accent. Her accent was much lighter than her parents, and sounded sort of sexy coming from her. Sometimes you really had to listen to find it, but it was worth it. Rachel worked for a small business in the town where we rented the apartment, but quit her job when she moved into the apartment. That, of course, gave the two of them even more time to spend together.

Our wedding day finally arrived. We were married in a local church and the reception was held at a small restaurant, not far from the church. I remember, it was a very windy day. My new wife got out of the car at the restaurant and, as she started to walk along the cobblestone path to the reception hall, her wedding gown became tangled in a bush. In our efforts to free her, the gown became badly torn. As a result of the tear, her gown was now not so much a gown as it was a mid-calf length dress. David served as my best man. Unfortunately, his love for wine got the best of him very early on at the reception. He was no longer capable of performing his best man duties, so Kevin, had to fill in for him. At the end of the day, Rachel and I went back to our apartment for the night. The following morning, we headed for Niagara Falls, our honeymoon. It was one week of driving, more than sightseeing, or at least so it seemed. We took the 'Maid of the Mist' ride at the base of falls and did some shopping on both sides of the boarder. There really wasn't much else to do.

When we returned home, we began to talk about Rachel going back to work. She didn't like the idea, but we needed more than just my income. She put some applications in at several local businesses and was hired as a secretary, at a local factory. That job lasted, all of maybe, two weeks and then she quit. After another couple of weeks with her not working, Tobias told me he was going out of business. I was going to be without a job. He said he knew some people and would try to help me get a new job. The day he told me he was going out of business, I left work in the middle of the afternoon, and went home. As I pulled into the parking lot of the apartment, I recognized a truck that shouldn't have been there. The truck belonged to one of Rachel's old boyfriends. Our apartment was on the second floor, with an exterior door serving just our apartment. Just before I got to the door, it swung open, and out came the 'ex'. He walked past me with a smile, and simply nodded on his way by. When I entered the apartment, I may have closed the door a bit harder than normal. The sound of the door closing brought Rachel running down the hall from the bedroom end of the apartment. She was wearing a pair of semi-shear panties and a sleeveless t-shirt that she had cut off just below her breasts. That was typical bedtime attire for her back then. She also had a very big smile on her face, as if the sound of the door closing would mean the return of her 'ex' for round two. When she saw me standing there, she stopped in her tracks, lost the smile completely and said, "What are you doing here?"

I told her, "I live here."

And she came back with, "Well, yeah, but not right now."

I didn't bother to ask if the 'ex' had been there. I already knew the answer to that. I wanted to hear why he had been there. I mean, except for the obvious reason, which I knew she wasn't going into. She said there was a plumbing problem with the kitchen sink and didn't know who else to call. Knowing that the 'ex' was not a plumber, I said, "If there was a problem with the apartment's plumbing, maybe you should have tried calling a plumber." During the long and difficult conversation that followed, none of which included my being out of work, she informed me that she thought it would be fun to have an open marriage. A what? What the hell was an open marriage? I had never heard of that. The way she explained it was, we would be married to each other but still be dating other people. Well I guess the obvious question would then have to be, "What was the point of being married?" She said we would still be living together like normal married people, but when the urge struck either one of us, we would be allowed to have sex with other people. I told her that I didn't think that was going to work for me. That was apparently not the answer she was looking for and that put an end to the conversation. All conversation, for the rest of the night.

A few days later, Tobias came through for me with an interview at a local cabinet shop. I went to talk to the owner and, with a good recommendation from Tobias, got the job. The shop made only one product; Formica covered plywood cabinets. It wasn't exciting work, but it was a job that paid a decent wage. Rachel not working, and still not trying very hard to get a job, was really starting to bother me. The fact that we needed more than just my income was bad enough; but knowing the potential of what was going on at home, while I was at work, added an enormous amount of stress to the mix. One day, I got a chance to speak to Izzy about it. She said that Rachel had never been very motivated about working. As for the sex thing, she was not going to get into that, after all Rachel was her friend. Over time, my parents seemed to warm up to Rachel, at least a little. So, without many options left, I spoke to my mother about the work issue and in less than a week, Rachel had a job at the same company that my mother worked at. They would be working in different departments, but Rachel would be working.

It didn't take long for Rachel to start to enjoy her job. She even began to look forward to going every day. With both of us working, we were able to move out of the apartment, into a rented three-bedroom house. The house was back in the same town where I had grown up. It was a small house with one large bedroom, two smaller bedrooms and a bathroom, on the second floor. The first floor consisted of a kitchen, with a side entrance from the driveway, a dining room, and a small living room. Off the back of the kitchen was a small laundry/mud room, with a door to the back yard. The house was on a corner lot, with the front door facing the smaller side street. There was a six-foot deep porch that ran across the front of the house, and the front door was a six-foot wide double door. The house was a somewhat simplified version of a Queen Ann Victorian, with 'fish scale' shingle siding in the front gable, and some of the typical gingerbread trim. The driveway entered from the side street, approximately 30 feet past the house. That gave us a nice wide, open, flat yard on that side of the house. The side street was the more private side as well. The lot next to the driveway entrance was vacant with just a few small trees on it. The house wasn't really ours, but I loved the house, and I loved living there. Being back in town also gave me more opportunity to join the, still being played, pick-up baseball and football games at the school yard and also to get together with some old friends.

The pick-up games were still being well attended. Most of the participants were the same old group that had been playing from years before. This posed what we considered a minor problem. The school officials, however, saw it as a much larger one. If you stood at home plate on the ball field, and followed the third base line, the left field ended approximately 330 feet away, with a ten-foot-high chain link fence. The field was built that way so that the football field would run from the first base line, into left field and stop about 30 feet before the fence. The problem was center and right field. The right field ended about 280 feet from home plate, with the back wall of the school. The back wall of the school was full of windows. Center field was marked by a three-and-a-half-foot high snow fence, the deepest point from home plate being just under 300 feet. Beyond the snow fence was the parking lot. Now that we were older, bigger and stronger, the windows in the back wall of the school didn't stand a chance. And any cars parked too close to the center field fence were equally at risk. We broke a few windows in the school and dented a few cars. After not much of a discussion with school officials, it was decided that softball was to be the game of the future. The occasional broken window and dented car still happened. The ball field no longer remains at the school yard. It has been moved to a 'Recreational Park', on land donated to the town, with no buildings on it.

Late one sunny Saturday afternoon, as I returned home from playing one of those fun filled pick up ball games with friends from town; I noticed a strange car parked in the vacant lot. When I went into the house I heard some sort of shuffling sounds coming from the second floor. I called to Rachel, and she came down the stairs, and went into the living room. She called to me to come in there with her. When I went into the living room, two thoughts came to mind. The first was tiny shorts and a tank top, which she had on inside out. And the second thought was that from that room I couldn't see the stairs or the vacant lot next to the driveway. Rachel did her best to keep me in that room as long as possible. She stood in front of me, hugging me and proclaimed her happiness that I was finally home. While she was doing that, I could hear some muffled sounds coming from the stairs, and then from the side door area of the house. When I was able to break away from her I went to a side window to look for the car in the vacant lot. I got there just in time to see it pulling out on to the street, and drive away. Rachel continued to swear there hadn't been anyone in the house.

When I started working at the cabinet shop, in 1974, there were four employees, counting me. Now in mid-1975, there were nine, and I had worked my way into being the shop foreman. We had also expanded the product line, to include plexiglass products and award plaques, for a marketing company in Boston. The owner of the company and I got along very well, and I was left to run the day to day operations as I saw fit. I, however, could see a small problem coming. My wife and I had just moved about eight miles east, and with the business growing as it was, it was being moved about 16 miles west. I had given up the very hungry Mustang when I got married, for a more sensible car, but still, I was going to be traveling about 24 miles to work each day. Having to open the shop at seven o'clock, six days a week, meant getting up and leaving the house before my wife was even out of bed. The significance of that was, I didn't know if my wife was going to work every day or not. It turned out to be 'not'. I was able to keep tabs on my wife's activities through the sister of a woman that worked with my mother.

Chapter Nine
Betty and Steve, Karen and Jim

I'm going to try to explain who my 'spy' was, and how she came to be. This gets a little muddy here, but pay attention. All of these characters will come back later, and play important parts in the story. My mother had a friend, Betty, who worked in the same department as my mother. I met Karen, Betty's friend, before I got married and we were very close friends, nothing more than that (In 1980 it would become more than that, but let's not skip ahead of the story). Karen got a job at the same Insurance Company as Betty, Rachel, and my mother. Shortly after starting there, she transferred to the same department where my wife worked. Now, Betty, Karen's older friend, was married to Steve, and Karen was married to Jim, Steve's best friend. Jim worked at the cabinet shop I worked in. All of us, the three couples, were very good friends. After transferring to my wife's department, Karen was able to keep very close tabs on my wife. The trick to getting all this information on my wife's activities, was to do it, of course, without Izzy knowing about it. Yes, Izzy is still very much in the picture. Through Karen I was able to find out, that in the last half of 1975, my wife had been sent home from work, on more than one occasion, for showing up dressed inappropriately. She had been told it was not proper office wear, but as Karen believed, she was also having an affair with her boss, so she never got fired or suspended. It seems Rachel had not given up on the open marriage thing after all.

Since Betty, Steve, Karen and Jim are all going to play important roles a little later, let's take some time to talk about them now. Betty, approximately eight-years older than me, was sort of an 'Olive Oil' type girl. She was about six feet tall, very thin, a rather plain face, with dark straight hair. Quite by accident, I can also say she had very small, but very nice breasts (An accidental displacement of her bikini top at the beach). She had a good personality, a good and quick sense of humor, and was fun to be around. Betty, like Karen enjoyed racket ball and tennis. I played both games with each of them many times. The three of us even joined a racket ball league in the 80s, but again, let's not jump ahead. Steve, Betty's husband, was about the same age and height as Betty. He had thinning, light hair and a very muscular build. He had a rugged, handsome look. And, no, don't try to read anything into that. At the time I met him, he was working in a local factory, a four-day shift, working 36 hours and getting paid for 40. There was a very laid-back feel about him, with a very good sense of humor. He was great fun to be around, and just made you feel as if life was so much better than whatever crap you were going through at the time. Steve was a bit of a heavy drinker, but always a happy drunk. He had an old Ford pickup truck that needed body work. I helped him patch up the holes and get it ready for paint. One day, I stopped at Karen's house and there was Steve, across the street at his house, painting his truck; using a roller with, what I think was, house paint. It was an ugly color brown, and when asked about it, he said he was going to call the truck 'His shit-brindle-brown-bile.' (An appropriate name, I thought).

Karen, Betty's younger friend, was one year younger than me. She was about six feet, six inches tall; with light brown, very curly hair. Karen, unlike Betty, had a very shapely and well-developed body. She was very athletic and played lots of sports, in high school. She went to a different school than I did. I met her in the very early 70s, through my mother and Betty, and we became very close friends; as I have said, just friends. We always kept in touch on the phone or would get together to play racket ball or tennis. We continued to do that even after each of us were married. She wasn't much of a drinker, until she got married. Like Betty, she had a good sense of humor, but was a bit more of a serious person. She was very intelligent, never went to college, but made very good career choices throughout her life. Jim, Steve's best friend and Karen's husband, was about six feet tall. He had a full head of light brown hair. Like Steve, he had a strong muscular build. When he got married to Karen he was working in a local factory. We had known each other for many years. We played Little League and Babe Ruth Baseball together. He was one year younger than me, so even though we were in the same school, we weren't in any classes together. Jim and I got along very well and were good friends since, we met, playing Little League baseball together. It wasn't until late 1976 that Jim came to work in the cabinet shop with me. I put him to work assembling the wood cabinets. He was good at his job and seemed to enjoy it. He got along well with all of the other employees. Since I had to go past Jim and Karen's house on my way to work, I would sometimes stop and give him a ride to work. Karen would have to come and get him at the end of the day. I almost never left the shop at the same time that everybody else did.

Okay, with those introductions out of the way, let's continue with the story. As you can imagine, at the end of 1975 and early 1976, things were not good at my house. I began taking side jobs; building kitchen cabinets, and doing some interior van conversions. I was allowed to do this at the shop, as long as I kept track of the materials I used and paid for them. I made very good money with the side jobs, but more important was the fact that it kept me out of the house. I worked 7:00 am to 4:00 pm at my regular job, and then would stay at the shop often until 9:30 pm or 10:00 pm; working, doing side stuff. On Saturdays, I worked from 7:00 am to noon at my regular job, and would work on side stuff until 5:00 pm, or so. Jim, Karen's husband, was not a night person. He was usually in bed by 9:00 pm or 9:30 pm, every night. Karen, on the other hand, was always up until midnight or a little beyond. Betty, Karen's friend, was the same way. Steve, Jim's best friend was up until 11:00 pm most nights. With the two couples living directly across the street from each other, the girls visited often. As I said, on my way to and from the shop, I had to pass by their houses, so I would occasionally stop at Karen's house on my way home. Betty, and sometimes even Steve, would come over and all of us would sit around the kitchen table; having a few drinks and visiting. These visits were when Karen would fill me in on the most recent activities of my wife. Betty, Steve, and I became very close friends during this time, not as close as Karen was, but very good friends.

Chapter Ten
A Car, Rachel, Izzy and Sex

Rachel's activities seemed to slow down during the early part of 1976. Karen was pretty sure that if there was an affair with her boss, it had ended and she was dressing properly for work. She was even showing up, almost every day. As the tension in our house eased a little, and having made some extra money, I started to do less of the side jobs. I took some of the extra money and bought a 1967 Mustang Fastback. It was in very good shape, for a ten-year-old car, back then. The bodies didn't last as long then, especially in the snow states, with the use of road salt in the winters. I ordered some Shelby body parts from an aftermarket catalogue; a hood, front air dam, side air scoops and a rear spoiler. I added those to my Mustang and did what little body repair work was needed, with the car at my house. Doing this meant that I was spending a lot more time at the house than normal. I also noticed that Izzy was spending what I thought was more time at the house than normal. Izzy always seemed to be drinking a bit more than she should, although she also seemed to be able to handle it well. She would sometimes come out in the yard and hang around the car while I was working on it.

About that same time, my boss had decided to expand the product line of the shop again. Before he made his final choice, he asked me if I knew anything about pattern making. I really didn't but said, "Sure, I can do that." He told me he had a chance to take over the manufacturing of a line of fiberglass body parts for cars, boats and custom van conversion parts. We were going to have to create our own patterns and molds, and wanted to be sure I would be able to handle that. After saying, "Sure, I can do that," he had a full-sized spray booth, complete with a heating system installed. He then added two fiberglass spray/chopper systems. I had never seen a fiberglass spray/chopper system before. I had some learning to do. Once we were completely set up to do the work, it began to flow in. I found myself making patterns for high top van roofs, light mounts, complete dash assemblies, with knock-outs for the gauges, and gull-wing style side compartment doors for vans. The work was easier than I had expected. I found that I could use plywood, plastic parts, body filler, bees wax and just about anything else I could get my hands on, to create a pattern. My boss hired a new employee, experienced with fiberglass lay-up work and the equipment, and we were in business. By that time there were fourteen employees working in the shop. This new work was added to my regular work duties, along with a nice bump in pay. It did mean a few more hours in the shop, before being able to do any of my own extra work, if I was going to do any.

Before the work on the body of my Mustang was complete, I took the car to a mechanic friend. He had his own auto repair shop, complete with a well-equipped machine shop. He was able to take the exhaust manifolds off the motor, grind the inner chambers and buff them a bit. That, along with a well-chosen muffler, gave the car a nice, smooth, mellow sound. Not that loud 'Rice Rocket' noise you hear on lots of the cars today. When I got the body work on my car completed, I took the car to the shop. I brought the car into the booth on a Friday evening, when no work was scheduled for the following Saturday morning. I worked almost around the clock, all weekend, only getting breaks while the paint was baking. Karen and Betty came to the shop and helped with the masking and prepping of the car. They came a couple more times to visit while I worked on the car. They brought me food and beverages, something Rachel never even would have thought of doing. When I was done, on Sunday night, Karen gave me a ride home. You could walk from their house to my house in about five minutes, so it was not as if it was out of her way. I had made arrangements with Jim to give me a ride to work the following morning. When I opened the shop on Monday morning, the car was still in the paint booth. It was now bright white, with Shelby blue stripes, and had four layers of clear coat finish baked on. The car was beautiful. All it needed now was the right set of wheels and tires to be finished.

In April, about the time I started working on the Mustang, the reason for Rachel's activities slowing down became clear. She told me she was two months pregnant. She also told me she had no intention of bringing our new child home to a rented house. We were going to have to buy a house before November. I knew as I was working on my Mustang, that in the end, I would have to sell it. But I wanted to finish it anyway, it would be worth much more when completed. Apparently as I was spending my time working at my job, and on my car, Rachel and Izzy were very busy working on something of their own. Rachel was planning to quit her job in July; I guess because she was pregnant, and didn't feel as if she could work and be pregnant at the same time. In the meantime, she had also not given up on the open marriage thing. She and Izzy had cooked up a plan, that she was sure would convince me of the benefits of having an open marriage.

On a Saturday evening in early June, of 1976, I was told that Izzy would be bringing her 'boyfriend' over for dinner and drinks, so I could meet him. Rachel, apparently, had already met him. I was surprised about the 'dinner evening' because in all the time I had known Izzy, I never saw her with a man. At the appointed time, Izzy and her 'boyfriend' showed up at the house. Dinner it would turn out, was nothing more than a few small appetizers and snacks. The evening was filled with liquor, lots of liquor, being almost forcefully fed, I noticed, to the 'boyfriend' and myself. Rachel and Izzy both spent lots of time making sure I got plenty of alcohol. At some point I began to question the motive behind the evening, Izzy wasn't spending a lot of time with her 'boyfriend'. As the evening wore on, and the liquor began to take the expected effect, Rachel leaned over to tell me, the plan was for me to have sex with Izzy. She then gave Izzy a nod, and

Izzy got up from her seat, took my hand and gave me a gentle tug. I, now being well liquored up, and Izzy being, well Izzy, went with her. We went to our bedroom, to the bed that Rachel and I slept in. Once in there, Izzy pushed me down to sit on the edge of the bed.

Izzy stood in front of me and very slowly, removed all of her clothes, except her panties. She had a very sexy body, more than I had ever imagined, given the type of clothes she always wore. Her very ample sized breasts were round, firm and maybe slightly larger than they should have been. Her nipples reminded me of oversized pencil erasers. They too were firm and very prominent. She was a little heavy, but she seemed to carry the extra weight well. Her legs looked smooth and strong, the kind you would expect a professional ice skater to have. She then came to me, removed my shirt, and pushed me onto my back on the bed. Izzy removed the rest of my clothes, slowly, the same way she had removed hers. But with me, she removed everything. As I laid on the bed, naked, she crawled up beside me. Izzy began to kiss me. I had never felt a kiss so passionate, and so full of love before. Rachel certainly had never kissed me like that. When Izzy kissed me, it was like she put her entire heart, soul and very being, into every second of that kiss. After kissing me for what seemed to be a very long time, she rolled over onto her back. She told me she wanted me to take her panties off, she made a point to tell me to do it slowly.

Laying on the bed in front of me, she opened her arms, and spread her legs, to beckon me onto her. She was beautiful and very sexy. I, being thoroughly liquored up and still knowing this was not right, was all too happy to comply. As I slid on top of her, and inside her, she let out a small cry and moan of pleasure. I felt her inner thighs clamp tightly against my hips, and her arms wrap tightly around my back. As I started to glide in and out of her, she began to move her hips. First in a sort of rocking, side to side motion, and then I think, in a more circular motion. I'm not completely sure of the motions, but I could tell she was using her feet to push on the bed to help make whatever the moves were. The motion was keeping perfect time with my rhythm. I had never felt anything like this before, certainly not with Rachel. Whatever she was doing, it was driving me crazy. As my rhythm began to get faster, her moans and the rhythm of her moves increased to follow mine. As I exploded inside her, she gave a gasp and a small cry of pleasure. Finished, and laying on top of her, I felt her legs wrap tightly around my back. She was holding on as if she thought I might disappear forever. As I was laying there she put her head beside mine, and said, "I have been waiting for this for a very long time."

Without thinking too much about it, I looked directly into her eyes and replied, "So have I, Izzy." I noticed, while looking very happy and content, she was crying.

About five seconds after saying that, I felt the sharp crack of a hand slap my ass. I was so shocked by the slap, that I tore myself from Izzy's grip, and rolled over onto my back. Standing next to the bed was Rachel, naked and smiling. I sat up on the edge of the bed and she said, "So, how was she?" Izzy giggled, maybe just a bit too loud.

I said, "Where's what's his name?"

"Him? Oh I just gave him a quick fuck and sent him home. I wanted to be up here with you guys. So how was she?" she asked again.

I decided to be honest and said, "She was amazing."

Rachel said, "I know," and then as I sat beside them, I watched Rachel and Izzy kiss each other, with the same passion Izzy had kissed me. If Rachel could kiss Izzy like that, why hasn't she ever kissed me like that? Then shocked, I sat and watched the two of them make love with great passion, love and caring for each other; as if I wasn't even there. I sat and looked at Rachel's face pressed tightly to Izzy's vagina, and listened to Izzy moan with delight. I felt Izzy reach up to pull my face down to hers to kiss me, but she lost her concentration to the orgasm Rachel was quickly bringing her to. As her moans became more frantic, she arched her back and pushed her head back so the entire upper part of her body was supported by her head. Then her entire body went stiff and silent for about four or five seconds. And then starting very low, and with increasing volume, a sound came out of Izzy that was, I think, un-Earthly, or at the very least inhuman. Then her entire body went completely limp. As I looked at Izzy's face, her eyes were closed with tears still coming out of them, but she had such a peaceful and content look on her. And I wondered if I was witnessing the look and sound of true and complete ecstasy.

Izzy got up and went home sometime during the night. The following morning, I got up with the previous night still vivid in my brain. I knew another long and difficult conversation between Rachel and me was going to have to happen. I started with, "Was last night all your plan, or did Izzy help come up with it?" They had worked it out together, I was told. The idea was, according to Rachel, that if I knew what Izzy was like in bed, and I knew I could have something like that whenever I wanted, well then maybe I would see that the idea of an open marriage wasn't so bad. I told Rachel that while Izzy was an amazing lover, better than I had ever had, Rachel's face darkened a bit, it was still wrong and if she was going to continue with the open marriage thing, it would be without me.

Chapter Eleven
Buy a House and Have a Child

I didn't see Izzy around the house much over the next couple of months. Not happy with the way things were going, but trying to hold it together, I sold my Mustang. I got almost $2,000 more than my total investment, so I guess that helped ease the pain of selling it. I started doing more side jobs again, to help with the house buying thing. Along with the side jobs, came more late-night visits with Karen, Betty, and sometimes Steve. Of course, more late-night visits meant more drinking with my friends. It was clear to everyone that I was not happy at home, but I felt again like I was trapped. Maybe, I thought, with the baby coming things might change (Hopefully for the better). We bought a small, five room house; about 12 miles east of the rental house. I never understood the need to buy a house, and leave that beautiful house with the mostly private yard. The rent was cheap, the location was a good one and it was about 12 miles closer to work than the new one. The new house had three small bedrooms on the second floor; a kitchen, living room and a bathroom, on the first floor. There was a washer and dryer hook up in the basement. The house was on a hill, with a very small flat area to the downhill side of it. There was a garage that had been converted to a workshop, without the garage door. The door had been removed, and a solid wall with a three foot wide door was put in its place.

Our first child was due in November, and we moved into the house in mid-October, 1976. About two weeks before Rachel's due date, the septic system failed. The system was located under that small flat area on the downhill side of the house. To repair it, meant digging the entire system up, removing all of the contaminated soil and replacing everything. This would be very expensive and very time consuming. Option two was to put a new system on the uphill side of the house. As we all know, shit runs downhill, so this option would require a pump system. More money spent. The third option was, for five hundred dollars and a small monthly fee, the town would hook us up to the city sewer system. They could have the work completed before the due date, and everything would be fine. It wasn't a difficult choice, the town got my five hundred dollars, and we got our septic problem fixed.

With the due date fast approaching, Izzy began spending more time with Rachel. Sometimes she would spend the night, as it was now about a 40-mile drive, one way, from Izzy's house. When the time finally arrived, Izzy and I took Rachel to the hospital. After a very long and hard labor, our first child was born, in November of 1976. I was in the delivery room with Rachel, and Izzy was in the waiting room like an expectant parent. Both Rachel and the baby were fine and healthy. After a couple of days, we were headed home with our new child. Rachel, however, was already showing signs of severe postpartum depression. Izzy stayed at our house for two days, to help me with both Rachel and the baby. I could only take a few days off from work and was going to have to get back. With Rachel's depression deepening, her mother suggested we move to her house for a week or so. She was not working at the time, and would be able to take care of the two of them while I was at work. One week turned into two. Rachel's depression only seemed to worsen almost by the day. She got to the point where she wouldn't get out of bed and didn't want to even see the baby. I asked Rachel's mom if Izzy had been around to help. The only answer I got was, "I haven't seen or heard from her since Rachel came here." Obviously she wasn't happy that Izzy didn't come around to help.

Five weeks after moving into Rachel's mother's house, I moved her and our baby back to our house. In all that time, Rachel had made no effort to improve her state of depression, and wanted little or nothing to do with her new child. Her mother was tired of trying, with Rachel not trying. She would come to the house during the day, as needed, only to help her. Rachel was going to have to be a mother now. Things got off to a rocky start, with Rachel calling her mother constantly to come over. Her mother on occasion would relay those calls to me at work. Izzy would come over once in a while, but it was too long a ride for her to make very often and still keep her job at the hardware store. Her parents were only going to put up with just so much as well. Rachel finally started to come around. She was calling her mother much less now. During all of this time, I had stopped doing side jobs again, and gave up the visits with Karen, Betty, and Steve. I guess I felt as if I should be home as much as possible to help with the baby. As Rachel began to get better and more confident, it seemed as if she would rather I wasn't there so much. I guess that was all right with me; I went back to the side jobs. Rachel became good friends with a couple of women in the neighborhood, and I think she was getting some help from them as well. Both of these women had very young children, and they all seemed to have fun getting together during the day while the husbands were at work.

We needed all of the money I was making on my regular and side jobs, just to meet all of those newly created living expenses. My side jobs were no longer side jobs, they were a second job. Of course, to help ease some of the stress of my new life, I went back to the late-night visits with my constant late-night friends. Some of the nights got very late, with lots of drinking involved. By the spring of 1977, I was not only doing my regular job, which had increased to 55 hours a week, along with the kitchen cabinets on the side, which had become very popular and were also keeping me busy; but I was also back to doing van conversions again. The van conversions were both interior and exterior, and getting the use of the paint booth was sometimes an issue. I was getting paid very well for all of the work I was doing, but it never seemed to be enough. Rachel always had a reason to be spending more than I could make. It seemed as if we always needed something for the house, the child, or the wife. I had to get a new truck for the cabinet work; using the company truck was all right with the owner, but I felt that it was becoming too often. Of course my getting a 'new' truck was out of the question, as far as Rachel was concerned. "Why should [I] spend money on something like that? Why couldn't [I] just get any old cheap piece of junk, as long as it runs?" I found a 1975 Chevy half-ton pickup that didn't look too bad, and seemed to run pretty well. Does anybody out there remember what happened to most of the mid 70s pickup trucks in the North East? That's right, the beds rotted and fell apart, and most of them got converted to rack body trucks. They became almost worthless. But yes indeed I had one, and within about a year of buying it, the bed started to rot apart (A fine investment, I told my wife).

I hadn't seen Izzy for a very long time now, and Rachel hadn't mentioned her. I think I might have actually missed her a bit. I asked Rachel if she had been in contact with her on the phone, and she said she had but not too much. I began to wonder if something had happened between them. They had always been very, very close. I know it was a long ride for Izzy to come to our house all the time, but there was no reason Rachel couldn't go to her once in a while. When the cabinet shop moved west a couple of years ago it wasn't too far from Izzy's parent's hardware store. I decided to take some extra time at lunch, one day, and go to the store to talk to Izzy. Her parents knew and liked me, and if the store wasn't too busy, it was all right for us to sit and visit for a bit. I asked Izzy what was going on between her and Rachel. She said things were still 'okay', but Izzy had found a real boyfriend. Apparently that didn't sit too well with Rachel. She had met him and did not like him. He was in the military and was going to be stationed at the base somewhere down south. Izzy's man had asked her to marry him and go with him. Rachel got mad at the news and Izzy said things had cooled off between them. She was hoping Rachel would still remain friends with her. She wanted Rachel to be a part of her wedding.

Chapter Twelve
And Another Child

In the summer of 1977, Izzy married her man. Rachel was her maid of honor and seemed to be really happy for her. The wedding was small, and the reception short. I don't remember if it was two or three days after the wedding, but it was about that time that Izzy's new hubby headed for his base down south. Izzy stayed back to finish taking care of a few things. Izzy left about three weeks after her husband did, and during that time I think she and Rachel got together only once, that I know of. That summer my parents sold their house, the 'fun' house we grew up in, and moved to a new house, one town to the West. The new house was at the top of a very steep, winding hill. I wasn't told of the move until after it was done. I guess they didn't need my help to move. Things between my parents and me had started to improve by that time. They enjoyed seeing and spending time with their new grandchild, fast approaching one year old now. My parents both now enjoyed seeing Rachel as well. She would often spend lots of time at their house on Saturdays, when I was working. On some Sundays, we would occasionally go over to their house for a large Sunday dinner. Kevin and his, soon to be, ex-wife would sometimes be there as well. After Kevin got married and left the house, his relationship with our mother dramatically improved. He never really got along with our father, right up until our father's death.

One night each month was grocery shopping night at my house. Now, to shop for food and all the other household necessities that go along with the food, once a month, was a very involved undertaking. First we had to get a babysitter, paid of course, and we had to plan on spending a very long time at the store. Naturally, we couldn't go to the store about half a mile from the house. No sir, we had to go to the store in the big city, 15 miles away. Picture it, a larger store with higher prices, and many more people. Now that you have that picture in your head, imagine the sheer volume of stuff being purchased for a month's supply. Besides costing a small fortune, we just couldn't fit that much stuff into a car. So my 1975 Chevy pickup truck was the obvious choice of transportation for these excursions. We could fill up the rear bed of the truck with all those bags of groceries and stuff, and that worked out just fine. My truck however, had an open bed, no top on it. With that in mind, we always had to plan on the possibility of rain or snow. A heavy tarp was the answer to that issue. Unfortunately the tarp wasn't always as effective as I would have liked it to be. Sometimes bags got wet and fell apart before we could go the 15 miles back to our house. Once back at the house, there was the ordeal of unloading all those bags from the bed of the truck and getting them into the house. Getting the bags into the house meant bringing them into the kitchen, and just setting them on the floor. Cold items were always put in the refrigerator or freezer. As for the rest of the stuff, well if I didn't put it away, it just sat on the floor in the bags until needed. I would start to put stuff away. Not getting any help with this daunting task was both overwhelming and, I felt, very unfair.

As time went on, and the winter of 1977–78 came, Kevin separated from his wife, and was now back living with our parents. Both of my parents were upset about the breakup. My mother didn't seem to mind having Kevin back at their house; dear old dad felt differently. Kevin was drinking very heavily at the time, and it was affecting his work. The company he worked for paid to put him in an inpatient rehab facility. The facility was located somewhere in Southern Vermont. The day he got out, my mother drove up and picked him up. She brought him back to her house, and after being there only a short time, he got into a verbal fight with my father. He asked my mother if he could borrow her car, and she gave him the keys. He showed up at my house, drunk. I let him stay the night and called my mother to let her know what was going on. I told her he would be going back to her house in the morning. Kevin's rehab didn't stick. It wasn't long after finishing the program that he started to drink heavier than before going into it. He began drinking while at work and that was the end of his job. He was still seeing his, now ex, secretary and moved in with her.

Back at my house in the summer of 1978, I was trying to take a day here and there to be home after regular work hours. I was doing that so I could spend time with my wife and child. Unfortunately, Rachel was content to sit on the couch reading soft porn paperback books, rather than spend time with me or her child. I would come home to a house with chairs full of some clean, and some dirty laundry; all waiting to be either put away or washed. If I was home, she refused to do either. Most of the time there would still be a few bags of groceries on the kitchen floor. She would always say she was emptying them as she used the food in them. The kitchen always had a pile of dirty dishes sitting in the sink, or on the counter. The mess and clutter drove me nuts. Not long after Rachel finally got over her postpartum depression, I told her that I didn't think I wanted any more children. I felt like one was going to be enough, at least for the foreseeable future.

In July of 1978, Rachel came to the cabinet shop with a gift-wrapped package for me. As it was not our anniversary, and not my birthday, I didn't like the look of that. She asked that I gather the other employees around and then open the package. With everyone standing around, I opened the package to find that it was a box of cigars. "I'm pregnant, pass the cigars out," she very proudly announced. I was so mad that I just threw the box of cigars on the assembly bench I had been leaning on. I started to walk out of the building with Rachel following, not too close behind. She knew I would be pissed about her getting pregnant so soon after the first one. She also knew I didn't want any more children, at least not for a while. Being so mad, and now alone with Rachel, I couldn't come up with the words to let her know exactly how I was feeling at the time. She kept coming to me and trying to get me to talk to her, but I just kept walking away. Finally, I composed myself enough to ask her why she had done that. Especially knowing I wanted to wait before having another, if any, child. She said that all she wanted to do now was to have more babies, and just stay home and be a mother to as many as she could. Without talking to her about it, I had a vasectomy about a month later.

During the fall and into the winter of 1978, knowing I had another child on the way, and not being all that happy about it; I began working very hard, very long hours. I began spending very little time at home. I would get up around 5:45 am each morning, get something to eat and head to the shop. I would have the shop open for 7:00 am, for the workday to start. At 4:00 pm, the shop closed and everybody went home, or at least left the building. All except me! I would start my second job; making someone's kitchen cabinets, or doing a van conversion. I would often work until 9:30 pm or 10:00 pm, as I had before. Most nights I would call Karen or Betty to see if they wanted some company. The answer from one or the other was always yes. Sometimes I would stop and pick up a bottle of Jim Beam Bourbon. That was the drink of choice at every visit, and I didn't want to be drinking all of theirs without contributing. I sometimes would stay at one house or the other until 1:00 am before going home. Once home I would shower, slide into bed, and at 5:45 am start all over again.

Our second child was born in late January, 1979. Rachel had almost no postpartum depression with this one. Just a few days prior to that, I traded the car Rachel was driving for a new leftover 1978 Dodge sedan. It was black with a powder blue leatherette interior, and was loaded with all the toys of the time. It was a large sedan, about the size of the Ford LTD. The front grill was a retro Cord style that I thought looked kind of classy. The car had been sitting in the local Dodge dealer's showroom for a while, and I would go past it on my way to work and look at it every day. One day, I just decided, "I want that car." So without talking to Rachel about it, I bought the car. She 'hated' the car. It was too big! She didn't like black; she didn't like the blue interior! She didn't like the front bucket seats with the center console and floor shift. It was an automatic. She just plain didn't like it. This was her car to drive, while I was still driving the 1975 Chevy pickup; with the, now, very rusty rear bed for work, and to deliver the kitchen cabinets I was still making. I took the truck to a local body repair shop to see if there was anything they could do for the truck, it was beyond my ability to fix, and it was apparently beyond theirs as well. I patched it up as best I could, and took a lesson from my friend Steve's auto painting guide, and rolled some paint on the bed; it looked good enough to get by for the short term.

Chapter Thirteen
The Seaside Adventure

In March of 1979, during one of my nighttime visits with Karen, Betty and Steve came over to tell us they had some news to share. They were both very excited and told Karen and me they had just bought another house. Karen was happy for them, but sad that they would be moving away. They told us where the new house was located and that eased Karen a little. The new house was on the street that I grew up on, and I knew the house well. It was not far from where they were living now. The house, up the hill from the one I grew up in, was a large farmhouse with maybe one and a half acres of land. It was an elaborate Greek revival style house; 'L' shaped with a large front 'Parlor room' jutting out beyond the rest of the front of the house, at one end. There was a large covered front porch that extended across the rest of the front. The porch columns were typical columns for the style of the house. The front door, located on the front porch, had wide trim with typical narrow Greek wood trim added. The first floor had the front Parlor room, a large dining room, and a rather small kitchen for the size of the house. There was a large walk-in pantry off the kitchen. The pantry had a countertop in it; I think most of the food prep must have been done in there. The second floor had three bedrooms, one larger than the other two. The bathroom was located at top of the stairs, on the second floor, above the front Parlor. If you were to walk all the way down the hall from the top of the stairs, past all of the bedrooms, to your right was another small hall. In that hall there was a set of stairs to the attic, and another set to the first floor that came down behind the pantry, almost as a hidden stairway. The house had been vacant for a number of years, and was in need of a lot of work. There was a large barn out behind the house that had long ago been used for horses. The barn had six stalls and a tack room on the first level, and a hay loft with drops to hay feeders in each stall below. The barn was in much better shape than the house was.

Steve said they got a very good deal on the property. Their plans were to gut the entire house, re-wire it and add as much new plumbing as was needed. Also in the plan was the addition of a half bath, and possibly a mudroom area off the rear entry door. The rear entry door was located in a small hall at the bottom of the main stairway. They asked if I would re-design the kitchen/pantry area, and build new kitchen and bathroom cabinets for them. I told them I would be happy to build all of the new cabinets for them. Then Steve asked if I could help with gutting and refinishing of the entire interior of the house. With things at home not being what they should be, a second child that had not been discussed first, the house being more of a mess than ever, and Rachel not interested in doing anything to remedy that, I said I would be happy to help. In April, Steve and Betty closed on the new property. Steve, Jim, and I immediately went to work gutting the interior of the house. Of course working on the house meant that I would have to again give up the side jobs that had become my second job. Rachel was going to have to make do with my not so meager day job income.

The three of us worked every day after work, well into the night, and on weekends as well. It didn't take long to have the house striped back to the open frame, wires and plumbing. Karen and Betty would stop by with food and beverages for all of us. Sometimes they would stay and visit which slowed things down, but it was good to get the breaks. With the work of gutting the house complete, Steve and I started the redevelopment of the first floor. We took part of the pantry and added it to the kitchen. We were unable to find room for a mudroom or half bath at the rear entry, so I took a small section of the front parlor by the stairway and added the half bath. During all that time working on the house, Karen and Betty continued to make their visits. When they were leaving, they would each give Steve and I a hug. Karen was in the habit of wearing a strong musk scented perfume. As she hugged me the scent of the perfume would get on my clothes. After weeks of working on the house, and Rachel smelling Karen's perfume on me, she asked if I was sleeping with her. I think she was hoping I would say yes. That would have opened up the open marriage thing again. No, she still had not given up on it. I told her it was from Karen and Betty visiting us at the house, and hugging both of us when they left.

While Steve and I were working on the house, Karen and Betty had been working on a plan for all three couples to rent a cottage by the sea. They found a nice three-bedroom cottage in a small seaside town. We were going to have to drive to get to the beach, but it was a short ride and nobody seemed to think it would be an issue. We all coordinated our vacations for the first week of August. My explanation of Karen's perfume being on my clothes seemed to ease Rachel's tension a bit. She knew Karen was a hugger, she even hugged her. She said she still didn't like the idea of all of us living together in the same house for a week. I told her that the two of us would be together all week, and if she wanted us to go off by ourselves for some time alone we could do that too. With Rachel feeling a little more comfortable about the arrangements, we began to look forward to our week at the sea.

Steve and I worked very hard in the weeks leading up to our vacation. The electrician had been working on the wiring, and had about one side of the first and second floors done. We did the plumbing ourselves as we got to areas that needed it. With the plumbing and wiring done on the one side, we began the job of insulating those areas. I hate installing insulation, especially in the warm weather. You have to wear long sleeve shirts and long pants, with gloves and a face mask. As soon as you start working, you start sweating. When you start to sweat, you start to itch. The more you sweat, the more you itch. Even taking a good long shower doesn't seem to get rid of all of the itching. We were able to get that one side of the first and second floors insulated. With that complete, we began to install the drywall over it before the first week of August arrived.

Vacation time! The first week of August was here. With our cars all packed, and everybody's kids attended to, we all met at Karen and Jim's house. Our two kids were spending the week with my parents. Karen and Jim had one child about the same age as my youngest one. Their child was spending the week with Karen's parents, and Betty and Steve had two children; one early teen and one preteen. Their children were staying with Steve's parents. Our three-car convoy headed off to our seaside escape. With me in the lead and the other two following, we headed for the MA turnpike and RT 495, headed north to Maine. Just over three hours later, we were at the cottage. It was on a dirt road, back away from the main tourist lanes, along with a few other cottages on the street. The area was very quiet and peaceful. All of the other cottages were occupied, but spread out nicely. As the three cars pulled up to the cottage, Steve parked next to my car and I could see he was drinking a can of beer. I asked Betty when he started drinking, and she said almost as soon as we left their house, at about 9:00 am.

Steve had obviously already had more to drink than he should have. We all went about the business of unpacking the cars and claiming our bedrooms. With the unpacking done, an inspection of the kitchen and the food each of us had brought with us was made, Karen and Betty decided some food shopping was in order and were going into town. They asked Rachel to come with them, but she said she was tired from the ride. We had reservations for dinner in town that evening, and she wanted to be rested up for it. We had also talked about going to a night club after dinner and she wanted to be able to enjoy that, too. So Karen and Betty left for the grocery store. As they did that, Steve decided that he needed to take a shower. The cottage had an outside shower stall as well as one in the bathroom. Steve decided to use the outside one. Jim and I took up seats on the screened in front porch to wait for the girls to come back with the food. As it was well past noon, and we were on our vacation, we too had started to hit the beer.

When Steve finished his shower, he came into the front porch with just a robe on, nothing else. The robe was untied and completely open in the front. There he was, with everything hanging out for all to see. He walked past us and went into the house ignoring our suggestions to close his robe. We both got up and followed him in, he was in the living room looking for a good place to sit. As he wandered around the room, Rachel was doing everything she could to stay in front of him. She was staring directly at his penis, as if it were dangling there just for her. Steve finally came to rest on a lounge chair and plopped himself down with his robe wide open and hanging to the floor on both sides. With Rachel standing directly beside him, and looking straight down at his penis, Jim and I could see it start to grow. Without taking her eyes off Steve's penis, Rachel removed her top to reveal her breasts to Steve. With no bra on, we all could see Rachel's nipples were extended and firm. Then she got on her knees and as Steve fondled one of her breasts, she took his penis in her mouth and began moving in the usual sucking motion. The two of them were doing all of this right in front of Jim and I, as if we weren't there. After making sure Steve's penis was fully erect, and ready for service, she stood up and while looking directly at Jim and me, she removed her shorts and panties. Steve made some sort of happy little sound as she straddled him and guided his penis into her vagina. Having successfully placed the head of his penis in her, she slid down onto him. As she did, she took the full length of his penis into her. They both made soft gasps and moans of pleasure. And, just as Rachel started to glide on his penis two car doors closed just outside of the cottage. The girls were back from the store.

With the girls back, Rachel jumped off Steve, grabbed her clothes, and ran into our bedroom and closed the door. Steve gathered his robe up and closed it. Realizing that wasn't going to be good enough to hide his obvious issue, he grabbed a magazine and opened it up to place over his penis. He then made believe he had fallen asleep while reading some in depth article in COSMO. Jim and I looked at each other in some kind of disbelief at what we had just witnessed. I said to Jim, "I can't believe she just did that right in front of me."

Jim shaking his head simply said, "Fuck me." And as we went out to help bring in the groceries, I looked at him and said, "Just wag your dick in front of her, and she just might." Nothing was said to anybody about what had just happened, but I knew my marriage was over at that point. I didn't want to ruin the week for everybody so I thought I would try to make the best I could of the vacation. Rachel spent the rest of the afternoon in our room; I did not. Steve, his issue sufficiently deflated, joined the rest of us for drinks and snacks on the porch.

Later, when Steve and I were alone for a few minutes he said, "I'm sorry, man, I didn't think she would do that." I told him I was only a little shocked that she would do it right in front of me, and I wasn't mad at him. I told him Karen told me (earlier that day) that Rachel had been doing it right along with other guys. I only knew about a couple.

As it got close to our dinner reservation time, I went into our bedroom to get dressed. Rachel had been lying on the bed still completely naked all afternoon. I decided to take that opportunity to tell Rachel that we were done, our marriage was over. She took the news with little emotion and said she was sure I would feel better about things in a couple of days. Neither one of us mentioned her little ride on Steve's penis. With all of us dressed for dinner, we took two of the cars to the restaurant. As most of the restaurants, this one was in the main tourist area of town. We all sat at a large table and ordered drinks. I didn't think Steve should drink much more; but he was a big guy, much larger than me, so I wasn't going to argue with him over a couple of beers. With the drinks now in hand we all ordered our meals. The food was good and the restaurant was nice enough. We talked about our plans for the up-coming week, some of which included some alone time for each couple. We also talked about where we would go after dinner. The drinks kept coming, faster for some of us than others. After our dinner was finished, we headed for a night club that we had all agreed on during our meal. The night clubs, for those of you that can't remember the summer of 1979, were standing room only. The noise (music), along with everybody yelling to be heard, was deafening. All of the girls were getting hit on. Sometimes they were being hit on by other girls. Even the three of us guys were being hit on, sometimes by other guys. The lights were flashing, and colored spotlights were swooping all over the crowd. The entire experience was awful. Steve decided to leave and just walked out. The rest of us followed and picked Steve up on our way out of the parking lot. We decided to just go back to the cottage and hang out, maybe have a few more drinks and some snacks.

We all sat on the porch, drinking some more, and having a few snacks and continuing to talk more about our plans for the week. After a while Steve and Betty got up and went to their bedroom. Rachel got up and went into our bedroom, I stayed out on the porch talking to Jim and Karen. A few minutes later, Rachel came back and went outside somewhere. None of us paid much attention to where she went. Karen asked Jim to go outside with her to talk about something. They went out and sat at a picnic table on the side of the house. I again stayed on the porch, just sitting and relaxing. Pretty soon I could hear the sounds of a very loud argument coming from Steve and Betty's room. A couple minutes later, Steve came out of the house and walked past me without saying a word. He went off the porch and headed off down the road in the dark. I could hear Betty crying in her room. About five minutes later, Betty came out of the bedroom and blew past me, and headed down the street. She was wearing nothing but a pair of panties. When she got off the porch she began to run down the street after Steve, screaming like a banshee with her arms flailing wildly above her head.

A short time later, Betty came walking back up the street to the cottage. She was alone and looked utterly and completely defeated. When she came up on the porch, she made no effort to cover herself from me. She was still crying very hard and mumbling incoherently. She went past me and on into her bedroom. Karen got up from the picnic table where she had been talking to Jim, and went into Betty's room to try to console her friend. Karen was with Betty for about ten minutes or so, and then went back to the picnic table. Karen and Jim continued to talk for another long time. They kept the conversation quiet and I couldn't hear anything being said. Suddenly Karen got up from the table and started to walk down the street. Jim got up and came onto the porch, but blew past me without saying a word. A couple of minutes later, Rachel came onto the porch looking very upset and angry. She looked at me and said, "So I was right about you and Karen. You must have been fucking her. She told Jim she is in love with you and wants a divorce." I told her I didn't know what she was talking about; I didn't know anything about Karen being in love with me. Rachel wasn't buying it and said she had been sitting behind a tree just a few feet from the table and heard their whole conversation.

She then asked, "Is that why you want to end our marriage? Is it so you can be with her?" I told her Karen had nothing to do with our marriage. Our marriage was over because she refused to give up on the open marriage thing, and I have been told about her continuing to screw every guy she could.

Rachel went into the house; I stayed out on the porch. After a short time, Rachel came back out and said we need to go find Steve. It's not safe for him to be out there alone. I agreed with her and told her we should also pick up Karen. I was less concerned about Steve, given his large size and very muscular build than I was about Karen, given her very well-proportioned body. As we got into the car, Rachel driving, she told me Karen was not getting into the car with her.

We headed down the road to look for both of them. At the end of the road was a 'T' intersection. Karen was sitting on the side of the road at the intersection, she was crying quietly. With the car stopped at the intersection, I got out to try to get Karen to get into the car. Rachel again said she would not allow Karen in the car. I told Rachel I couldn't just leave her there like that. Rachel then gave me an ultimatum. "You either get in the car with me, or the both of you can stay here." Without saying anything to that, I sat down next to Karen. As Rachel started turning the car onto the next street I could hear her say, "You fucking bastard!" We sat and talked for a little while and Karen told me about her conversation with Jim. When she told me that she told Jim she was in love with me, she rested her head on my shoulder. With my arms wrapped around her, I told her that I loved her too. It was true that I did love her, but I didn't tell her that I never thought of her in a sexual way or as a wife. After a short time we got up and went back to the cottage and sat on the porch talking.

Maybe about an hour, perhaps a little later, Rachel came back to the cottage. She had found Steve and he was with her. As Steve came onto the porch, he had a sort of funny small smile on his face and just walked by us into the house without saying anything. When Rachel came onto the porch she stopped and looked at both of us, and then directly at me and said, "Steve and I finished what we started in the living room in your car, and it was the best sex I have ever had!" She then went into the house and our bedroom and closed the door. Karen and I spent the rest of the night out on the porch. We talked about the wreck that our lives had become. I told her that I had ended it with Rachel. Neither one of us knew what we were going to do now. She thought she might have to go back to live with her parents; I said I didn't feel like that was an option for me. We both agreed that our week at the seaside was, after one day, over.

As the sun started to rise, Karen and I went in and made a pot of coffee. The smell of the freshly brewed beverage floating through the house began to bring the others, one by one, into the kitchen. Each person, as they entered the kitchen, grabbed a cup and filled it. Betty and Steve said that they had decided to split up along with the rest of us. Everybody was sitting at the table when Rachel finally came in. For whatever reason, she decided that a pair of shear bikini panties, and a way too small tank top would be appropriate that morning. The other two girls, in perfect harmony and raised voices said, "Go put some fucking clothes on, you fucking pig!" With that, Rachel turned around and went back to the bedroom. When she came out she was wearing a pair of shorts and a partially unbuttoned semi see-through shirt. Ignoring Rachel, Karen and I announced our decision to leave that morning. Everybody agreed with the idea. After we were done with the coffee, the re-packing of all of our stuff began. We had all chipped in for the food bought on Saturday, so it got divided up among all of us. We were all going to have to go into town and get a cheap Styrofoam cooler for the cold stuff.

And so on that first Saturday of August, 1979, three couples arrived at a small seaside town cottage, for a week of anticipated fun and relaxation. Six individuals would leave that cottage the following Sunday morning. The ride home was long and uncomfortable; neither Rachel nor I saying a word to each other. We went to our house and unpacked the car and put away the food. All of the food! I got Rachel to change into more appropriate clothes and we headed to my parents' house. I had called them before we left the house and of course they were upset. When we got to their house to pick up the kids, my mother took Rachel aside to talk privately. My father just started yelling at me like everything wrong in the world was somehow my fault. When my parents felt like they had lectured/yelled at us enough, they told Rachel and me to get together and talk it out. That didn't go as well as my parents had planned. I was done. I was done on Saturday afternoon, and I was still done. As the talk with Rachel was only making things worse, I left the house and started walking in the direction of my house. When I got to Karen's house, I saw that Jim's car was gone but Karen's was still there. I went to her house and she was in the process of packing some of her clothes. She said I shouldn't be there because Jim had just gone to get their kid, and would be right back. I saw that the 'Shit-brindle-brown-bile' was still at Steve's house. I went over to find both he and Betty sitting at the kitchen table talking about what had happened the previous day. I don't think the part about my wife trying to ride Steve like a wild horse was part of the conversation.

Chapter Fourteen
The Breakup

I sat and talked with Betty and Steve about the whole mess. I also did not add anything about Steve and Rachel to the conversation. After talking with them for a while, I asked Steve if he could give me a ride to my house. I was going to need to do some packing of my own, and retrieve my truck which was still at the house. On the ride to my house I asked Steve if I could stay at the house where we were working. All we had to do was set the toilet and vanity sink in the upstairs bathroom; the tub had already been installed, and there would be a complete working bathroom. He said he was planning on staying there and would like the company. We talked briefly about him and Rachel. He said he remembered her trying to mount him and ride him in the living room, but he said he really didn't think anything else happened between them. I told him I didn't really care; and if he screwed her brains out in the back seat of the car, it didn't matter to me. We both agreed to continue working on the house while we were staying there. Steve said there would be a good chance the house would be sold if they got divorced.

When Steve dropped me at my house, Rachel was already there. I knew that meant my packing and getting out of there was going to be a bit messy. I met Rachel in the kitchen; she seemed to be calm but somewhat reserved. She tried to give me a hug and told me she was glad I was home, as if nothing had happened. I told her it wasn't going to work, and I was just there to gather some clothes and get my truck. I told her where I would be staying and she just exploded. "I suppose you're staying there so you and Karen can fuck yourselves crazy? Is she staying there with you?" she asked. I told her I had never touched Karen, and didn't know anything about her being in love with me until last night. I told her that Steve and I would be staying at the house and that Karen said she was going to her parents' house. Jim was going to stay in their house for a while, but it was going to have to be sold with the divorce. Betty had said the same thing. Every few days I would go back to my house to pick up more of my clothes and other stuff. I began to notice lots of missing clothes and tools. When I asked Rachel about the missing items, she simply said, "Prove that you ever had them." I found out from the lady across the street, that she was giving my clothes and other things to her brothers, and friends on the street.

In the months that followed, Rachel was spending a lot of time at my parent's house. I don't know what she was saying to them, but my relationship with my parents began to improve. Eventually she stopped going to their house, and I became much more welcome there. I asked her why and she just said that they were my parents and she didn't feel right spending so much time with them. I asked my parents about it and I was told that they had stopped at her house one day, and were appalled at the mess she had those kids living in. There were dirty clothes and dishes spread out all over the place, and old food just lying around in the kitchen. They had a bit of a falling out with her after that. From that point on my relationship continued to improve with both of my parents. Steve and I continued to live and work on the house (no visits from Karen or Betty). Things at the cabinet shop were a little tense between Jim and me. As his boss, I tried to give him as much space as possible, but we still had to work together. We took some time one day and went out to lunch. We sat and talked about everything, including Karen telling him she was in love with me. I told him that I found out the same time he did, and he said that she told him she never said anything to me about it. He did say that he was enjoying watching Rachel trying to ride his friend like a bucking bronco. I said I was done with her when she did that right in front of us. After talking things through a bit more, the tension between us seemed to ease a little, and we both agreed we would be able to work together without having a problem.

Rachel found a very good attorney. He worked at one of the big powerhouse firms in the city. He seemed to take Rachel's case very personally. He treated me as if I were a war criminal, responsible for all sorts of major human atrocities. My attorney, on the other hand, turned out to be a meek little mouse that cowered at the very sound of her attorney's voice. I'm not sure about this, but I think after a meeting between Rachel, myself and the attorneys, there may have been a wet spot on my lawyer's seat when he got up to leave. Strong demands and accusations were being made by Rachel's attorney almost weekly. I wasn't aware of this, but apparently, according to Rachel, I had been sleeping with Karen on a regular basis for the past two years (It made me think of all the fun I could have been having, instead of doing all that work). While all of this was going on, I would try to see my kids, one day, each weekend. Rachel made things as uncomfortable as possible when I was at the house. After she stopped going to my parents' house, I would bring the kids over there so they could see them. That time was not only spent with them visiting with their grandchildren, but with us trying to mend the broken fences that was my childhood. They had both seemed to mellow considerably. My mother was drinking much less now. My father, while still drinking heavily, may have slowed some.

One of the demands made by Rachel's attorney was that I take the less than one year old Dodge back, and provide Rachel with comparable, reliable, transportation suitable to Rachel's needs and desires. Since I wanted the car back anyway, I readily agreed to that one. Of course that meant I was going to have to use my 1975 roller painted pickup truck as a trade in to buy another car. Having made the trade, I delivered Rachel's car to her. What I got in return was a less than one year old car, with small dents on all sides, and not one panel being without a scratch of varying degrees. The interior had cigarette burns, crayon marks, small punctures, and dried old crusty food stuck to the seats. I asked my lawyer to appeal to the court for compensation, but he said, "That would set a bad precedent, and turn the court against me." So, in complying with the demand, and giving Rachel a car she wanted, I was left with a new car, with a high monthly payment, that was almost worthless. When I was picking up the car, Izzy was back for a visit. When she got me alone for a couple of minutes, she asked if I would like to 'Hook up' with her. Apparently her views on marriage were the same as Rachel's. We didn't 'Hook up'.

Steve and I had been working very hard on his house. Shortly before Christmas, 1979, we had finished the kitchen and bathrooms. All of the drywall finishing had been completed. No paint was going to be applied. The interior trim had been installed and the floors were sanded and finished. Steve announced that he was moving out, and the house was going up for sale. I was going to have to find another place to live. Steve found a nice little apartment a couple of towns over and invited me to visit often. Visiting Steve generally meant meeting at the apartment and then going out somewhere to drink, usually too much. Karen and I had been keeping in touch occasionally by phone through that whole time. She was at her parents' house and we never made any effort to get together. She said she had visited Betty a couple of times, but also kept in touch with her mostly by phone. Steve and Betty's first house went up for sale the same time the renovated one did. The first one sold quickly and Betty had to move out. She bought a house trailer in the same town, and moved herself and her two kids into it. I went to visit them once in a while. She and the kids all seemed to be happy living there.

Chapter Fifteen
The Divorce and Other Things

Rachel's attorney somehow pushed our divorce through very quickly. We came before the judge the first week of February 1980. Her attorney went in front of the judge and stood there growling and bellowing all sorts of accusations about the cold hearted, godless, philandering, husband that I apparently had been. He pleaded with the court to meet the many demands he had laid out on behalf of his client. When it was my lawyer's turn to get up and answer all of those nasty accusations and demands, I was sure he would make the judge see how ridiculous they were. Now, my memory may be a little cloudy here, but I seem to remember looking for him, and finding him under the table, with his brief case held over his head, shaking violently. There may even have been some small tears on his cheeks. He stuttered and stammered like a child for a few minutes, and then sat down. Now having no hope, I was sure I was doomed. And I was right.

Rachel got the house. The 18 or 20 thousand dollars' worth of improvements I could prove had been made, and paid for by me, over the short time we owned the house made no difference to the court. If she sold the house for a profit she would not have to split the money with me. I was to keep health insurance on all of them, including Rachel. I was allowed to take the kids freely one day every second weekend for visits; holidays were up to Rachel's discretion. The car I had supplied was to be kept in good running order by me, with regular scheduled maintenance, and repairs as needed. And then there was the money. Oh yes, we can't forget the money! Even though I had not done any side work since starting to help Steve with their house renovation, and there was no record of any side work ever having been done; apparently 'potential' was a consideration. Along with my regular work income, a random number for 'potential' additional income had somehow been arrived at. The judge decided that it was reasonable to take that number into consideration when declaring my child support. The standard one third of the gross income from my daily job was not going to be enough. One third of that 'fictional potential' number was going to be added to it.

Doing the math in my head as I walked out of court, I realized I was going to be paying just over fifty percent of my gross weekly income to Rachel. Allowing for the roughly thirty percent I was paying in taxes, that left me with less than twenty percent of my income to live on. I promptly fired my meek ass, cowering lawyer. I think I remember him hiding behind his briefcase, and going into a fetal position as I yelled at him and told him what I thought of him. Again,

I was under some stress, so my memory may be a little cloudy about that. The money I was left with wasn't going to be enough to make the payments on my car, Rachel's car, and the insurance on both. Something had to be done, quickly. I was still living in the renovated house, but it was up for sale and people were looking at it. I started doing side jobs again, as fast as I could to get enough money to hire a real attorney, one from the city that knew Rachel's attorney, and how to deal with him.

Karen called me at work, one day in late February. She said she was planning to move into an apartment, but the money was going to be tight. Then she asked if I would be interested in moving in with her. Thinking back to her telling Jim that she was in love with me, I had to think this wasn't just about the money. I told her I would meet her at the apartment to talk it over with her. I wondered how that would affect Jim. It had been more than six months since all of us split up, but still we had all been friends. When I talked to Jim about it, I found that he had already moved on; he had someone he was seeing. He told me that he had been thinking about asking me if I would consider hiring her to work in the shop. That was a conversation for another time, I wasn't looking for any new help at the moment, but I would keep her in mind. With Jim not having any problem with me moving in with Karen, I went to see her at the apartment. The minute I saw her, I realized just how much I missed her and our nighttime visits. I also came to realize that at some unconscious level, there must have been more of an attraction than I was letting myself admit to. We fell into each other's arms comfortably, and we were moving in together.

Betty and Steve's renovated house finally sold. They did very well with that one. They split the money from the sale of the house, and they each had a nice bit of cash on hand. Jim and Karen had put their house up for sale and were having some trouble selling it. The house was a two-family house with a tenant on the second floor. It was a nice house, and in very good condition. The problem was, they needed to get more than the house was now worth, due to a slide in the market. They ended up selling it for what they paid for it. At least it was done and they didn't owe money on it. Jim moved into an apartment not far from where their house was.

Not having any money to live on, I knew I had to get rid of my high car payment. Karen had a car that we could share, but our work schedules were going to make it difficult. I couldn't sell the Dodge in the condition it was in, and it was too much for me to repair properly. The only thing I could do was to give the car back to the dealer. So one day Karen followed me over to the dealership. I explained my situation to the owner of the dealership, while he stood looking at the car. After giving it some thought, his response was that if he were me, he would get in the car and drive to Florida and just disappear. Not really liking that as an option, I left the car there and went home with Karen. I felt better now having at least a little money to live on. I began to get letters from the bank stating that the payments on the house, Rachel's house, were not being made and that my credit was in bad shape. That was going to be a problem because I would need to buy a car sometime soon. So I called the bank and explained the situation to them, telling them that Rachel was now the sole owner of the house. The bank said my name was still on the mortgage, so it was still going to affect me. I called Rachel about it and she told me she stopped paying because the house was for sale. I told her she still had to make the payments; she hung up on me. Still not having a good lawyer, and not being able to afford one, there wasn't much I could do.

When we moved in together, neither Karen nor I, had much in the way of furniture. So not being able to go out and buy some, I started to make pieces we could use at the house. My boss saw some of the things I was making and said he thought it might be a good idea to start a small line of accent pieces to sell. So along with everything else going on, we built a small showroom in part of the shop. We started a line of oak and pine accent furniture. He and his wife would take care of the sales and I would build the furniture. That was a great idea on paper. I would get fifteen percent of the gross sales, along with my regular salary. While the money began to add up, so did the time required to build all of the furniture. I needed help. I took Jim from his regular job and had him helping build the furniture. To replace him in the shop, I hired his girlfriend. Both were good at what I had them doing, and it eased the burden on me. The furniture was selling very well, almost too well. My boss was asking for new designs all the time.

Running out of ideas for Early American pieces, I moved into the Victorian period. I liked the look of the heavy, more detailed Victorian furniture, but had one small problem. Most of the pieces that had doors on them, had glass panels in them, leaded stained-glass panels. So to solve that little problem I taught myself how to make stained glass windows and door panels (I needed something else to do anyway). I found a place to get the materials, at wholesale prices, and bought the tools required. The panels for the doors were done as part of the furniture. Any window panels or hanging panels, I made, were sold separately as mine. The stained-glass panels sold slower than expected, but the furniture with glass door panels sold very well. My boss and his wife had been out on a selling spree, and we now had commercial accounts with furniture stores in MA, CT and NY. With the furniture moving so well, my boss told me he would like to give up the fiberglass business. Most of the parts were custom and I had to make the patterns, and the whole process was expensive and time consuming. It was okay with me. Giving up the fiberglass was going to open up some time for me to spend more time making kitchen cabinets, on the side. I could make more money doing that on my own.

Rachel sold the house for more than twice what we had paid for it. The bank got paid and she walked away with a pile of money. She moved in with a guy that I knew from high school; he was in a couple of my classes. He was a tall thin guy; John was his name. I found out that he was divorced, and owned his own house. I don't know what John did for work, but every time I called to make arrangements to pick up the kids, the oldest one would answer. When I asked to talk to his mother the answer was always the same, "John's in bed taking a nap and Mom is in there with him." Nobody needs that many naps, and Rachel most certainly wasn't in there napping with him. Karen and I began to refer to him as 'old tired Johnny'. Getting the kids was difficult; Rachel would always make me meet her in different places, never at John's house.

Chapter Sixteen
Build a Jeep and the Client's Daughter

As all of that was going on, I had picked up a kitchen renovation job back in the town where I grew up. Spring had spun into early summer. With the new renovation job, I was going to need some sort of my own transportation. Not having much money or credit, thanks to Rachel, I got a small advance on my salary and bought a 1972 Jeep CJ. That old Jeep was a mess. The guy I bought it from had a seven-foot plow on the front of it that, I think, must have weighed half as much as the Jeep did. It was so heavy that the front springs were bent in reverse of their original form, and the drive shaft to the front transfer case was rubbing on the frame. The body was in very bad shape and the floorboards had large holes in them. The front fenders were rotted out, the side panels had large rust holes in them, and the tailgate was held on with rope. I got it cheap!

The first thing I did was to remove the plow and its frame. I thought the front springs would come back up; I was wrong! I knew a guy whose family owned a spring and brake repair shop for large trucks. We brought the Jeep in, took the spring off and he re-sprung each leaf of all of the springs. We then added one extra leaf to each corner. That made the Jeep sit a little higher and ride a little harder, but I liked it. The floorboards were next. I patched the holes in the floor with ¾ inch plywood and sheet metal, supported by angle iron ribs screwed to the frame. I removed all of the rust on the frame, and replaced areas as needed with new metal plates welded on. Once the frame and underside of the floor had been cleaned and repaired, I coated it with new automotive undercoating, lots of it. The next step was the body. The Jeep came with a hard top and metal doors, none of which I wanted. I removed those and started to repair the body. Now, being a cabinet guy, more than an auto body guy, what do you suppose I chose to do here? That's right folks; one wooden Jeep body coming up.

I started in the back with the tailgate. That became a twin raised panel piece, stained a dark oak color, and coated with several coats of marine varnish. It looked great! As I worked my way around the rest of the body I replaced rusted steel with plywood and body filler (body filler works very well with plywood because it's fairly stable). When I was done with the body work, the only metal parts left were the hood, part of the driver's side front fender, the front grill, and windshield frame. While I was working on the body, I went to a junk yard, well three or four junk yards, and got the front seats out of a 1972 Mustang, and a roll bar out of a 1970-something Jeep, that would fit my Jeep. I ordered a new soft top that was supposed to be medium blue; it was a little light for medium, I thought, but we'll call it that. The top came with removable fabric doors of the same color. I took the junk yard seats and one of the new doors to the auto upholstery shop that did the upholstering work for the vans I worked on. They re-upholstered the seats to match the color of the door and set me up with a set of seat belts, which the Jeep didn't have.

With the body work done and the seats being worked on, I took everything out of the dashboard. I made a new oak applique' slightly smaller than the original dash, I wanted to see some of the original metal, and inlayed all of the gauges, knobs, and vents into it. The oak was stained and finished to match the tailgate. Before putting the dash back together, or the seats in, the Jeep had to be painted. After giving up the fiberglass business, we still had the spray booth. We used it for the spray staining and finishing of the furniture. I brought the Jeep in, and applied a good heavy coat of primer with a little thinner in it, to help it get into the plywood parts. After sanding that, I painted the Jeep a deep metallic midnight blue and added a couple of coats of clear coat over it. With that done, the tailgate was added, and the interior and dash were put back in. The roll bar, front and rear bumpers, and tailgate hinges were painted high gloss black. The headlight rims, and hood lock downs were sent out to a metal plating company. I had them plated in polished brass. Before installing them I gave them a couple of coats of clear lacquer to keep them shiny. The knobs on the dashboard for the radio, heater, lights, and windshield wipers were replaced with brass and porcelain cabinet doorknobs. The roof and seats were added, white spoked wheels, one size up from the original, and a new set of white lettered tires finished the Jeep. When it was done, it was impossible to tell what parts of the body were wood and what was metal; it looked like a factory Jeep.

While working on the Jeep, I was slowly working on the kitchen renovation I had picked up. The homeowner was doing all of the gutting of the room on his own. He was moving all of the plumbing from an inside wall, to the back wall with the sink under a window facing the back yard. He was very busy with his own work, so the work on the house was going sort of slow. The homeowner, Tom, was a big guy. He seemed like a nice guy, and he had a good sense of humor. He was married with two daughters, the oldest fifteen. By the time he had the room ready, I had his cabinets waiting. I used the company truck to deliver their kitchen; they had a lot of new cabinets and countertop area. It took a few nights of working after my regular job to get all of the kitchen installed. It came out great, and the owners were very happy. The following weekend I called to make arrangements to come by and make sure everything was working and no hinges broken or doors fallen off. Really, I just wanted to be sure they were still happy with everything. Tom and I had a couple of beers as I visited. When I was leaving and got to the Jeep in his driveway, Tom's fifteen-year-old daughter was leaning against the side of it. She was very pretty, and could probably pass for a twenty-year-old. I'm sure you know what I mean here. She was wearing a loose dress that was maybe a little too short for her, but looked good on her. As I approached her she tried to hug and kiss me, while telling me that she loved me. When all of that was going on, I felt her grab my wrist and try to force my hand between her legs, and up her dress.

While I was just about to turn twenty-seven and she was fifteen, the age difference may have been a small factor. However, the larger factor here, was that we were standing in her father's driveway, and SHE WAS FIFTEEN! The fact that she was actively throwing herself at me, and trying to get me to touch her in all the wrong places, was making it hard to get her to understand what was so wrong here. As I tried to get her to understand, she began to cry. At that moment, an ugly thought slammed into my head. What if she gets mad and turns this around on me? What if while she was hurt and crying, she goes into the house and tells them I was the one doing the attacking? I stood out there in the driveway talking to her for a very long time to get her calmed down. She began to agree that her being fifteen was an issue and I told her if she were older maybe things would have been different. As she still seemed sad but in control, and understanding the situation, she went back in the house and I finally went home. The police weren't knocking on my door later that night, so I guess things were good at Tom's house.

Chapter Seventeen
The Mailbox Caper and the Kid on a Leash

Life with Karen was going along very well. The apartment we lived in was on the second floor of a two-family house. The first floor was occupied by the homeowner. Both Karen and I got along well with them. My parents liked Karen, which was a help. We visited them and spent some time just becoming friends. I was getting more comfortable with my father, and he was getting more comfortable with me. Maybe my childhood was what it was because he just didn't like kids, and took it out on my mother and all of us kids. I'm not sure my mother liked kids either. As summer rolled into fall, I had been doing a few more side jobs and saved some money. Karen and I both agreed it was time to get a new lawyer and try to fix some of the mess that was my divorce settlement. She had moved up in the company she worked at, and was making very good money. She felt that if it cost a little more than I had saved up, she was willing to help. I found an attorney in the city that not only knew Rachel's attorney, but really didn't like him. And about ten years later, I would find out that he was related to my third wife. Yeah, I know you're saying I skipped one. I didn't; I just jumped ahead in the story. Let's get back to Karen who becomes number two, soon.

My new attorney was expensive, but as it turned out, worth it. He got me back in court with Rachel and her attorney, and he knew how to handle him. I had taken pictures of the Dodge when I got it back from Rachel to show the judge in the divorce case. Because of my wimpy lawyer, they were never seen by the judge, and the condition of the almost new car was never mentioned. My new lawyer got them front and center and made a very big deal out of it. He made the judge understand that because I was made to pay such a high amount in child support, I couldn't afford to keep the car and it couldn't be sold in that condition. I was forced to give the car back, and it was listed as a repossession, not suitable for resale. The car company wanted their money and I couldn't give it to them. The Judge ruled that since Rachel was given the house and allowed to sell it and not split the enormous profit with me, along with my reduced income at the time, my child support was reduced to just forty dollars a week.

Just before Thanksgiving, Steve called and invited me over to his apartment. When visiting Steve, it was always without Karen, she would go visit her sister. As I said before, visiting Steve was meeting at his apartment, and going someplace in the area to sit, drink, and pass the time with each other. That particular Saturday evening we went to a place that Steve liked to go to a lot. He was well known there. Steve had made other friends there, and he introduced them all to me. They would all buy us a round of drinks as we sat and chatted. By the end of the night, both Steve and I had had maybe just a little too much to drink. Well, maybe more than that. Steve drove us back to his place, where I had left my Jeep. I didn't stay when we got there, I just got in the Jeep and headed home. In the morning, Steve called me and the conversation went something like this, "Hey Steve, how you doing today?"

"Hey, Shawn, did you run over my mailbox last night?"

"I don't know. Do you think I ran over your mailbox?"

"Well, somebody ran over it, and I thought I heard a noise like you hit something when you left my yard last night."

"Well," I said, "I did hear a noise, but it didn't sound like a mailbox getting run over. Let me go check the back of the Jeep to see if there are any marks on it."

"Okay, you do that," Steve said. "And while you're out there, why don't you pick up a new mailbox and post, and bring them over, oh, and don't forget to bring a shovel with you."

"So I guess we're pretty sure I ran over your mailbox then?"

"Yup, I'm pretty sure."

"Okay, Steve, I'll see you in a bit." I don't really know if I ran over his mailbox, and there were no marks on the back of the Jeep. But I replaced the box and post anyway.

On one other occasion being out with Steve, we stopped at a fast food store for something to eat. It was sort of late at night, maybe 11 pm or midnight. We went in and placed our orders at the counter. There was a surprising number of people in there for that time of night, I thought. There were other people at the counter as Steve and I stood leaning against it. Steve and I were facing each other, with other people behind me. A tray of food was set on the counter, sort of next to me, but slightly behind me. I was thinking that it was my tray, and we were just waiting for Steve's food to come up. As we stood there talking, I was taking a few French fries and popping them into my mouth. Still talking, not even looking at the tray, I noticed a silly, smirk sort of grin, on Steve's face. Then he started to make this sort of half giggle/laugh kind of noise. Then I saw the girl behind the counter was looking at me, too. Not yet realizing anything was wrong, I reached for another French fry, but the tray was gone. I turned around to see a man standing behind me now holding the tray that I was taking the fries from. He was just staring, and never said a word. It took me a second or two, but I finally realized it was his food I had been eating. I apologized for taking his food; I said I thought it was my tray. The girl behind the counter gave the man a new bag of fries and he left without saying a word.

As 1980 turned into 1981, things were going pretty smoothly. I was making good money at my regular job, plus the money from the furniture sales, and I was still doing some side jobs. The stained glass was selling well as door panels in some of the furniture, and I was getting some custom orders for that. The window panels and hanging panels were selling slower, but they were selling. Karen was thinking about changing jobs. She had put out her resume' and had a few offers come back. She ended up taking a job as the administrative assistant to the head of one of the medical departments at a large teaching hospital in the city. She liked the job, and said it was a bit challenging, but very interesting. It was all new stuff to her. Rachel split up with 'Old tired Johnny' and moved to a town in Western MA, about a two-hour ride for me to see the kids. Visitation was still the same. So a two-hour ride to pick them up, and bring them to my parents' house for a visit, and then a two-hour ride to return them made for a short visit. I think she was ordered by the court to get a job, to help support the kids, I don't know if she did or not. She had a way of finding people that would support her and the kids.

Not much of note happened in 1981. Karen and I moved into a duplex, in a small development. They were nice, almost new, two-bedroom, one-bathroom units. We tried to get to know and be friendly with the couple in the unit next to ours. They seemed to be a little standoffish. The wife seemed to be a little friendlier, but she was also a bit strange. They had a child. The wife did not work, and she would apparently put a harness and a long leash on the child, and connect it to a large stake she had put in the ground in the front yard. She could often be found napping on the couch in the living room, while the kid was on the leash out front. One day, she locked herself out of her unit. As it happened, she never locked the second-floor windows. All it took for me to get into her unit was a ladder, and to pop the screen in the window of her bedroom. After popping the screen and opening her bedroom window, I got ready to crawl through the window. Just as I started to do that, I heard her say from the bottom of the ladder, "If you stop to look at anything in the bedroom, I will call the cops on you." Now, the fact that I'm helping her get into her unit and she threatens me like that is one thing. But what do you think must be going on in that bedroom that she felt like she needed to threaten me like that? I didn't stop to look at anything, but it did make me wonder.

Chapter Eighteen
Get Married and Quit My Job

Late one summer afternoon, my father showed up at my apartment. I was heading out for something, I don't remember what, so I met him in his car in the driveway. I could tell he had been drinking, a lot. As I stood beside the driver's side door talking to him, I could also see two six packs of beer and a .22 caliber semi-automatic handgun on the seat beside him. I tried to get him to come into the apartment with me, but he wasn't getting out of the car. After talking to him for a while, he said he was going away and may not see me for a long time. I tried to reach in to get the gun, but he pushed me away and rolled up the window. While he was doing that, he started to drive away saying he would see me again sometime. When he started to move the car, I don't think he realized how close I was, and as a result, he ended up running over my left foot. The trunk was empty at the time and the car was not a very heavy one, so no real damage was done. I think the most damage was that he just kept on going, not pausing to ask if I was okay. I knew where he was going. I knew where he always went at times like that. He owned an eight acre 'wood lot' as he called it, a few towns north of us. The land wasn't good for much other than harvesting firewood, and that's what he did with it. He would go and cut down a couple of trees, cut them into stove lengths, and fill the trunk and back seat of his car and then drive the six or seven miles back to his house with the back end of the car almost dragging on the road. He had, over the years, cut a small road back into the woods so he could get his car off the street.

When I was talking to him in the driveway, he was saying some very sad things and I was worried about the gun. Not knowing what else to do, I called a friend that was a police officer. He told me to pick him up at his house and he would go with me to try to get my father to either go home, or at least give up the gun. We drove to the wood lot, and sure enough he was there. He had backed in his car off the street, but not very far in, so I just pulled to a stop with the side of my Jeep in front of his car. My father wouldn't roll his window down to talk to us even after Sam identified himself as a police officer. He refused to go back home, and said if we didn't leave him alone, he would use the gun on himself. I tried to break the window, but didn't have anything hard enough to do that. After trying the doors on the driver's side and finding them locked, I went to the passenger side to try those. They were also all locked. As I moved between the front of the car and side of my Jeep, the car lurched forward. He had apparently started the car, and was going to try to get away from us. What he did was pin me between the two cars. I knew my left leg had taken most of the hit and I could hear Sam still yelling at my father. The car moved back just enough for me to fall to the ground under the front of it. I heard Sam call to me to see where I was, and if I was okay. I told him I was under the car, and don't let my father move until I was able to free myself.

I felt Sam grab me by my arms and pull me out. When I tried to stand, I couldn't put any weight on my left leg. I thought it might be broken. Sam helped me to the Jeep, and as he was going around to the driver's side I could tell he was very upset with the whole thing. He stopped at the side of my father's car and told him to go ahead and use the gun if he wanted to. We left my father there and Sam took me to a local hospital. After x-rays and some painful poking and prodding, I was told I had a lot of soft tissue damage, and torn tendons around the kneecap, which had caused it to be out of place. The doctor moved the kneecap around, (ouch) to get it back in place, and then put a brace from my hip to my ankle on the leg. I was going to have to wear the brace and use crutches to walk for a few weeks. I took a few days off from work and then went back to mostly office work. Karen was very upset with everything and wouldn't talk to my father for a long time. He did, by the way, go home the following morning.

Nineteen eighty-one ended as it came in, with not much going on. Early in 1982, Karen and I decided to get married. We set a date for a spring wedding. As our wedding time approached, I began to talk to Karen about quitting my job and going out on my own. She was a little apprehensive about it but said she would support my decision if that's what I wanted. We got married in early May (So for those of you counting, that's wife number two). It was a small wedding, with just a few friends. We took a trip to Newport, Rhode Island for a couple of days. In June, I told my boss of my plans to leave the company. I had found shop space and would continue to supply him with the furniture as he sold it. He agreed to keep trying to sell some of the stained-glass windows and panels in his showroom for me. I would continue to work for him at the company until the end of July, but on a part time basis. He told me he had some extra machines he would be willing to sell to me, and that worked out well for both of us. Through June and July I was talking to Karen about the move I was making, keeping her up to speed with all that was happening. By the end of July, I was all moved in and producing furniture.

Working alone in my new shop was a bit daunting. It was a lot of work for one person. I also needed a truck to deliver all the furniture to the showroom. My ex-boss would sometimes, in the beginning, come and pick it up but he didn't want to have to do that for long. So I had to sell my very nice old Jeep, and buy a truck for the business. I was very busy for a while and I needed help. While my mother was upset about me leaving that good job I had, my father supported me. He said he could take a leave of absence and come help me at the shop. I wasn't sure if that was going to be a good idea, but I needed some help fast. A few days into my father working in the shop, he cut off three fingers. In the rush to get him to the hospital, I could only find two of them. They were able to re-attach the two fingers they had, and close the end of the other one. My father's leave of absence was going to be extended. Now I had to hire somebody to work for me.

With the furniture still selling well, the stained glass seemed to pick up in sales as well. I also landed a very large commercial furniture account for office furniture; tables of all sizes, small cabinets, and fancy oak wood file cabinets. I had enough space in my shop to do all of that, but now I needed two people to work for me. I was growing too fast. Then I found out that my ex-boss had lost interest in keeping up his commercial furniture accounts, and they began to dry up. My workload began to get much smaller, quickly. In the meantime, my old friend, Steve, quit his job and moved some place down South. He wanted to work with horses again, and had a farm that would take him. With work slowing down, I was back to just one employee. We finished the office furniture and delivered it. I waited a couple of weeks without hearing anything from that account, so I went to visit them to see how my products were selling. They said nothing was moving very fast, it was just that time of the year. I had been doing some advertising, with some response, but not enough. My business was drying up, and I didn't have enough reserve capital to float it. I let my one employee go and did whatever work came in by myself. It still wasn't going to be enough.

Chapter Nineteen
Karen and the Covered Bridge Lady

By the beginning of 1983, I was not doing much work at all. Karen was telling me that if she knew I was going to quit my job, she wouldn't have gotten married. I know she was in the room for all of those conversations about it. She was the one I was talking to about it before I quit. Somehow she must have forgotten about that. She was not happy. She didn't want to have to use any of 'her' money to pay household bills. That was supposed to be up to me and I wasn't able to do it. She didn't like the fact that over the past couple of months, I wasn't making the kind of money she was used to seeing come in. In November of 1983, Karen asked me to leave the apartment. I went to stay with Kevin, at his apartment. He lived just outside the city, and was doing some small graphic arts jobs on his own. He was making enough money to get by, but that was about it. He was drinking heavily at that time, and he had some favorite bars he liked to go to. He would introduce me to some of those bars and the friends he had at them. While I was staying with him I was looking for work, and got a job designing kitchens. I hated that job. It didn't pay very much, but it was work. The one real positive thing that I got from that job was a contact that, in the next two or two and a half years, would come back in my life, and play an important part in the story.

One night, in early December, Kevin and I went to one of his favorite places. While there, I met a young lady by the name of Gretchen. She was a nursing student at one of the teaching hospitals close by (No not the one Karen was working at). Gretchen and I hit it off right away, and before long, I was living with her and her mother at their apartment. Her mother didn't seem to mind, as long as I was going to chip in for the bills. Designing kitchens was boring me to death. I kept looking for other work, but not finding anything suitable. So I did what any red-blooded New Englander, with a residential design and home building education from the distant past, would do. I decided to start my own building company. Of course doing it is much easier said than done. And if you don't already know, the middle of winter is not a great time to build things in New England. Even though I was living with Gretchen, and getting along very well with her, I was still married to Karen. I was hurt and still mad about the way she turned on me over the money and work issue. I did still stay in touch with her, and told her I would like to try to make our marriage work. She knew about my situation with Gretchen and didn't really say too much about it. She just asked me if we were having sex. I told her we were living together; I think she figured it out from there.

The middle of March 1984 came around and I had started to advertise my, as yet not real, building company. I was looking for work in the mostly wealthy parts of Eastern MA. I thought maybe I would have a better chance of making faster money that way. I had been buying some small tools that I knew I would need for the new business, but couldn't afford the larger, more expensive ones I also knew I was going to need. Those were going to have to come from deposits on jobs. Now, if you're thinking of going into business, don't take that as a lesson in starting a business; it's not really a good way to do it. I just didn't have any other options. As time had passed from November to March, Karen had begun to soften her approach to 'her' money and 'my' money. She was beginning to try to ask me to come back to her. I explained about starting the new business, and still had no money. I was just starting to get some small jobs, but again they were small jobs. I think people were testing me and my abilities. There wasn't any money to play with yet. She said she was all right with that, she just wanted us back to being a family again. When I spoke to Gretchen about it, she said, "If your wife wants you back, then go to her." I thought Gretchen and I had more than that going on. So in the middle of April, I went back to Karen and tried to pick up the pieces and start over.

Before long, my building company was growing. I was getting the kind of work that was fast, in and out type of renovation work, but also paid very well. I met a family in one of the very wealthy Boston 'Burbs'. They had a large old Colonial style house that needed lots of work. I stayed busy on that house for a couple of months and made very good money. That family also had a house cleaning service that came in once a week. The lady doing the cleaning wanted an addition put on her house, and wanted me to give her an estimate. I got the job, and that was my first real building job. I started the addition in early September, and had it closed in and ready for the interior work before it got too cold. The nice wealthy Boston 'Burb' lady called in December and said they were buying a house in the mountains of New Hampshire. The house was going to need some work, but there was something that was going to have to be done as soon as spring would allow. She wanted me to go to the house and take a look at it with her.

A covered bridge! That's what she wanted built as soon as spring would allow. She didn't ask if I knew how to build a covered bridge. She just said that's what needed to be done. And oh, by the way, the bridge was going to have to span 26 feet, and be capable of allowing the passage of a standard UPS truck for deliveries to the house. The house, a log home, was about 3/10 of a mile up the side of a mountain beyond the river the bridge had to span. That was going to be a very well- paying job. However, it was about a three-hour ride to get there, so it meant there would be some overnight stays. Karen again was not happy. The money was great, but now I was going to be away for a couple of days at a time. I think she still had Gretchen in the back of her mind. I told her I was going to need help with the bridge job, and wouldn't be there alone. I also told her Gretchen and I were completely finished. She still didn't seem too comfortable, but it was a good job, and I wasn't going to give it up.

In February 1985, Karen and I went to Hawaii for a one week stay on Waikiki Beach in Honolulu. It was beautiful, and far less crowded than we had expected. We spent lots of time on the beach, enjoying the sun and the water. As it turned out, Karen bore a striking resemblance to a young actress popular at that time. She, too, happened to be staying in a hotel on the same beach, at the same time. People were running up to my wife and snapping photos of her, as she was laying on the beach in her bikini. I think she liked it for a little while but then got tired of it. She wanted to go for a drive around the Island. Heading west we passed Pearl Harbor. We didn't stop, and then we turned north into the Dole pineapple fields. For miles, as we drove, all you could see were pineapple plants. We ended up in a park in the mountains overlooking Waialua Bay. It was very beautiful, exotic plants and trees, and several waterfalls; some with small pools you could swim in at the base of them.

After leaving Hawaii, we stopped in San Francisco to see David. He was living just outside of the city, and going to one of the colleges there. He was married now. I wasn't fond of his wife; she seemed to be very bossy and controlling. She was also going to one of the colleges out there, and they each had part time jobs. He seemed to be happy enough, and we spent almost a week with them. They took us around the city, and showed us all the normal tourist things and places. David seemed to enjoy having us there. I'm not sure if his wife enjoyed our company as much as he did. I didn't really care; it wasn't her I was there to see. With February drawing to a close, it was time I got back and pay attention to my business and my work.

As I was making preparations to get started on the covered bridge, I got a call from someone looking to have a house designed and built. Another great job! However, up to that point I hadn't really been doing work in the state that required a builder's license. I would need one for the new house job. The work in New Hampshire was so far back in the woods, and up in the mountains, that I wasn't worried about permits. I knew if I was going to be building houses and additions in Massachusetts, I was going to have to get a Contractor's License. I got all the necessary information and paperwork required, and went to Boston to take my test. When I got there, I realized I could take the test for a Contractor's License, or a Construction Supervisor's License. I decided to go all in and take the Supervisor's test. About ten days or two weeks later, I got my License in the mail. I guess I passed. I met with the people for the new house and started working on the design. It was going to be a simple Cape Style house, no garage. It was now early April, and I had to get to work on the bridge.

My father said he could work weekends for me if I wanted, and he had another guy that he worked with that was also interested. I told him that would be great, and we agreed on payment. The first thing that had to be done was to remove the existing log and plank bridge that was apparently built when the house was built. I had a load of lumber delivered, to start building the new beams and floor sections. We went up for the first weekend, Karen included. While my father and his friend were busy ripping up the old planks on the bridge, I was assembling the new built-up beams that would replace the old logs that had been used as beams. For some reason, the old planks being pulled up were being placed in the middle of the bridge, as the two of them worked from one end to the other ripping them up. That put the pile of old planks behind them as they worked. Just as I was about to tell them I didn't think it was a good idea to place all of the old planks in the middle of the span of those old log beams, because they would have to move them again anyway, my father's pry bar lost its grip and he fell back onto the pile. He broke three ribs and was going to be out of commission for some time.

I got Kevin, to come up and help with the removal of the existing bridge. Both Kevin and my father's friend were heavy drinkers, and it was like watching two stooges work completely against each other in their efforts. They did, in spite of themselves, get the old bridge removed. I had ordered a couple of new concrete lintels to be placed on new concrete piers at each end of the new bridge. The piers, three on each end, would be poured-in-place. And we would do that part ourselves. With the new concrete piers in place, and the built-up beams, four of them made to span the river completed, we were just waiting on the concrete lintels. They were going to be ready in the middle of the week, so it was just going to be me and the truck driver there. The concrete company assured me that the driver could put them in place for me. They were right. He set them in place and they were ready for the new floor beams. The truck driver was not allowed to help me with them. I was going to have to find someone local, with a backhoe.

Meanwhile, back at the drawing board, I was having trouble making my new house clients happy with the interior layout of the house. As work went on with that, I continued up in the mountains. Kevin came and worked some days with me. He was sort of a help. With the use of the local backhoe guy, we got the new beams set and began putting the floor frame together. The bridge was coming along nicely. I was getting paid as I was billing, and the homeowners didn't bother me too much. The floor was framed, and the two side walls were built and standing before Mrs. Homeowner came to see how it was coming along. Mrs. Homeowner, Angela, was a very nice Italian lady, maybe six or eight-years older than me. While she was very happy with her bridge, she also noted that she thought it was moving a little slow. I explained that since there wasn't any electricity close by, everything was being cut with either a hand saw, or a chain saw. Besides, all of the materials we were using for the frame were too big for a skill saw. She seemed okay with that, and decided to be a little more patient. It was the first week of August, when the bridge was finished. It had a gate at each end that could be locked, and four windows, two on each side. All of the windows had shutters that could be closed and locked. The homeowners seemed very happy with their new bridge, and would think about what they wanted to do with the house.

Having finally made my new house clients happy with the plans for their house, it was time to get that started. I had to hire two new employees, both with building experience. I did some advertising, and while waiting for that to pan out, I got the foundation for the house put in and backfilled. I got a couple of young guys, from my ad, that seemed eager to work. With my new help, and Kevin still tagging along, we started building the new house. My mother was happy to see that Kevin was working for me. She was more comfortable seeing my business growing as it was. One day, she told me that she didn't think Kevin was going to make it on his own and asked if I would sort of take care of him. I told her I would try to do that for her. We worked on the exterior of the house through the fall so we could work inside during the winter. We finished the house in late January of 1986. And, as we finished it, I got a call from the covered bridge people and from the contact I had made while designing kitchens. That was to turn out to be a very good contact indeed.

Chapter Twenty
Karen, Angela and Angelo

Meanwhile, back on the home front, Karen told me that Betty had a new 'boy-toy'. She had left the insurance company and got a job in the administrative office of a factory. The new young man was about nine or ten-years younger than her, and they seemed to be very happy together. Karen said they were planning on buying a house together and had found one a few towns over. Karen also said that she had heard about a Racquetball League that was starting up at a local golf and fitness center. She wanted to join and wanted to know if I would go with her. I had been playing Racquetball with both Betty and Karen for a few years. I had never played against anybody else, but since I liked the game I said I would give it a try. Betty and her new young man, Ron, were also joining. The League played on Thursday nights, and it was there that I first met Ron. He seemed like a very nice and likable guy. The league was broken into teams, on different levels based on ability and quality of play. The better you played the game, the higher level team you were on. As you got better, if you wanted to move to a higher level team, you had to play and beat, the lowest ranked member of the higher ranked team. I started in the lowest level team, as one of their lowest ranked players. By the end of the first season, I was the next level up, having defeated two of the members of that level team. I liked the game, and was having lots of fun with it. After the games were finished for the night, some of the players would gather in the bar of the golf club for food and drinks.

Having finished the new house, I met with Angela about the work they wanted to have done to the log home in the mountains. It was going to be extensive. Starting at the basement level, I would be adding a new concrete floor, a full bath with a whirlpool type tub and a walk-in shower. Off the bathroom there would be a sauna, large enough for six people. The rest of the basement would be finished as a large game room, with stairs being added to the first floor. Work on the first floor was really no more than re-working space for the stairs to the basement and sprucing up the bathroom. The second floor had two bedrooms and a bath at one end, with a high cathedral ceiling above the family room and attic area above two first floor bedrooms and a bathroom. They wanted to use the attic area to add another bedroom, with a dormer and balcony looking out at Mt. Monadnock. To get to that bedroom they wanted a bridge built from the existing second floor area, to the new bedroom. I said, "Sure let's do it, why not?"

About that same time, I was meeting with my contact from the kitchen design place. As it turned out, he was about my age and was a very wealthy young man. Angelo was half owner and had seen some of my work. He was now looking to get into house building and development, and wanted me to work for him. I told him I had my own building business now, and while I couldn't work for him, I would be more than happy to work with him. He said that would be fine with him. So, in the summer of 1986, along with the mountain house, I began to build new houses with Angelo. By September of 1986, I had two six-man framing crews and one two-man finish crew, working five-and-a-half days a week. As the houses were being built, I was stealing weekends and whatever time I could during the week to work on the mountain house. Karen couldn't have been happier. There were expensive dinners out, and lavish gifts for Christmas', birthdays and anniversaries. I had a new truck; she had a new car, and she got to do whatever she wanted with 'her' money. I finished the mountain house a little later than I wanted to. Angela had a habit of showing up with a bottle of her favorite whiskey, making a pot of coffee, and having the two of us sit and visit, drinking coffee with whiskey in it. Not much work got done at those times. My electrician said he thought she was trying to get me into bed. She did seem maybe just a little too friendly and touchy sometimes. I never took the hint. Those things can be bad for business (Marriages too). It was late November or early December, and I had to go and finish up a few small details and it would be done.

Besides having my work truck, I also had a Subaru GL. On the day that I was going up to the mountain house to finish up those few little things, I drove that up. I didn't need much in the way of tools, and the car got much better gas mileage than the truck. There was an ice storm that turned to snow the previous night. With only about one or two inches of snow on the ground, driving in the area just prior to the covered bridge was easy. However, after passing though the bridge and starting up the side of that mountain, things got a little rough. I got about halfway up that twisting little road to the log house and my car lost traction and began to slide backwards down the side of the mountain. Not having any control, there was no way to keep the car on the twisting road. Before I knew it, my car was off the side of the road, and stuck in the woods with no hope of getting it out. I had bounced off several trees and over lots of small rocks and other debris before coming to rest against another small tree. I didn't know it at the time, but Angela was also on her way to the house. She parked her car at the bottom of the hill and walked up. As she was climbing the hill, she found me sitting in my car backed into the woods off the road, maybe a little dazed. With the help of a tow truck we got my car out of the woods. All of that took some time, so I ended up calling Karen and telling her what happened, and that I would be staying the night at the log house. She didn't ask how I was. What she asked was, "Is Angela staying the night with you?"

My Subaru was a mess, but drivable and I drove it home the following day. And yes, Angela did stay the night at the log home, and no nothing happened between us. I made that sort of stuff clear before. I sent my Subaru to the body shop and it came back looking like new. With the log home now complete, Angela told me they also had a beach house on Cape Cod that was going to need some work. She also gave me her sister's name and phone number. They were looking for a very large addition to their house. Simone, Angela's sister, lived in the same 'Boston burb' that Angela lived in, and not too far away. They too had your basic big box Colonial Style house, and wanted to add a three-car garage, with the master suite above. I was going to have to hire more help to get that, and all the houses we were working on, done. Simone said she had another friend that was looking to have an addition put on their house; I told her if she wanted me to do it, she was going to have to wait. Angelo was keeping me very busy building new houses.

With the coming of March 1987, just as I was starting Simone's addition, Angelo told me he had purchased a large tract of land just outside the city. His plan was to develop it into a small neighborhood community. He also had some sort of business going on in Florida, at the same time. So he was going to want me to handle everything; roads, drainage, underground electrical, and all of the landscape work. He wanted that along with getting the houses designed and built on some sort of schedule. Since most of the houses being built were in or very near the city, I was going to have to have constant contact with subcontractors and suppliers and I needed a new toy. I had something called a 'mobile cellular telephone' installed in my truck. That phone cost about $1,250.00, and was hard wired to the truck. As long as I was in or close to the city, I got really good reception. Get too far from the city, and there was no reception at all. Cellular phones had only been around for a couple of years at that time, and there was only one carrier in our area. The phone was mounted on the dashboard of the truck and looked like a regular phone handset, with the numbers on it. It also had a small digital display that identified incoming calls.

Also that spring, I began doing small things that Angela wanted done at the house on Cape Cod. I would take one or two of my guys, along with Karen and the guys' wives, and spend a weekend working there. All of the wives would go off shopping, or doing something, for the day while we worked. We worked like that on her house through that spring and most of the summer. Angela would occasionally come and stay for the weekend in the summer while we worked. The house was right on the beach, so Angela and the wives would spend a lot of time by the water. Karen seemed a little uneasy with Angela. She never came out with it, but I think she thought Angela and I had an affair while I was working on the mountain house.

Most of my employees were good, honest, hardworking men that knew what they were doing. I was confident that if I gave one of the framing leaders a plan, the house would get built as planned and on time. However, there was on occasion the guy that would slip in through the cracks. I had run another ad for experienced carpenters for the new development. One of the people that responded was a young guy, with a truck and lots of tools. He said he had been working in the business for about five years, the condition of his tools told another version of his story. Most of the tools that I could see were new, or almost new. I decided to give him a chance. One of the houses being framed at that time was a tri-level Contemporary Style house, with several skylights on the south side of the roof. I asked him if he was okay with height and he said he was.

91

Hearing that, I sent him up to help apply the roof shingles on that house. About ten minutes later, one of the other guys working on the house came to me and said there was a problem with the new guy on the roof. When I went over to the house and looked up; what I saw was my new guy, on his stomach, with his legs and arms spread out, and his fingers trying desperately to claw though the roof to hold on. It took three of us about a half hour to get him off the roof. I also got him back in his truck and off my work site.

Chapter Twenty-One
Cape Cod

Karen and I bought a house in the summer of 1987. It was one town over to the east from the town I grew up in. I thought I might be able to reconnect with some of the old friends from the pickup ball games. That never happened. About the same time we bought our house, Rachel decided to move to some small town in the mountains at the corner of MA, NY and VT. I don't remember the name of the town, but I think it was somewhere East of left ass cheek, and just South of ball sack MA (Hmm, does that sound a little bitter? Well, maybe, but I'm going to leave it in anyway). What I do know was it was more than a three-hour ride to see my kids. There wasn't going to be much in the way of picking them up, going to my parents' house for a visit and then bringing them home again. She moved there to live with some older man with lots of money that would take care of her. Without going back to court, Rachel was not going to let me have the kids for a weekend. Seeing them was getting more and more difficult.

Also in the summer of 1987, Karen and I, Betty and Ron, rented a cottage on Cape Cod for a week. The week went fine, and we all had fun. Betty brought her two kids with her, so the cottage was a bit crowded, but it reminded me of the summers at my grandfather's cottage when I was young. One afternoon we all went to a local ice cream shop. We all got either an ice cream cone, or some sort of ice cream drink. As Betty's youngest son was sitting at the picnic table along with the rest of us, he had gotten an ice cream soda, and with it just sitting on the table it exploded. I don't know what made it explode like that, but it got all over everybody. Sitting right in front of it, the poor kid got the worst of it. He didn't want to replace it; he just wanted to go home.

Simone's addition went smoothly, but took a little longer than I planned. The drive from the housing development to Simone's house was about an hour, and I was glad to see all that running around come to an end. By the end of 1987, the addition was done and we were working our way through the development at a very good rate. The houses were selling before we could get them built. The road with all of the underground drainage, and electrical and sewer work had been completed. As each new house was built, all they had to do was make the necessary connections to the underground services. Having to be on site at the development, all day, meant that I would go home and spend my evenings designing the new houses. There were nights that I would be up until two in the morning working on a design. I remember the nights visiting Karen, Betty, and Steve until 1:00 or 1:30; I thought those late nights were behind me. While designing all of the houses in the development, I also found myself now designing houses for other builders. The year had been a very good one. However, 1988 would look much different.

As 1988 got started, things were going along just fine. We had the exterior framing complete on several houses and made them weather tight. So now my framing crews could work on the interior frames of the houses through the really cold weather. I liked to work with the framing guys, so sometimes when time allowed, I would jump in and do some of the framing work. I supplied my framers with pneumatic nail guns to speed things up, and to make the work a little easier and faster for them. While doing some interior framework, I shot a nail into the base of a wall stud. The nail apparently hit a nail underneath the stud, and came back out, and into my hand. I couldn't get the nail out of my hand so I had to go to the hospital to get it removed and my hand patched up. When I got back to the work site, I saw Kevin sitting on the deck of one of the houses. He had a bucket of old rusty, bent nails, that I would occasionally pick up off the ground with my hands, rather than with my tires. He had dumped out the nails, and looked as if he was trying to sort through them. I asked one of the other workers how long he had been doing that and he said almost since I left. When I asked Kevin what he was doing, he said he was looking for good nails to take out of the trash. As calmly as possible, I explained to him that I wasn't paying anyone to sit around and play with a bucket of old nails. I told him to get back to the work he was getting paid to do.

One day, my father's car broke down. The truth was he was using it as a truck to carry firewood. He would load the trunk and back seat until the rear springs bottomed out, and then drive it six or seven miles back to his house. He finally broke a rear spring going over a bump. The weight of the overloaded car came down on the rear axle and broke that as well. Because he couldn't afford to go out and buy a new car, I gave him my Subaru. The Subaru had a five-speed manual shift. I knew he could drive a standard shift, what I didn't know was he didn't think you needed to shift it. He would get the car into forth gear and drive along at 5500 or 6000 rpms, and never get to fifth gear. He would then have to slow down to a point where he should be in second gear, and not down shift the car. The poor little engine would be coughing, and sputtering, but he still would not shift it. If I told him he should be in some gear other than the one he was in, he would get upset with me, and tell me the car was doing just fine as it was. I was sure that was going to be the end of my Subaru.

I had given the Subaru to my father sometime around the end of February. About a week after giving him the car, my truck got t-boned by a car. As I was going past the exit from a small shopping center, a car shot out of the parking lot, and drove right into the driver's side of my truck. The car pushed the driver's side door in, along with the rocker panel beneath it. Since my truck was still moving forward when it got hit, the car slid down the side of the truck also taking out the corner post of the cab and the side of the rear bed. The car had four young people in it, three late teenaged boys and one girl. I had to climb out the passenger side door of my truck. When I got out and made my way around to see the damage, all of the kids were out of the car looking at the front of it. I could hear the girl telling the driver there wasn't much damage to the car and they should get out of there. I told the driver that I wanted his driver's license and insurance information. To my surprise he gave them to me quickly and without an argument. With his information in hand, I got back in the truck and called the police.

A police car was at the scene within minutes. I gave the other drivers information, along with mine to the officer. As the officer was walking around looking at the car and the truck, he turned to the young driver and said, "So were you planning on stopping?"

The young man, still looking at his car, turned to the officer and said, "Well, yeah!"

"Well, when?" asked the policeman. The young man never answered him. A report was filled out and we all went on our way. When I got home and Karen saw the damage to the truck, she began verbally attacking me as if I had been the one at fault. When I got her to listen to what had happened, she began to calm down but for some reason continued to be mad at me about the accident. It took over a month, but the other drivers insurance company finally paid to get my truck fixed.

The Racquetball League was still going on and by now, I had worked my way up to the second highest level. I was playing really well and still having a great time with it. On a Thursday night in the middle of April, I twisted my right knee very badly. I had torn tendons and damaged my knee so much that I was going to have to wear a brace on that knee for the next two or two and a half years. I was still able to play, but was never as good after that. By early May, we were working on framing more new houses in the development. With new materials being delivered almost every day, there was a lot of plywood and framing supplies on site all the time. One of my framing crews said that they seemed to be losing plywood at night. I began to keep a daily inventory, and sure enough eight to ten sheets of plywood seemed to go missing every night. I had the local police come out to the site to talk about the problem and what we could do about it. The only solution we all came up with was to get a box trailer on site, and keep the materials in it. Having to do that was a pain in the ass. We spent the first half hour each day pulling out the materials we would need for the day. But it did solve the theft problem. While the police were still there, I heard someone scream, and other guys start to yell. I, along with the police officer, went to see what was going on. Apparently Kevin had fallen off a step ladder and broken one of his ankles. An ambulance was called and Kevin was off to the hospital. I sent one of the other workers to the hospital to give Kevin a ride home when he was done there. The houses were still selling, but by late May or June, I began to see sales slow down a bit. By the fall of 1988, sales had all but stopped.

The housing market, in late 1988, came to an absolute standstill. You couldn't sell a house no matter how hard you tried, not even for half of its value. I don't remember the reason but nobody was buying anything. I had to finish the houses that we were already working on, but I couldn't start anything new. So again, that meant I had to let several people go. Having promised my mother I would look after Kevin, I had to keep him. By the start of 1989, Kevin and I were the only two left. I was scrounging for any work I could get. Back when I finished Simone's addition I never got back to her about her friend's addition. I knew she had gotten someone else to build it for her. I called Angela to see if she had anything that needed to be done. She had some things at the mountain house that she wanted to do, but her husband had talked her into waiting for a bit. By mid-spring of 1989, I had only picked up a few small jobs here and there. By now Karen and I were not getting along very well, again. Money was getting tight but Karen and Betty still wanted their week at a cottage on Cape Cod. Karen knew we couldn't afford it, but that didn't seem to matter. She wanted it, and she was going to have it. I finally had to let Kevin go.

Kevin was able to get a job at a local factory as a janitor. With the housing market not moving, and me having to pay for a week in a cottage on Cape Cod, I too got a job at a local factory but not the same one where Kevin was working. I was going to start my new job as a machine operator's assistant on the last Friday of our Cape Cod vacation. That meant that I would come home on Thursday and Karen would come home on Saturday. My job was a weekend shift. I worked Friday, Saturday and Sunday for 36 hours and got paid for 40. That was a good shift for me, because it allowed me to continue to look for other work during the week. My starting pay at the factory was $7.25 per hour. I hadn't had a job that paid that little, since I graduated high school. It was a job! It did bring in some money, but Karen was very unhappy with the situation. As you can imagine, Karen and I were not getting along very well, again. All of the money from my new job went to Karen just so she could be sure I wasn't wasting it on things not needed. She gave me money for gas and that was it.

Chapter Twenty-Two
Angela, Again

When I started my new job at the factory, my supervisor told me that he was one year behind me in high school, and that he remembered me from the National Honor Society meetings when I was a senior. He assigned me to the best machine in the factory. It was the only one in an enclosed, air-conditioned space. He spent a lot of time in there just visiting with me. Another frequent visitor was the quality control tech. Her name was Diana, and she was one year older than me. Her job was to monitor and test the material coming off the machines. She worked in a lab that was at a second-floor level, above the supervisors' offices. From the entry door to the room my machine was in, you could look up and straight into her lab. She was very often standing in the lab window looking at the door to my room. It always made me happy to look up there and see her looking back at me. I was finding her very attractive.

Around the end of September, Angelo called. He had another house for me to build. That was great news for me, except I didn't have anybody to help me build the house. Angelo said he was only going to have me frame, roof and side the house. He was going to leave it that way until someone put a deposit on it. At least it would be some extra work for a little while. After looking around a bit, I found a contractor that had three men working for him, and he was looking for work. I got together with him and between the two of us, we came up with a deal that would allow me to use his men to build the house. He of course was going to get some money out of the deal as well. It was a good deal for both of us; his men were working, he was getting some money for the use of his men, and I was building my fiftieth house as a building contractor. I would build just one more house on my own, and that would be my own house, later in the story. We got the house closed in, and we were done with it by the end of October. I was back to looking for something to do during the week.

In the second week of November, Angela called about her covered bridge. It wasn't there anymore! Apparently they had one of those one hundred year floods up in the mountains. She and her husband had gone up to check on the house, and couldn't find the bridge. The river flooded and swelled so much that it washed out the bridge pilings, and the bridge was later found a couple hundred yards downstream. It was stuck in a tangle of downed and broken trees. Angela said they were unable to get to the bridge to see what condition it was in, and didn't know if it could be reused or was going to have to be rebuilt. She asked me how soon I would be able to meet her there to take a look at the situation.

Since she was calling on a Sunday night, I told her I would be there the following day. Karen again was not very happy about the arrangements. I simply told her to just keep thinking about the money. That reply didn't seem to make her any happier.

When I met Angela, we stood at the side of the river, which was still quite high, and moving very fast. I could just see the bridge downstream. With the help of a chain saw, we were able to cut a path along the edge of the river to get to the bridge. Once there, I was able to get on the bridge to check out the parts that were still above water. Most of what I could see looked to be in good condition. I told her that if I could get the bridge free from the broken trees, and get it back up to the road, I would be able to check out the beams beneath it. Getting the bridge back up to the road was not going to be easy, but the high water would be a help. The fact that it was moving so fast away from road, would not help. We went back up to the site where the bridge had been, and looking at the ends of the road on each side of the river, a larger problem began to surface. Because the sides of the river had washed out, the bridge, built to span twenty-six feet, was now going to have to span about thirty feet. Angela started to cry and said that her family had planned to have Christmas at the mountain house. As I gave her a hug, I told her I would try to think of a way to fix it. She went back to her car, and came back with a large thermos of coffee and her favorite whiskey, and said "I know you can fix this". As we sat consuming the hot beverage, I was already coming up with a plan.

Later that evening when I got home, Karen came to me for what I thought was a kiss. Silly me, she just wanted to see if I had been drinking with Angela. Somehow my having a drink with a client, while looking at the situation at hand, translated to the two of us having sex all day. I was really getting tired of her accusing me of having an affair with Angela, so I told her to think whatever she wanted, I wasn't going to get into it again with her. I called the local backhoe guy I had used before at the bridge, and after explaining the situation, we agreed to meet the following morning at the bridge site, with his backhoe. That morning I grabbed several auto tow chains with hooks on both ends, and met the backhoe guy. After looking things over we decided to cut a wider path along the side of the river to get his backhoe down to the bridge. Standing in very cold waist deep, fast moving water, I connected chains to the front two corners of the bridge, and then to the front bucket of the backhoe. The driver decided the only way he was going to be able to pull the bridge up the river, was to back his way out, digging the rear bucket into the ground to help pull him along. With the backhoe keeping tension on the bridge, I cut the broken trees and brush from around it. Now with the bridge free and floating, the backhoe driver's idea was working very well. It didn't take us too long to get the bridge back up to the road, and lined up ready to slide right back in place. With the bridge on the road again, I was able to get under it to check out the original beams. Everything looked in very good shape, it was just going to be a matter of putting the bridge back in place. Of course there was that pesky matter of the extra four feet the bridge was now going to have to span.

I had a plan for that, too. When I got home later that day I called a steel salvage yard in Northern Connecticut, about twenty miles east of my house. After doing some quick figuring I told the yard man what I was looking for. He didn't have it, but he had two steel beams that were going to be close enough. With the yard holding two steel beams for me, the next issue was getting them from Connecticut, to the mountains of Southern New Hampshire. I called a commercial truck rental place and put a hold on a twenty-six-foot cab-over flatbed truck to be picked up the next morning. When I got to the truck yard, I was given several papers to fill out, and then I was asked for my driver's license. The young lady behind the counter, mid thirty something with a tight sweater, a very short skirt and what looked to be three or four inch heels on, took my paperwork. In very short order she gave my license back to me, and said she would need to see my commercial driver's license. I did not have a commercial driver's license. That was apparently an issue for her, a much larger one for me. I needed that truck! After explaining the situation and begging and pleading, and promising to have the truck back before the end of business the same day, she agreed to give me the truck. Just as long as I would also promise not to leave the state (MA) with it. With me standing in front of her not saying anything, after an awkward moment or two, she threw her arms up and said, "I don't want to know." She asked if I had ever driven a truck with air brakes before, I said I had. I was sure I would be able to figure it out as I drove.

Driving the truck was easy, and I got to the steel yard quickly. As we were loading the beams on the truck, I found that it did not come with any hold down straps. With a hefty cash deposit, the beams were on the truck and secured. I drove the truck up to the mountain house road. However, the truck was too big to make the turn down that small winding dirt road to the bridge site. I ended up backing the truck all the way down the road to the river. The plan was for the backhoe guy to be there, and take the beams off the truck and put them next to the bridge. That way, we could just slide them into place when I got the new bridge abutments made. Mister backhoe man was nowhere to be found. Not having a lot of time to play with, I just pushed the beams off the back of the truck to the ground, and headed back to the truck rental yard. That night I called the backhoe man. He had been called to an emergency water main break in town, but would be there the next morning. On my way up that morning, I stopped and picked up several sheets of plywood, some two by fours, and concrete form ties. The next step was to make the forms for the concrete abutments. We used the backhoe to divert the water away from the plywood forms with stones, logs, brush, and anything else we could find. We got the form built on one side of the river, but it was now Thursday night, and I had to go back to my factory job for the weekend.

I made arrangements for concrete to be delivered the following Monday morning. I had built the abutment forms with two pockets at the top to drop the ends of the steel beams in, and with a lower shelf sticking out far enough to set the ends of the original wood beams on. With the first abutment complete, we began to remove the forms. I didn't want to have the back side of the new abutment back-filled without first building a stone rip rap in front of it. The rip rap would keep the new abutment from moving while the other one was being completed. A rip rap, for those of you that don't know, is a pile of rocks, placed against a bridge abutment, or riverbank, to reduce erosion and movement, from the river constantly passing by. It took all of that second week to get the other abutment in place, and then back to the factory. What a pain in the ass.! Karen was also being a pain in the ass. She kept wanting to know if Angela was at the site with me. When it was obvious that Karen thought Angela was with me all of the time, I stopped telling her I hadn't seen her since I started the work. The following Monday morning I was back at the bridge. I spent some time, with a little help from the backhoe, building the rip raps. Once that was done, the new steel beams were put in place, and the back side of the abutments were then filled in with gravel. The gravel was kept down about four or five inches from the top of the road surface, so I could install new concrete approaches at each end of the bridge. The new approaches would become concrete ramps to take care of the fact that the bridge was four feet too short. The bridge was then put back in its proper place. With a little cleaning up, the job was done. The following week Angela met me at the bridge, with money and that favorite hot beverage of hers. She was a very happy young lady. Christmas was going to be held at the mountain house after all. Karen and I were invited. I politely declined and never told Karen about the invite.

Chapter Twenty-Three
Breakup Number Two, and Diana

Shortly after the first of the year, 1990, Angelo called and wanted the framed house finished. He had a buyer and had gotten the house ready for the interior trim. One day while working on the house alone, I had an accident in which all of the soft tissue of my left hand got crushed. It was an odd sort of thing to happen. A piece of wood got stuck in the table saw, and shot back, catching my hand just right. For some reason no bones were broken, but my hand and arm, up to my shoulder began to turn almost black, and swell unbelievably. I went to a local hospital and they had to cut my wedding ring off. My left hand was completely useless, and I had to have hand therapy for a couple of months. During that time they had to glue hooks on my fingernails and tie my fingers forward to my wrist to get them to bend. Karen accused me of hurting my hand on purpose. She never gave me any reason she thought I would do such a thing. It did not help our relationship. The house was finished in late March of 1990. Through all of that time I was still working at the factory each weekend.

While I was working on the house, and still working at the factory, I was promoted to head machine operator, in control of that nice air-conditioned machine. Over time Diana began to spend more and more time in my machine room. She clearly was spending time in there just to visit with me. I was in one very bad relationship, and I wasn't sure I wanted to start anything else at the time. But Diana was very pretty, and very friendly. When I hurt my left hand, my Supervisor put me on light duty work, and gave me an extra assistant to help me. With me hurt and having extra help, Diana would of course have to spend extra time with me, (yeah, that was a shame) and pay extra attention to the materials coming from my machine. She was beginning to wear me down. She was not just beautiful to look at, but I was starting to feel an inner beauty in her that I had never felt with anybody else before. Karen and I were not doing well at all. At the end of April, my father called and said my brother, David had moved to Virginia and bought a house. He said David needed to have an oak floor installed, and had asked my father to come and help him. Dad knew nothing about installing hardwood floors, and I didn't think David did either. I told my father, with my hand now better, I would drive down with him, and we would install the floor together. When I told Karen of my plans with my father, she said if I left for a week with my father, probably drinking more than working, she may not be here when I get back. After all, I should be out looking for real paid work, not taking drinking vacations with my family. I took Sunday off from my factory job, another thing to piss Karen off, and my father and I drove to David's house. The drive took about eight hours, but wasn't really that bad of a drive.

When we got to David's house, we rested for the rest of the day, and started his floor on Monday morning. By early Wednesday, the floor was done. David's wife was working, so we didn't see much of her, except in the evenings. That was ok with me; I still didn't like her. David had taken the week off from work to help us with the floor. He mostly watched, as did my father. I called Karen once from David's house. She didn't really want to talk to me, and said that she had found an apartment, and was planning on moving into it the next weekend. I would be back at my factory job at the time. Now, if you think back, you may remember that Karen had a son from her marriage with Jim. She had custody, and he had been living with us all this time. Jim made little effort to see his son. Karen said the apartment was in another town, and she didn't want to take the son out of school so close to the end of the school year. She asked if I would keep him with me until school ended. Realizing none of our problems were his fault, I agreed so he could stay in the same school until the end of that year. Meanwhile, Diana and I had become very good friends. I would talk to her about all the crap with Karen. She understood; she too had been married twice before we met. With Karen making it clear that we were done, and me making it clear that I was fine with that, Diana and I started to see each other. That would turn out to be the best move of my life.

Having a house involved in the divorce, with me not having any money and Karen not being able to keep it, we tried to sell it. The house was not selling, and the bank was demanding their money. Bankruptcy seemed to be the best answer for us at the time. The bankruptcy was handled quickly, and we were done by the end of July. Now needing a place to live, Diana was very quick to ask me to move into her house with her. The house was a small four room Summer Cottage that had been converted to a year round home, and was across the street from a very large lake, in a very small town. Diana had a daughter from a previous marriage. She was almost twenty and had a baby. She lived with her husband in an apartment in another town. I moved into Diana's house the first week of August, 1990. Diana's daughter and her husband were in the process of buying a house, and the lease on their apartment was going to be up at the end of the month. The house, as it turned out, was not going to be ready. Her daughter, along with her husband and newborn child, moved in with Diana and me. It was only supposed to be for a couple of weeks, but it turned into a couple of months. Things were a little tight and uncomfortable at the house.

Right after I moved in with Diana, the builder that gave me the use of his men called. He had a house to build and needed more help than he had. I told him I would work for him Monday through Thursday every week. He said that would work for him, and oh, by the way, the house was in Boston. Hearing that I said I would still do it, but I would want to leave my truck at his house and ride with him. It was about a half hour ride to his house from mine, and another hour and a half to Boston. He said that was ok. One of the other guys was doing the same thing. Working in Boston all week and then working at the factory all weekend was beginning to be too much for me. At the end of August, I quit my job at the factory, and just worked five days a week for the builder. Having built as many houses as I had, I quickly became the lead carpenter, and was in charge of the work when my boss wasn't there. The work was going well and we were making good progress on the house. Of course, driving a total of three hours a day from my bosses, cut a lot of time out of the workday. By the time cold weather set in, we were ready to start working on the interior of the house.

Diana's family finally moved out and into their new house just before the end of October 1990. Now, we all know what happens at the end of October-that's right! It's Halloween! Apparently Diana had a Halloween tradition, and she couldn't wait to make me a part of it. She, along with her daughter, son in law, and a couple of their friends would dress up in Halloween costumes, and go out toilet papering some of her friend's cars, and maybe a little in a tree, here and there. Diana assured me that she always let the victims know ahead of time, to avoid any issues. This year would be a special year because they had a newbie with them. So, not wanting to break anyone's tradition, I allowed Diana to dress me up as "Beetlejuice". But, not just any old Beetlejuice! No, I had to be Beetlejuice with a nice bright, glow in the dark, face. Diana dressed as a little girl, with a tiny little skirt and ruffled, polka dot panties. I may not have mentioned this before, but I can't see in the dark. So as we were out there toilet papering someone's car, I had to be led around by the hand. Not being able to see the actual fun we were all supposed to be having takes a bit of the "fun" out of fun.

This year, one of the son-in-law's friends was in charge of getting the rolls of toilet paper. He showed up at the house with several of the industrial size rolls that you might have seen in restaurants, and other commercial settings. The rolls must weigh about five pounds each. When you throw one of them up into a tree, two things happen. The first is, the roll doesn't get very far up the tree, and second, it makes a loud "thud" when it hits the ground. Neither of those things are conducive to the art of toilet papering. The fun was that while all of the victims knew we were coming, they wouldn't know when we were there, and would not be able to catch us. One of the first stops was at Diana's best friend's house. She had promised not to make too much of a mess, so we were only going to throw some toilet paper on their car and van. As a roll of paper was rolled across the roof of the van, it made a loud thud, thud noise as it went over the raised ribs of the roof. So much for not knowing we were there.

Having made a couple more planned stops, Diana and her daughter thought it might be fun to visit her son-in-law's family's house. Before I go any further with that wonderful decision, I should tell you that the son-in-law's father was the Chief of the town's police department at the time. I'm pretty sure that this stop was a spur of the moment decision. There are two more things worth mentioning here. The first is, Diana and the son-in-law's father are not exactly friends, to say the least. The second is the man was a raging homophobe, and his son was dressed as a drag queen. Parking the cars down the street from the house, we made our way to the front yard and, with the very first "thud" of a paper roll, head lights and light bars lit up the entire area. Police cars came from every direction. All of the kids scattered, leaving Diana and me alone. Not being able to see anything other than lights and a black background, I was no help in making our getaway. Diana was trying to pull me down the side of the house, when I had a very bright light in front of my face. As the two of us stopped, I heard a voice say, "I have the perps on the side of the house!". "PERPS!" Did I just get called a "PERP?" I looked in the general direction of Diana and said, "I have never been called a PERP in my life!"

As the police brought Diana and me to the front of the house, the rest of the kids all came back to be with us. I thought that was an excellent idea. We were all brought into the police chief's house, and made to do the "Perp. walk" for him. When he saw Diana, he said that he should have known she had something to do with it. Then he saw his drag queen son! Everybody was told to go out and clean up whatever mess we had made, all except the son. Given the fact that we only had time for one "thud" of paper, there wasn't much to clean up. We stood around outside waiting for the son to come back out of the house. As we stood there, we could hear lots of yelling, mostly from the father, but I couldn't make out what was being said. That bringing an end to our good clean Halloween fun, we got in the cars and went home. Even now, Diana tells people that even after all that, I still stayed for more. And she was right, I wasn't going anywhere.

Chapter Twenty-Four
Your Truck's on Fire

Diana's mom lived one town over, and by late Fall her health seemed to start failing. After taking her for some tests, she was told she had lung cancer, the really bad kind that was fast moving, and often didn't respond to treatment. Right after Thanksgiving, we moved her into our house with us. Diana was, at the time, going to school during the week to become a massage therapist; she would be graduating in the Spring. With me working all week in Boston, and her going to school, she thought she would have to drop out. To my great surprise, my father offered to come to our house and be with her mother while we were away. It seems both my mother and father had taken a liking to Diana. That arrangement worked out fine for a while, but as the spring of 1991 came along, Diana's mother was getting very sick. After Diana graduated, she was able to be with her mother during the week, and I would be with her on the weekends. For her graduation, I built Diana a folding massage table. She was able to get some work doing massages at the house during the week, so she could stay with her mom. She was having a lot of trouble seeing her mother as sick as she was, and her heart wasn't really into doing much in the way of massage at the time.

To help me pass the time on the weekends, while looking after Diana's mom, I bought a 1949 Willys pick-up truck to work on and restore. Well, let me be a little clearer here. What I bought was a Willys cab, with a broken frame, no rear bed. The seats and gas tank were just thrown in the cab, and all of the windows were broken. All of the gauges from the dashboard were on the floor of the cab. The truck had a 400ci motor and matching transmission from a 1970 something Pontiac Firebird. The hood and front fenders were piled on the frame behind the cab, all were in very bad shape. The truck had four tires on it, but they were all of different sizes. While we're talking about cars and trucks here, remember that Subaru I gave to my father, and was sure it would be the end of it? Well I was right, the Subaru was no longer of any use to anybody, and my father was now driving a new Dodge pick-up truck that Kevin had bought, and didn't want to keep. Anyway, back to Willy. I didn't have much in the way of tools left, so working on the truck was going to be slow and hard. Finding parts for the old beast was done through catalogs and the mail. I was able to find a radiator repair shop that said they could repair the gas tank and then line it with some kind of rubber that was impervious to gas.

As I worked on the frame and body, I bought new windows locally. They were all flat automotive panels, so that was an easy fix. The window gaskets had to be ordered from some place in New Jersey. I was able to clean up the hood and front fenders and reuse them. The rest of the cab wasn't too bad. There were only minor rust holes to fix, and lots of surface rust, but it cleaned up nicely. I took the seats over to the upholstery shop that did the van work when I was at the cabinet shop. I had the seats done in gray vinyl, with a red fabric inlay, in the middle of the seats and backs. They looked really nice. I also bought some matching gray vinyl and gray vinyl buttons from them. With that material, I made a new vinyl headliner and rear wall panel, with a button tufted diamond pattern. The dashboard I treated the same way as the Jeep. I made an oak applique' and inset all of the gauges, vents, and knobs. Diana's brother came over with a welding set and repaired the frame after I had gotten all the rust off.

The unmatched tires and wheels were taken off, and new proper sized wheels and tires were installed. The entire brake system had to be replaced, from the master cylinder, to all of the brake drums. With all of that taken care of, I had gotten the gas tank back and re-installed it. Before installing the new window glass, gaskets, or any of the interior stuff, the truck was ready to paint. So without having a spray booth handy, I spray painted the truck right there on the grass, beside the house. All of the body work and whatever interior metal was going to show got painted a very deep metallic maroon. The frame was painted glossy black. Not having the rear bed for the truck, I did the standard thing. I built a rack body for it. The gray and red seats, along with the gray headliner and rear wall panel went nicely with the maroon color of the truck. There were no interior door panels and no interior handles to open the doors. I made new panels out of 1/4 inch plywood, and upholstered them in gray vinyl, with red fabric inlay to match the seats. The door handles were going to be an issue. I couldn't find them anywhere. I ended up making new arm rests out of oak for each door. For the handle to open the doors, I made push buttons at the end of each arm rest, and upholstered them with the gray vinyl material. To open the door from inside the truck, you just had to push in the gray button, and the door would open. I only paid two hundred dollars for the truck. Doing all of the work myself, repairing and finishing it, my total investment was about eleven hundred-fifty dollars. I sold the truck right after I finished it for eighteen hundred dollars. It gave me something to do, and I made money on it.

The house in Boston was coming along, and by late spring of 1991, we were just about done with it. There were a few small details left to do, when my boss told me he was going to be out of town for a few days. He gave me the keys for his truck and said I could use it while he was gone. Now, to get to that house you had to take Rt. 128 just south of Boston. So one other worker and I would take the truck, an early 1980 something Ford pickup, to the job each day. One day, as I was driving along in the far-right hand lane, a car pulled up beside me, and a woman dressed in business clothes was yelling something at me. I rolled down the window so I could hear her. She was yelling that my truck was on fire! I looked in the rearview mirror and saw a small wisp of smoke trailing the truck. Just about then, flames started to shoot up inside the cab, behind the seat. We had to get out of the truck! For those of you who have not driven on Rt. 128 South of Boston, and I must admit I haven't since the mid 1990s, let me try to explain what that was like. The road is a multi-lane road with bumper to bumper traffic going 60-65 miles per hour. There are breakdown lanes if you need to get out of traffic. However, during rush hours in the morning and evening, the breakdown lanes become travel lanes. So if you need to take an exit, or your car breaks down, you have to merge with the traffic in the breakdown lane and look for a place to get off the road completely. I was fortunate enough to have a state police car about to pass me on the right, in the breakdown lane. The officer must have seen the flames and the smoke coming from the truck. She put her emergency lights on and slowed down to block the breakdown lane traffic for me.

As I pulled the truck into the breakdown lane, I saw a spot just ahead of us where I could get off the road completely. Just about the time I was pulling off the road, along with the flames inside the truck, flames started to shoot up between the cab and the rear bed. Stopping and getting out of the truck as quickly as possible, I saw the state trooper, (a woman) already out of her car and heading to the truck with a fire extinguisher. I folded the seat back down away from the back of the cab. The flames inside the truck were coming from several rolled up blueprints. Looking under the truck I could see the flames coming from old built up grease and oil. More importantly, I saw the flames licking the side of the gas tank. I told the trooper what I saw under the truck, and she immediately got down on the ground and started spraying those flames. Both the fire under the truck, and the one inside were extinguished quickly. After surveying the damage, I thanked the trooper and said we would be on our way. The trooper however was not about to let me drive the truck. She called for a tow truck from her car and sat there until it showed up.

The tow truck driver gave us a ride to his shop, where I called Diana and told her about the problem. She was going to have to come and get us. She had to call my father and ask him to come and be with her mother, and then drive all the way to Boston to pick us up. Diana does not do well with heavy traffic on major highways. When she finally got to us, she was chewing what looked like an entire package of gum, and her hands were white and frozen in a steering wheel grip shape. Needless to say, I drove the car home. The truck was going to need some repairs done before we could drive it. I called my boss and told him what happened. He was very upset. He wanted me to bring the truck back to the shop that he used for service, but the police officer told the tow truck driver the truck was not to be driven until the repairs were made. The truck was repaired quickly and ready to be picked up when my boss got home. I took Diana's car and brought my boss to get the truck and from there we went to the house to do the final little things left to finish.

The following day my boss brought his wife to see the house. We had maybe one hour of work to finish up, and then we were done. After cleaning up the site, we loaded all the tools on one corner of the wrap around porch. My boss was going to back the truck up to that corner so we could load everything in the back of it. With his wife standing by the corner, he asked her to tell him when to stop. He ended up using the "touch system", backing into the corner of the deck and damaging some of the decking and the column at the corner. Very upset, he got out of the truck and asked why she didn't tell him when to stop. His wife replied with "I couldn't tell you because I was eating a plum." Now we had a little more work to do before being done. After finishing the house, again, my boss didn't have any more work lined up. I was out of a job once again.

Chapter Twenty-Five
The Start of Business

Now with both of us home during the week, and trying to deal with Diana's mom, we were losing ground with her, and we knew it. I was trying to help Diana deal with seeing her mother like that, as well as help with the care of her mother. We were able to get a home health aid to come to the house for a couple of hours, a few days a week. She was a very nice and very caring young lady, and understood what we were dealing with. One day when she came, we went out and bought a "lake yacht", a rubber raft just big enough for the two of us. When the weather was nice, and the health aid came to the house, we would sometimes pack a lunch and go "yachting". We would carry our little raft across the street to the lake, throw it in the water and row out into the lake and have a picnic. Sometimes there would be speed boats running up and down the lake, and we would try to get them to go past us so our little raft would bounce and roll over the boat wake. It was a simple pleasure, but a very much needed diversion.

Needing a job and not being able to find one, I did what I had done before. I started a new business designing additions and new houses. I was able to work from home, only having to leave to gather information for additions to existing houses, or meet with builders or clients to discuss plans for new houses. The business was slow getting started, but any money I could bring in was a help. To add to the business income, we also started to sell drafting and engineering supplies. We got a couple of commercial accounts, and a little walk in traffic. By that time, around the middle of fall 1991, Diana's mother was in and out of the hospital quite a bit, and becoming very frail and much more sickly. Diana was having a very difficult time with that. Her grandson was also very sickly as a baby. Her daughter's husband was one of those men that felt all of the childcare was simply up to the wife. As a result of that, she was constantly calling us in the middle of the night to come over and help her with her son, or to take them to the hospital. We made those trips often.

Diana's mother passed away at our house in April of 1992. It was in the evening, and her brother was there with us. Neither one of us could do anything to console Diana. She called her daughter and she came over. The two of them just sat hugging each other and crying. My father, now retired, came to the funeral. He tried talking to Diana to help her through her grief, but she just had to do it on her own. It took a long time for her to get to a point where she wasn't crying all the time. With her mom not being at the house anymore, we decided to move our little business to the main shopping area of a much larger town. We were now getting a lot more business selling supplies. We had a local newspaper do a small story about our business, and that helped bring in lots more business. We both worked at our little store during the week, and I worked there on weekends. I was doing my house designing at the store, and with Architects and Engineers coming in to buy supplies, I was able to make some good contacts. When we moved into the store, we also bought a blueprint machine. There wasn't anybody in the area doing blueprinting, so that paid for itself very quickly. We added fine art supplies to our stock, and in the winter of 1992, we hosted watercolor painting classes. The idea was, that besides getting paid for the classes, the students would buy their supplies from us at discount prices. Most of the students, for some reason, went into the city to buy their supplies, the very same brands that we were offering to them at much lower prices. The painting classes were not working out for us, so we ended that part of the business.

When I moved in with Diana, she had a dog. She was a large mixed breed, and weighed about seventy pounds. For a large dog, she was very hyper and barked more than she should. She was also a digger. We would put her out on a run during the day, and she would dig holes large enough to hide in. When digging the holes, she would tunnel under the ground so she could get into the hole, turn around, and be completely out of site. Sometimes she would get into one of the holes and stay there for hours with just her head sticking up above the ground. We called the holes her condos. During the Fall and Winter of 1992, she began to get visits from a stray dog. I don't know where the dog came from; it just started to show up. The dog was a male, with a very skinny body and a very large head. He looked like a German Shepherd, possibly mixed with something else. He made it clear that he loved Diana's dog and wasn't going away, but he was very timid and wouldn't let us near him. So when winter came around, he started to hide under our front porch at night. We would put food out for him, but he would never take it if we were out there. One morning as we were getting ready to go to the store, we heard some strange noises coming from the front porch. When I opened the door, I found the dog lying on the porch with at least three bullet holes in his face. He had one bullet coming out of his head, just above his eyes. He had also been shot in one of his front legs.

We didn't really know what to do with him, and we had to go open the store. We got him to come into the house, and locked him in the bathroom, he was a bloody mess. When we got to the store, we called the Veterinarian that Diana used for her dog and explained the situation. We also explained that he wasn't our dog, and having just moved the business to the new location earlier that year, we didn't have a lot of money. The Veterinarian said she wasn't going to be able to help us with the dog, so we called another one. He said get the dog to him as fast as possible. That Vet took the dog in, and did all of the surgery required, along with the follow up visits for free! He saved the dog's life, and for that we sent his office a very large gift basket, and became customers for all of our Veterinarian needs. The Vet told us that there had been a lot of similar shootings that fall. He told us a story about a local police officer that was running his dog in a public park, and the dog was shot with a cross bow bolt. He wasn't able to save that one. We called one of the local newspapers and they ran a story about our dog and the many others that were being shot that Fall. They put a picture of the big guy (we didn't have a name for him, so we just called him "the big guy"), in the paper, and talked about the Vet doing what he did for us. We kept the dog on a run in the yard after that, and he stayed with us until his death in 2003.

In the summer of 1993 we decided to close our store. It seems that no matter what we had in stock, people always wanted something else. We could get whatever they wanted, but we had to make up minimum orders and would end up losing money. I kept designing additions and houses, but I still wasn't getting enough work. My developer friend, Angelo, had a brother that bought a thirty-six-foot fiberglass boat. The boat was basically sound, but the exterior was a mess. Knowing my background with fiberglass, Angelo's brother called and asked if I could help him restore the boat. I said I could, and then he told me where the boat was. It was in a marina in Fall River, MA about a two-hour drive for me. I decided that I would still do it, but I would need to buy a small truck to carry the tools. I found a 1980 something Chevy S-10 that was in pretty good shape for not too much money. The truck was very close to the same color as that old "shit-brindle-brown-bile" that Steve had roller painted several years ago.

One day when I arrived at the marina, one of the men from the office came to the boat and told me there was a message to call home as soon as I got there. When I called, Diana told me that a raccoon had attacked her dog. She said it was on her face, and won't let go. Diana said she ran out of the house, grabbing a shovel by the driveway, and tried to beat the raccoon of the dog. Being unsuccessful with that, she grabbed the raccoon and pulled it off the dog. Of course the raccoon, not wanting to be cuddled by Diana, began to fight her and she let it go. The raccoon ran off into the woods, but the dog had several scratches and bite marks on her face and head. Diana also had blood and saliva from the raccoon on her hands and arms. It was then that she realized she was standing in the front yard with just a t-shirt and panties on. The noise of the fight brought some of the neighbors out to watch, and were now just standing there looking at her. (We always felt good about being able to entertain the neighborhood). She said she didn't need me to come home, but she sounded so upset that I told her I was heading home as soon as I got off the phone. When I got home, Diana had already cleaned up the dog, and herself. We now had to tell the local animal control officer about the incident. I knew it was not going to be a good conversation. The dog was going to have to be quarantined for six weeks, and Diana was going to have to undergo treatment for possible rabies. We were able to talk the officer into letting us kennel the dog at our house, away from the other dog, as long as we monitored the dog daily, and gave him updates of any changes.

After giving the situation some thought, I'm pretty sure what happened was that the raccoon crawled into the dog condo at dawn, thinking it looked like a nice place to nap. When the dog was put on her run, she must have gone into the condo and come face to face with the raccoon. I never thought the raccoon was rabid. It just seemed to me that it was in the wrong place at the wrong time, as was the dog. After the quarantine period was over, and the dog showed no signs of rabies, the officer gave her a clean bill of health, and we were able to go back to treating her as part of the family again. Diana's dog went on to live what seems to have been a happy life, until the late 1990s when she developed severe hip dysplasia and became unable to function on her own. We had to have her put down; that was a very sad day indeed.

I finished the boat I was working on in mid-September. From there, I went back to just doing my house designing. A large pharmaceutical company was moving onto a property a couple of towns over. It had been an old farm at one time, and the old farmhouse was still there. The manager of the company got my name from the local building inspector. He called and asked if I would be interested in restoring/converting the old farmhouse into a guest and conference center. I was very interested, and met with him a couple of days later. The house was a very large classic example of Greek Revival architecture. There were no rooms on the first floor large enough to serve as a conference room, so walls had to be removed, and second floor areas re-supported. Using old interior and exterior pictures from the local Historical Society, I was able to return all of the woodwork to its original style. The kitchen and bathrooms were upgraded out of necessity. There were four guest bedrooms on the second floor, and three other bedrooms for the manager and his family. The house was also going to serve as their residence on the property. The company moving onto the old property got lots of local media attention. I was able to work in some good coverage of the renovation of the old house as well.

After the article about the renovation came out, I was getting more calls from builders wanting me to work with them. I began to get pretty busy and making enough money to live on. I was never happy with the color of my "Shit-brindle-brown-bile", so one day I pulled it to the side of the house and borrowed an air compressor and spray gun from Diana's brother, and painted it Cayman green. It came out great and looked almost new again. I have always heard that being in business, image is very important. The first job I had to go to after painting the truck, was to meet with a builder that I had been doing a fair amount of work with. One of the first things he said to me was, "Did you get a new truck?" I guess the paint job helped. The late Fall and Winter of 1993-94 was a very busy time for me at the drawing board. With Diana still working her weekend job, I was able to stay busy right through the weekends working at my job. It didn't really feel like a job; I was having fun and loved what I was doing.

Chapter Twenty-Six
Three Queen Ann's and Another Wife

In the spring of 94, I began to get more calls from homeowners looking to have additions designed, along with the occasional new house. Asking how they were getting my name, the answer was always word of mouth. They either got it from a local building inspector, builder, or someone I had done something for in the past. Now having been in the business for a few years, I did learn that I wasn't going to make everyone happy all of the time. I had a client come to me for a new house plan. I met with her to talk about the style of house, rooms, and also important was the budget. Most people wanted more house than their budget would allow. The woman was a real estate broker, so I was pretty sure she knew what she could afford. She wanted an authentic Queen Ann Victorian house, complete with the front turret, and all the trimmings. I designed the house just as she wanted. I gave it wrap around porches, bull nose gable roofs, that big tall front turret, and of course all the gingerbread typical to the style. She loved the plan and set out to find a builder. After a few months, with the house now well under way, she called me one day and said that I designed a very expensive house. When I asked her what she meant by that, she said the house was going to cost several thousand dollars more than I told her it should. Asking for more details I found that she had hired a builder to build the entire house, by the hour! I told her that nobody hires a builder to do that. I said she may as well have given him a blank check and walked way. She said she liked the builder, and that she still felt that I may have misled her on the cost estimate.

When the very overpaid for house was finished, I saw an article about it in one of the major local papers. To my surprise, my client gave me credit for the design work, and never mentioned how she felt about the cost estimate. About two days after that article came out I got a call from another real estate lady. She said her son had been looking for someone that could design an authentic Queen Ann, and now she felt his hunt was over. I met with her son's family and found that they wanted a very large, very authentic Queen Ann. It was so authentic to the point that they were going to send a copy of the plan to a company in the Mid-West. I had never heard of such a company, but what they were going to do for my client, was look at the plan and come up with authentic paint colors, to turn the house into an actual painted lady. A painted lady is a Victorian house with five or more authentic colors on the exterior of the house. I cautioned my client about the extreme cost of building such a house. He told me he was a builder, and would be building it himself. And yes, he said, he understood the cost involved. The plan and the actual house both came out great. The last time I saw it, they were still waiting for paint colors from the Mid-West company. I don't know if that ever happened.

When we had our little store selling drafting and engineering supplies, I made two very good contacts. The first was a local retired engineer, and the second was an architect living in MA but registered in NY. If I had a plan that I was working on that was going to require an engineer's stamp, my new engineer friend was always willing to help me with that. One day he called me and said that he was working on plans for a new baseball field for the town that he lived in, and asked if I could help him with the design of the dugouts. I told him I would be happy to design them for him. I didn't know anything about designing dugouts, but after looking them up found that there wasn't much to them. When I gave him the plans, he wanted me to give him a bill for them. I told him that since it was his job, and for a good cause, I didn't want to get paid for them. He was very happy about that, and said he would let the people in town know what I did. He came to me another time with a project someone had asked him to do, but he wasn't sure what to do with it. The problem was a mobile home that had a very leaky roof. The homeowners were a young couple with a small child and they couldn't afford to do much. The engineer said he wanted to put a roof over the mobile home, but didn't know how he was going to support it. I designed a new roof system to cover the entire building, but to be supported completely by beams, and decorative columns. It also allowed them a six-foot covered front porch. I did not accept any payment for that one either. Since then I did at least two projects every year for which I would not take payment. I felt blessed that my business was going so well, and that was my way of giving a little back. The projects were always for towns or less fortunate people.

The second good contact was the Architect registered in NY This was a young lady that was working out of her house, and seemed to have a small but active business. After the newspaper articles about the renovation of the old Greek Revival and the first Queen Ann house, she began to bring me some of her addition work from NY. She started with small stuff and when she was more comfortable with me, she started to bring me good projects that paid very well. One job she gave me was a very large addition to a mid-1970s colonial house. She hadn't given me all the information I was going to need, so she sent me to the house to get the rest of the info. Both Diana and I went to New York to visit the house. It was a nice looking house from the outside, but things changed rapidly when we went inside. Both of us began to turn bright red, almost immediately. I started to get lightheaded, confused, and disoriented. We decided to go out of the house through the garage. That made it even worse. The house was built on a bluff overlooking the old Erie Canal. That entire area apparently has a very high Radon rate. It was the effects of Radon exposure that we had been feeling. We went back in and got just what I needed, and nothing more. She became a steady client, and remained with me until September 11, 2001.

With the business growing and making very good money now, Diana and I started to talk about doing a little work on her house. It definitely needed it. The house looked like the Summer Cottage that it once was, and I was doing my work

114

on a drafting table in the living room. I began plans for a completely new house for us. I would take that little cottage and turn it into a one and a half story Queen Ann Victorian cottage, with of course an office for myself. Because of construction restrictions around the lake we lived on, we could only remodel the existing house, and could not expand the footprint of it. I was ok with that, as long as I could go up, I could add the extra space we were looking for. I worked on the plans for our house in between paid projects. By the end of February 1995, the plans were ready. Work had slowed just a bit for the winter, and so for the last week of February and the first week of March, we drove to Florida. Diana had a cousin there who was just a few years older than her. We drove to Orlando and would be staying there for a few days. When we arrived at our hotel, the room wasn't ready for us. It was hot that year in February, with higher temps than normal. Since we couldn't get into our room, we decided to go to the hotel's pool to pass the time. Diana changed into her bathing suit, and I just had on shorts. When we got to the pool, it was jammed! There wasn't room for one more person in the pool. We decided to leave the pool and go find something else to do. As we were walking along the concrete pathway, Diana stepped off the edge of it, and twisting her ankle, she fell down. I was behind her and started to go to her assistance, when all of the sudden I was pushed out of the way by a very large black man. He bent down, grabbed Diana, first by the hips, and then around the chest, and picked her up asking if she was alright. I think he may have held onto her, maybe just a little too long. Once she was up, he was holding her very tightly against himself. Diana was mortified. We both laugh about the incident now, and I heard Diana chuckle a little when she read this.

In our time in Orlando, we visited some of the theme parks, and other attractions. We didn't go to Disney World on that trip. Diana wanted to go to see her cousin instead on the gulf coast. Diana had gotten directions to the apartment complex her cousin lived in and it was pretty easy to find. When we drove into the parking lot, we saw an old woman sweeping the sidewalk wearing heavy long pants, and a very heavy wool sweater. We just sat for a few minutes watching her, and saying to each other "But it's 85 degrees out." The old woman dressed for December in New England was Diana's cousin. The two of them were happy to see each other, and of course Diana had to rib her cousin a bit about the way she was dressed. Her cousin went along with the ribbing and just said she had been a little sick and seemed to get cold easily. We stayed at the cousin's apartment for a few days, did a few touristy things, and they just enjoyed seeing each other again. We knew it was going to take us a couple of days to get home, so, just before the end of the first week of March, we headed north.

In the time that I had been with Diana, I came to know her as the most caring, honest, giving, and selfless person I had ever met. I also began to understand that the love I felt for her, was, for the first time in my life, true love. The feeling I had for her made me realize that I never really loved my first two wives at all. I had asked Diana three or four time to marry me. She said no each time! When we got back from Florida, and were getting ready to start the renovation of her little cottage, I asked one more time. This time she said yes. So, before we started the work on the cottage, we got married. For those of you still counting, yes this is number three. The wedding was small, and held in my parents' back yard. My mother was a very capable gardener, and had beautiful flower gardens all over her yard. Diana's daughter was maid of honor, and my brother Kevin was best man. The wedding day was a bright sunny day in the middle of May, and the ceremony went very smoothly. The reception was something else. When we got to the reception hall, the band was not there, and the catering wasn't ready. Diana's son-in-law went to their house to get a CD player with some disks, that helped the music situation. The caterers were still setting up, but finished quickly once we got there. After about an hour into the reception, the band showed up. They said they thought they were getting there on time. With the food and music now taken care of, things got a little less tense.

There comes a time at all wedding receptions when the best man must get up and give a toast to the bride and groom. Ours was no exception, and when that time arrived, Kevin got to his feet and gave us his most heartfelt toast. "Well let's hope the third time's the charm." Yes. That was it! He then sat back down and the reception continued. Diana was furious with him. The rest of the day went smoothly and everyone seemed to have a good time. We didn't take a honeymoon since we had just come back from Florida. I guess that turned into a pre-wedding honeymoon. It was ok with both of us. We had to get back to work and I wanted to get started on the house. I also had several design jobs waiting for me by that time.

Chapter Twenty-Seven
We Won the War

At the beginning of May, I had applied for membership in a national organization for building designers. I wanted to join to get to meet other designers, and see what kind of work they were doing, and how busy they were. Along with the application, I had to send three complete sets of plans that I had done. I was quickly accepted, and I became the twelfth member in Massachusetts. Now having twelve members, the state was allowed to form our own State Society. We had to pick officers to run the Society. Being new, I was not eligible for any of the office posts. The State Society would have four regularly scheduled meetings throughout the year. I found that most of the members in MA were from Cape Cod or the areas around Boston. As a result of that, all of the meetings were going to be held at the same location, just off-Cape. That, I guess, made the most sense for most of the members. I also found that there were several other designers all over the rest of New England, other than CT that were called "At large members". They were in states that didn't have enough members to form a State Society. They were all paying dues to be members, but had no representation. If I were one of them, I'm not sure that I would have stayed as a member.

Sometime in June I got a call from the Vice President of the National Organization asking if I would go to the National Convention as the delegate representing Massachusetts. The Convention was being held in Charleston, South Carolina the first week of August. Every year they hold a National Convention, and every year it has a different theme. The theme that year was the Civil War. As hard as people are trying to erase it, it did happen and will always be a part of America's history. I agreed to go and do whatever it was that the delegates do at those things. Diana was coming with me, and we counted that trip as another honeymoon. Part of the Convention included a dress up dinner party. We were all given a choice of costume to wear, all provided by the National Society. The choices of costume were, Southern General, Southern Soldier, Northern General, or Southern gentlemen. For the ladies they had Southern Belle dresses, complete with all the dress hoops required.

All of the costumes had to be ordered in advance of the Convention, and were given to us when we checked in. I, being from the North chose Northern General. The costumes were complete and authentic looking, right down to the saber hanging from my hip. Diana looked very nice in her Southern Belle hoop dress. I went to all of the meetings that required my attention, and voted on whatever issue was on the table at the time. The meetings took up most of my time there, but Diana got together with some of the other wives and toured the city. At some point during all of the meetings, I had a private meeting with the National VP. We talked about all of the members in New England that were not getting any representation. I suggested that we open the MA State Society to all of them. She said she would have to put it before the National board, but would get back to me. On the day of the dress up dinner party, the city was once again swarming with Union and Confederate Soldiers. Before the party began, about fifteen or twenty members wanted a group picture of them on the steps of one of the old municipal buildings in the center of the city. I told them I would take pictures for them, and I was handed several cameras. With the members all standing on the steps in a variety of different uniforms, and me across the street taking pictures, it looked like a page out of a history book. As I was taking pictures, people began to stand around looking at us. One woman came up to me and asked what was going on. I replied by saying "Haven't you heard? We won the war! It's over now." The woman, looking very confused asked, "What war?" I said, "The one between the states. But, don't worry, it's all over now." She just shook her head and walked away. As the evening went on, the ladies began to find that wearing those big hoop dresses, while looking very nice, were a very big problem when trying to use a modern toilet. Just try to picture it, trying to sit on a small modern toilet, in a regular size rest room stall, with all those large stiff hoops not wanting to bend or allow the skirt to move in the manner needed for the women to complete their task.

I don't know how many of you have been to Charleston in August. I can tell you that it's hot there, and very humid. After the dinner party, several of us got together and walked along the streets in search of a good bar. We found one, and it had live music playing at the time. Now, when a group of Civil War Soldiers and Southern Belles walk into a place like that, there is going to be an almost one hundred percent chance that you're going to have to get on the stage. We did and along with the band, we agreed to sing "Dixie Down," I think we all did a pretty good job with it. Walking back to the hotel later that night, sometime around midnight, other groups of Soldiers could be seen wandering the streets. Even at that late hour, the air temp was still close to one hundred degrees, and the humidity must have been close to that, too. Being from New England, I was very uncomfortable with the weather there. Overall, Diana and I had fun at the Convention, and I got to meet designers from all over the country. Then it was time to get back home. We still had half a house to build, Diana had used all of her vacation time, and I again had several design projects waiting for me.

When we started the work on our cottage, several friends all said they would be glad to help. There was no help when the time came, except for one of the guys that worked for me as a builder. We had remained good friends and saw each other often. He came every weekend to help me with the house. Diana's daughter came to help do whatever she could, from time to time. That little cottage was turning into a small Victorian cottage, with the main part of the house being one and one half stories with a very steep pitched hip roof. There were bumped out windows with gable roof areas cutting into the hip roof. I had designed two front facing gables on the main part of the house, and another on a bumped out window in the family room. As we were building the house, people would gather in the street to watch the transformation of the little cottage. (Here we go entertaining the neighborhood again). When it was done, it had the high-pitched main hip roof, and seven gables placed all around the house. I gave the two front gables "fishscale" shingle siding, and the rest was clapboard. We painted the house five different colors to create our own "Painted Lady". The lady that lived across from us was not fond of all the different colors, and she made sure we knew that. It didn't change anything for us.

The office that I had designed into the house was on the driveway side of the house, with a private entry. I didn't want people to have to go through the house to get to the office. In September, my old developer friend, Angelo, called. He had bought a piece of land on Cape Cod and wanted a house designed. The house was to be approximately five thousand four hundred square feet in size, with eleven rooms. All of the rooms except one would have ocean views. The lot he had purchased had three hundred feet of beach frontage, and the house was going to sit about two hundred feet back from the water. Because of height restrictions in that location the house had to be less than thirty feet high. A house that large, with that many square feet needs a lot of roof to cover it. To compensate for the large amount of roof, I dropped the roof down, so the second-floor walls were only six feet high. The house was twenty-nine feet, eight inches tall. I added balconies from the second-floor bedrooms, and a large open entertaining deck on the ocean side of the house. On a clear day, you could see Martha's Vineyard from the deck and most of the rooms in the house.

Later that fall, with the house not quite finished, but having to pay attention to my business, I bought my first computer, and computer aided design software. The software was geared specifically to residential design. I had some trouble trying to teach myself how to use it, but did. At first the computer wasn't helping that much with the speed of completing the plans, but it helped a great deal with the changes that would need to be made to preliminary plans. As I got better and more comfortable with the software, that began to change. By the end of 1995, I had completed my first house plan using the computer. Early in 1996, with business really starting to pick up for me, I hired my first design employee. He was a young guy that was going to school to be a Civil Engineer. He was very good with the computer, and it didn't take him as long as it took me to become comfortable with the design software. I started him out doing preliminary plans, while I was doing the final construction documents. Business was going great.

The first official meeting in 1996 of the State Society of Building Designers was in March. The National VP came to the meeting to help get us started, and she told us that we could accept designers from other states in New England, as long as their state didn't have a State Society in place. That opened us up to all of New England, except CT After reaching out to all of the "At large" members of all of those states, our membership almost doubled in size. Now with members coming from all over New England, we began to spread out the locations of the meetings. At each meeting we would have some sort of educational seminar dealing with building code changes, or different solutions to design problems that come up in the design of additions or buildings with strict code regulations, or lot sizes. As I began to get to know some of the other designers, and see how they approach different issues, I think I began to become a better designer myself. Having been a builder for several years, and now a designer, I began to see some of the other designers start to use much of the same format that I used in preparing their plans.

Chapter Twenty-Eight
What? Do You Want It Perfect?

Sometime early in 1996 my parents bought a new car. That car was the first car they ever had that came with power windows and door locks. I have to assume that the salesperson went over all of those new high-tech toys with them when they picked up the car. If that was the case, they must have glazed over and completely forgotten all of the information given to them. When they got home with their new car, with all those miracles of modern technology, they pulled into their driveway, got out and locked the car. I'm not sure if they used the key fob to lock it, or if they just hit a button on the door by accident. At any rate, they later decided to go out to dinner to celebrate their new purchase. When they got to the car, however, they couldn't seem to figure out how to unlock it. After apparently trying without success, my mother called me. She was very upset and thoroughly pissed off. Diana and I made the thirty-five-minute drive to their house to see if we could help. When we got there, I asked them to show me what the problem was. With my father at the driver's side door, and mom at the passenger door, I watched as they both grabbed the door handles and pulled as my father was pushing the unlock button on the key fob. I told them to let go of the handles and push the button. By some miracle, the driver's side door unlocked, all by itself.

Happy now, my father opened his door and got into the car. Meanwhile, I could see my mother still frantically pulling on her door handle. The door would not open. Again thoroughly pissed she began yelling at the car door. I told my father that to open more than just the driver's door, he would have to rapidly push the button twice. He got back out of the car, closed the door and then quickly pushed the button twice. The passenger side door still would not open. I went over to see what was happening on that side of the car. I saw my mother standing at the door, pulling on the handle. I said to her, maybe a little too forcefully, "Get your hand away from the handle", and then told my father to push the button twice quickly. With my mother's hands at her sides, that miracle of modern technology took over, and the door unlocked all by itself. I had them lock and unlock the doors a few times to make sure they had the idea of how it was supposed to work. Before leaving, I also explained that they could still stick the key in the key slot on the doors and unlock the car the old fashion way. They said they were under the impression that because the locks were automatic, that was no longer an option.

As long as we're on the subject of cars, we also bought a new car around the same time as my parents. Our car was not "new"; it was just new to us. It was a 1995 Ford Thunderbird. The car had very low mileage, was very clean, and had lots of options in it. As we were driving the car home from the dealership, Diana put the sales papers on the dashboard. Within a few seconds of that, the head lights came on. Not thinking about the papers on the dashboard, we couldn't figure out why the lights came on. So, thinking we had some sort of electrical problem, we promptly turned around and went back to the dealership. When I explained our problem to the salesperson, he said he had forgotten to tell us the car had automatic lights, and the paper on the dashboard was covering the light sensor. Satisfied that the car was problem free, we went home and enjoyed having our beautiful Ford Thunderbird.

Angelo's house got started in May of 1996. The construction was going very slowly, and he would call me often with concerns that would come up in the construction. By the end of June, I think he was second guessing his choice of builder. Meanwhile, Diana was still working in the quality control lab at the local factory. There was a young man that worked there that she was friendly with, and would talk to from time to time. One day he told her that he liked to do karaoke at a bar in the city. He said he was quite good at doing Elvis Presley songs and invited her to come see him perform. On a Saturday night Diana and I went to the bar he would be singing at to see his show. We were sitting at a table about in the middle of the room, with a table to our right that had a large party at it. When it was his turn to get up and sing, he sang a rather poor rendition of "Steamroller". Diana and I laughed through much of the song, and then we found out the table next to us was his family. His wife leaned over to us and said she didn't think he was all that good either, but it was something he liked to do. He quit working at the factory soon after that to become a builder. I don't think it had anything to do with his singing, I think it was his plan all along.

After Diana's friend did his "Steamroller" debacle, two girls got up and were introduced by a man claiming to be their manager. He said this was to be their first performance in public. The girls were in perfect harmony, and had some very well-choreographed moves. I don't remember the song they sang, but it was clear they had done it before. When they finished their performance, their "Manager" took the floor to sing a song by himself. As he started to sing "I've been waiting for a girl like you", he started very slow and very much off key. When he got to that main line of the song, his pitch and voice went up so much I really thought the glasses on the table were going to break. From that point on that guy became known to us as "The Screamer".

Angelo was living in a house near-by the construction of the new one. He would visit the site often to see how things were going. He kept finding things that had been done incorrectly, but was trying to deal with it on his own. One day in August, he called me and said that there was a large hump in the first-floor hall between the dining room and his home office. He also said it looked like the corner of the house overhanging the garage entry was sagging a bit. Even though the house had been started in May, they were just now getting to frame the second-floor system. Angelo was concerned that the extra weight of the second floor was going to cause that area of the house to collapse. He asked if I would come to the house and do an inspection of the construction. When I got to the house I found that many of the first-floor trusses had been installed backwards, and the bearing points of the trusses were in the middle of the floor, not holding anything up. I stopped construction of the house and called in a Structural Engineer to try to help me fix the situation without having to take down the house and start over. With the Engineer's help, we got the first-floor system fixed. The second-floor trusses that had been installed backwards would have to be removed and installed properly. With that done, the construction of the house could continue. For some reason, Angelo was reluctant to fire the inept builder, and let him continue working on the house.

By late September, Angelo's house was about ninety percent framed. There was still the matter of a barrel vault ceiling in the master bedroom, along with some bumped out windows with seats in them. The builder said he didn't know how to frame any of those things. Angelo was on the phone to me again. I agreed to go to the house and finish the frame for him, but I was going to have to have some help, and stay in a motel while the work was going on. Angelo agreed to all of that, and Diana's friend "Steamroller" turned builder said he would help. The first thing I wanted to do was build the barrel vault ceiling. The ceiling would have another barrel vault coming off it into a bumped out window seat, to form a groin vault. To begin, I measured the room to be sure it was the same size all the way across. It was not. The room was about four inches wider at one end than the other, and the bumped out window seat had been placed at the wrong location. I also noticed that the top plate of the second-floor exterior walls had high and low spots in it. Angelo had the builder come back to explain the discrepancies. When he was confronted with his mistake, his reply was "So what, do you want it perfect"? Angelo's wife burst into tears, and I thought Angelo was going to throw the builder out the window. I asked the builder about the waves in the top of the exterior wall plates. I knew that was caused by the top of the foundation not being flat. But I also knew that it was easy to fix with a few shims when framing the first-floor system. The builder said he had never shimmed a floor system in his life. I was sure he was telling the truth right there.

While we were working on the house during the day, Diana and my helper's wife made the rounds to what must have been every Christmas Tree Shop on the entire Cape. On Saturday night we all went to dinner and then to a bar that, you guessed it, had Karaoke. The first thing that happened was, as we opened the door to go in, a very strong gust of wind came up. The wind was so strong that it literally pushed the four of us through the door into the bar. Now, having made our grand entrance, we found a table and settled in for an evening of fun watching people try to sing. To our great surprise, one of the very first to get up were the two girls with the "Manager" that we had seen after "Steamroller" man. They did the same bit that we had already seen, and then the "Screamer" got up and did the same thing he had done. It was just as ear piercing and funny as the first time we saw him. We couldn't help ourselves; we sat there roaring with laughter.

Over a three-day weekend we finished the frame of Angelo's house. The barrel ceiling was not going to work because of the discrepancy in the width of the room. Instead we added a two-step tray ceiling, with the higher tray extending into the bump out window area. Angelo and his wife were happy with the house again. Once the house was finished, they invited Diana and me to come see it. The setting of the house was perfect. It had a bluff behind it that was almost as tall as the house, and on the ocean side the house sat with about twenty yards of scrub brush, and then nothing but beach sand and ocean. The house had wood shingle siding that was left to weather naturally. The house looked like it was supposed to be there, and nothing else that I could have designed would have fit like that house did.

1997 came and my business was getting much busier. My two NY Architects were sending me a lot of work now, on top of all of the local work. I was thinking about hiring a second employee. I knew I needed the help, but my office wasn't designed for three designers and one support person, it was going to be too tight. Not wanting to start turning work away, I felt as if I didn't have any choice. I had to get more help. After wrestling with the idea, I decided to hire the second person, and allow my help to work from their homes. They would, of course, have to come to the office to review their work, and pick up new assignments. Concerned about paying them to work from their homes, I came up with a percentage pay scale plan. They would get a certain percent of the cost of the plan for doing the preliminary plan, and a higher percent for doing final construction drawings. The bigger or more complex the plan was, the more the client was paying, so the more they would make off that plan. The system worked very well. They were happy; I was happy, and the work was getting done in a timely manner, so my clients were happy.

Chapter Twenty-Nine
Mostly Cars

Early in the spring of 1997 I was told about a national organization that went around the country testing building designers for national certification. They were going to be at one of the colleges in the city of Worcester, MA. I got the paperwork to apply, and bought all of the books required to study for the test. So on top of my normal workload, I spent many hours studying. The test was given over two days, approximately ten hours each day. The first day was a question and answer day. It covered subjects like business ethics, electrical and plumbing systems, solving design problems with minimal space or code restrictions. It even covered the history of architecture. One of the subjects was a section on structural analysis. That was a two-part section, the first was a question and answer section; for the second part of that one, they gave us a cross section of a building. We had to identify and calculate every load from the roof to the foundation footings. The second day, we were given a plot plan and a list of code requirements. We had to design a house using the codes we were given, place the house on the lot, and show the septic system and a well in their proper locations as directed by the codes we were given. The house we designed had to include all of the floor plans, with the rooms identified, and all of the exterior elevations. We also had to provide a cost estimate for the house.

There were three members from Massachusetts, two from Maine, and two from Pennsylvania taking the test. Both members from Maine passed, one from Massachusetts passed, and I don't know how the others made out. I was not the one from MA that passed. I failed the structural analysis section. The good thing was, they would let you retake sections that you failed, as long as you did it in a certain number of months. I went back and studied structural analysis, and I, along with the other failed member from MA, went to an office near Hartford and retook the sections needed. We both passed and she became the sixth Certified Professional Building Designer, and I the seventh in the state of MA. That test was the most stress I have ever put myself under on purpose in my life. For passing the test, you were given a stamp with your name and certification number on it. You also were now allowed to design houses in forty-six states. Having that stamp and keeping my Construction Supervisor's license current seemed to make a big difference in my business. I was now getting to the point where I had no choice; I had to start turning work away.

That summer, two bad things happened. The first was that my father was getting sick. Tests showed that he had emphysema and lost about thirty percent of his lung capacity. He was going to need an operation to remove the dead parts of his lungs. The operation was scheduled for early that fall. He was now on oxygen, and would remain on it for the rest of his life. The other bad thing that happened was somewhat less tragic, but sad just the same. I had a job near Boston, and the turnpike was the best way to get there. I was driving our Thunderbird at about sixty-five miles per hour, and as I approached the exit I was to take, I reached for the toll ticket and accidentally hit the overdrive button on the side of the shift lever. The rpms instantly went from about 2,600 rpms to about 5,800 rpms. The motor roared, and the car shuttered and slowed a bit on its own. I saw a small puff of blue-white smoke come from the tail pipe. I quickly re-engaged the overdrive and the motor calmed down, but I noticed a distinct lack of power, along with some unpleasant noises coming from the motor. Getting off the turnpike, I went to my appointment and then went home. I took the turnpike back home, but the car just didn't feel right.

After getting home I called the dealership to make an appointment to have the car looked at. I was pretty sure what they were going to tell me. We had to wait a couple of days to get the car into the dealer. That night we had a very bad rainstorm with very high wind gusts. During one of those big gusts of wind, a tree branch next to the driveway broke, and came straight down, like a spear, and landed almost dead center on the hood of the car. It had made such a deep dent in the hood that the metal had started to collapse around the stump of the branch. I had to get up on the hood and pull, while twisting the branch to free it from the hood. As I stood looking at what had been a very nice looking car, all I could come up with was, "Well, besides having a bad motor, the car was also seriously aerodynamically flawed." I was very sad about the state of our car. When the time came, I took the car to the dealership to have them not just check the motor, but now also the body damage.

Diana didn't come to the dealership with me, so while they were going over the car, I was out looking at other cars. At the back of the lot I saw a 1996 Lincoln Mark VIII, LSC. It was black and loaded with all of the toys of the time. It even had a telephone in it. It was beautiful. When I went back inside, they were finished checking my car. I was right it had two blown head gaskets, along with some valve and timing issues. The motor repair, plus the body work was going to be in the thousands. The only thing my insurance was going to cover was the body work, and I had a five-hundred-dollar deductible on that. Almost as a joke, I asked how much they wanted for the Lincoln. The price surprised me by being much lower than I thought it might be. I decided to see what kind of a deal could be worked out with the dealer. I called Diana and told her I was still at the dealership, and may be there for a while longer. I didn't say anything about the Lincoln.

After a little haggling with the dealer, I made a very good deal. The Lincoln, he said was a Ford buy-back car under the lemon law. The previous owner had brought the car back several times because of a vibration in one of the speakers. He said they took all of the speakers out, and remounted them with foam around them. The previous owner still said he could hear a vibration. Before making my deal for the car, I took it out for a ride, and turned the radio up as loud as I could stand it. I could not find a vibration anywhere in that car. I was able to get the Lincoln for ten thousand dollars, plus my Thunderbird, with the two blown head gaskets and large dent in the hood. The dealer gave me the original window sticker; the car listed for just over forty-five thousand dollars when it was new.

I drove the Lincoln home, and I went in the house and told Diana that it took so long because they fixed the car while I was there, and oh, by the way, I had them paint it black when they were done. Diana's brother owned a body repair shop, and she sometimes worked there for him. She knew I was not driving a car that had just been painted. She went to the front door, and when she looked out to see the Lincoln sitting in the driveway, she couldn't believe it was ours. To this very day, of all the different cars we have had together, that Lincoln still remains her favorite. My personal favorite has to be a 2004 Cadillac CTS; that too was loaded with all of the toys of its time. We bought that one new, and that's another part of the story.

Shortly after buying the Lincoln, my mother called and told me that they were involved in a very bad accident involving two other cars. Apparently the car driving in front of my parents' car was hit almost head on. The car doing the hitting was going so fast, that it spun around the first car, and hit my parents' car in the driver's side front corner. The car then rolled up and over my parents' car. My parents' car was totaled. People were injured in the accident, none of them being my parents. My parents got a check for their now destroyed car, and set out to buy a new one. They got another car with those pesky power windows and locks, but this time added front wheel drive to the mix. Now you have to remember that my parents were, at that time, in their early seventies, and late sixties. They grew up in New England, always driving rear wheel drive cars and trucks. Every winter, you would add cement blocks, or bags of sand to the trunk of the car, or the back of the truck. By doing that, you would get better traction from the rear wheel drive cars. If you will remember, my parents were living at that time, at the top of a very long, steep hill.

One snowy, winter day, while I was working in my office, I got another frantic call from my mother. That new front wheel drive car, that new wonder machine of the snowy roads, would not go up the hill to get them home. Diana and I again made the drive to my parents' house. Getting to the bottom of the hill to their house, the car was sitting off to the side of the road in a bit of a snowbank. Driving a four-wheel drive truck, (I never drove the Lincoln in the winter) we went up the hill to my parents' house. I asked what was happening when they tried to come up the hill, and they said the front of the car just slipped on the snow, and then the car would turn sideways. I took the keys and walked down to the car. As I tried to get the car up the hill, they were right. The car did just what they said it was doing for them. After thinking about it for a few seconds, I got out of the car and looked in the trunk. Guess what I found there? Yup, four cement blocks, and two 80lb bags of sand. I took all of that added weight out of the trunk, and drove the car up the hill to the house. My parents were amazed, and wanted to know what I did to get the car up the hill. I took my father and my truck down to retrieve the blocks and bags. When we got back to the house, I also explained the principal of the front wheel drive feature of the car, and that adding all that weight in the trunk simply took away any advantage the car may have had. They never had trouble getting up the hill again.

Chapter Thirty
That's Not Mud You're Going to Land In

I had a client come to my office to have a house designed. He came with pictures, sketches, and a wish list for every part of the house. We signed my standard design contract. He gave me the required deposit and I got going on the preliminary plan as soon as possible. When we got together with the preliminary plan, both he and his wife were there. They had some small changes they wanted to make, and then they would be ready for final plans. Having a very heavy workload, it was going to be a couple of weeks before I could get back to working on their plans. During that time they had apparently changed their minds about the style of house they wanted. My client came back to my office with pictures, sketches, and another wish list, for a completely different type of house than we had been working on. I told him he would have to sign another contract and leave another deposit for the new plan. He got very upset and didn't understand why he was going to owe more money. I tried to explain that the first deposit was to cover the hours needed to prepare the first preliminary plan, along with a few minor changes. He still didn't get it, and demanded all of his money back. He said I had not performed the service he had paid me for. I told him he wasn't getting any money back, and he said he would see me in court.

The client did file a suit against me. When the case came up, he was there alone, without his wife. I thought that was a little odd, I thought she had some interest in this along with her husband. The case went before a Magistrate and he was to present his side of the case first. He sat at the desk and told the Magistrate his version of what happened. His version was pretty close to the truth, but he had nothing with him to demonstrate what he felt the problem was. When it was my turn, Diana came with me in support, but it turned out she wasn't needed. I told my side of the story, and gave the Magistrate all of the paperwork that had been generated for the work I had done for the client. The Magistrate listened to both of us, and then went through the papers I had given him. When he was done, he looked at my client and told him never to waste the court's time like that again, and then told him to get out of his court. Judgment was for the defendant (Me) with no damages or money owed. Diana and I ran into him and his wife while shopping at a mall. He acted as if he wanted to be my best friend. I brushed him off saying "You sued me over nothing. We are never going to be friends!" and then we just walked away from them.

Diana has always been very creative when it comes to birthday and anniversary gifts. For my birthday in 1997, she bought me a ride in a hot air balloon. The ride was to start in another town, and we had to be there very early in the morning to help get the balloon set up. It was interesting to see how that's done. I didn't know that there were a series of wires that went from the gondola, up inside the balloon to various flaps to help control the balloon. There were five of us plus the controller in the balloon. Diana was allowed to ride in the chase car. The object of the chase vehicle was to follow the balloon, and pick it and the passengers up at the end of the ride. All was going well. The balloon controller had radio contact with the chase vehicle to help them follow us. Unfortunately he did not like the chatter on the radio, so he turned it off. Very soon after liftoff, a strong gust of wind took the balloon in a direction apparently not anticipated. The chase vehicle lost site of the balloon, and not being able to talk to the controller, they began driving wildly in the direction they thought was right. Diana said later that it was the scariest ride she had ever had.

Somewhere in Northern CT the controller began to look for an open field to land. He thought he found just such a field, but as we got lower and closer to the ground, I recognized the unmistakable pattern of manure spreading, and told him he really didn't want to come down in that field. He brought the balloon back up, and we began the search all over again. We found a corn field that had been harvested, and the stalks cut down. From the air it looked like the stalks were no more than an inch or so high. When the balloon was about two or three feet from the ground, a gust of wind came up and pushed the balloon to the side. When we hit the ground, the gondola tipped over on us and everyone fell out. Fortunately we had all put helmets on before we landed. With some of us having some small scrapes and bruises, we had to get up and collect the balloon, so the corn stalks didn't tear it. The owner of the field apparently saw the balloon come down, and drove out to meet us. He helped get the balloon rolled up and into the gondola, and then gave us a ride to his house.

The balloon controller gave the field owner a bottle of champagne for the use of his field, and his help. The farmer gave all of us a small bottle of real maple syrup that he produced at the farm. The chase vehicle was contacted, and after a short wait, they arrived at the farm to pick us up. The balloon controller then took all of us out for a breakfast, including champagne. I had heard that you don't feel movement in a hot air balloon, and now I know that it's true. You really don't feel much of anything. But the ride is wonderful and you can get some spectacular views from them.

My father's lung surgery finally came up some time around Thanksgiving. My brother Kevin, Diana, and I stayed at the hospital with my mother during the surgery. It was going to be a very long operation of several hours, but she wanted to be there the whole time. I don't think I could have blamed her for that. The rest of us felt the same way. The operation was very serious, and it was quite possible that any number of things could have gone wrong. After several hours, the surgeon came out to see my mother and to tell her that the surgery went fine, but the damage to his lungs was greater than they thought. Taking one third of his lung tissue out was going to help him but it wasn't going to buy him as much time as originally thought. After a few more hours in recovery, they moved him to a room in the intensive care unit, and we were allowed to see him one by one for just a few minutes each. He seemed to be doing pretty well: uncomfortable but not in a lot of pain. I think they had him pretty well drugged up. My father stayed in the hospital for about a week, and then they sent him home. Kevin moved back in to help my mother, and Diana and I spent as much time as we could at their house to also be of some help. My father recovered from the operation nicely, but remained weak, and on oxygen.

Over that summer, my parents had new high efficiency vinyl windows put in their house. The window in the dining room was a large sliding window. One day my mother decided to clean the windows, and when she was working on that one, it fell off the track. She called me while I was busy working in my office at my house. She was again frantic, and needed my help with the window. So, again stopping work we made the trip to their house and, in about one minute, maybe a little more, the window was back in the track. As we were standing talking to my mother, Kevin came out of a bedroom down the hall. I looked at my mother and asked her why, if Kevin was right there, she didn't have him put the window back. She said he was sleeping and didn't want to disturb him. Since I was home, she thought I could come and fix it for her. This, folks, is just one of the problems with having your business office in your home.

Chapter Thirty-One
Easter Sunday and Blueberries

It was Easter Sunday! For years Diana and I had been going to my parents' house for Easter Sunday dinner. Many of those years I would drive with my father to Springfield MA to pick up my mother's two elderly aunts and bring them to the house to have Easter with us. Easter Sunday 1998 was to be no different, except that this particular Easter fell on one of those ridiculous weekends that we were to turn the clocks ahead one hour when we went to bed Saturday night. Diana and I had forgotten to do that. We were supposed to be at my parents' house by about noon time, so I could drive my father to get the Aunts. Kevin had by now moved back out of the house, so it was just my mother and father there at the time. Having failed to turn our clocks ahead, we were running one hour behind everyone else. Now, if I knew someone was supposed to be at my house at a certain time, and was as much as a half hour late, I would pick up a phone and call them to be sure everything was alright. Not my parents', not either of them! They had our house phone number, and they had our car phone number, but for whatever reason, not calling seemed the best thing for them to do.

When we arrived at my parents' house, thinking we were on time, we very quickly found out we were not on time. My father, after waiting until 12:45, decided to drive to the city by himself to get the aunts. My mother was so mad at us, that she would not talk to either of us. We tried to explain that we simply forgot to set the clocks ahead, but my mother wasn't going to hear any explanations. When I asked her why she hadn't called to check on us, she didn't say anything. When my father got back with the aunts, the tension just got worse. He was not talking either. As we were sitting at the table for dinner, my mother and her aunts were talking, and you could feel the tension there as well. While passing different dishes of food around the table, Diana ended up with the basket of rolls. Holding them up to my father, knowing he always had bread or rolls with his meals, she said, "Here, have a roll!" Without looking up he said, "I will take a roll when I am damn good and ready!" He never had a roll at that dinner.

My father refused to let me bring the aunts back to Springfield for him. After he left we tried again to soften things with my mother, but it just wasn't working. We helped clean up and just went home. My parents didn't talk to us for several weeks after that. Knowing that my father was a big fan of old western movies, for Father's Day we got him a collection of movies featuring John Wayne and Clint Eastwood, two of his personal favorites. When I went over and gave them to him, he opened that package, looked at the videos, and just threw them on the table, without saying a word. That display pissed me off so much, that I looked him straight in the eyes, and said, "Well fuck you too!" My reaction must have shaken my mother to her very core, and as I stormed out of the house saying, "I'm done with all this shit!", she ran after me and apologized for his behavior. She wanted me to come back in the house and visit for a bit, but I told her I wasn't going to be able to do that. A few days later, my mother called to ask Diana if she would go with her to pick fresh blueberries.

We drove to my parents' house, and while Diana went with my mother for the blueberries, my mother driving, I had a somewhat uncomfortable visit with my father. Easter Sunday and the video gifts never entered the conversation. My mother told Diana that she knew of a farm not too far away that let you pick your own berries, and that was where they were headed. They were gone for a very long time. In reality I'm sure it felt longer than it actually was. When they got back, Diana helped my mother pack up the berries for the freezer, and then we left. It was then that Diana began to tell me the tale of the hunt for the blueberries. I have known for many years that my mother was a very bad driver, but Diana had until then never had the pleasure of the experience. She began to tell about my mother apparently not really knowing where the farm was, and driving around doing more sightseeing than driving.

That was typical driving for my mother; she didn't want to miss anything. Diana said there were several near misses with other cars, and fixed objects on the sides of the road. She said that at one point, when my mother thought she had found the right farm, she pulled completely sideways in the road, blocking both lanes, and stopped. Diana asked her what she was doing and my mother said she now wasn't sure that was the right farm. As they sat there in the middle of the road, with Diana looking out the passenger side window, she could now see traffic coming straight at them. Diana said she began yelling at my mother to move the car into the driveway, or they were going to get hit by oncoming cars. While my mother would panic over some very small and simple things, four thousand pounds of killing machine coming at her at forty miles an hour was not one of those things. After repeated yelling, Diana said she did finally pull into the driveway, but not until the oncoming cars had to come to a loud horn blowing stop.

Early in the summer of 1998, my parent's fiftieth wedding anniversary came up. We held a large party for them at a local restaurant that our family had used for many parties and occasions over the years. All of my mother's siblings and half siblings were there. Many of their friends that were still around also came. David came up, just for the day. He was divorced now and had been for a few years. My mother, being mildly religious, Irish Catholic after all, I made arrangements for the priest from her local church to come to the party and give a blessing. My father was failing a little more now, but he seemed to enjoy having the party. When making plans for the party, I spoke to Kevin and David about it, and we all agreed to split the cost among us, and to try to keep the party short for my father. At the end of the day, I paid the bill. Kevin later gave me some money, David never did send any to me. It was ok; David had other bills to deal with, and I was probably better equipped to cover the cost than the others were at that time.

In September 1998, there was a wedding on the Cape. My mother's eldest brother had a daughter getting married, and for some reason, it had to be three hours away, on Cape Cod. My mother and father were invited, but my father was too sick to make the trip. My mother called me and asked if I would take her. That brother was one of her siblings that told her when I was a child, that in their opinion, I would never amount to anything in my life. He was a lawyer, a very wealthy lawyer, and made sure that everyone knew that he leased a new Lincoln Continental every three years. As we pulled into the parking lot the timing couldn't have been better. Most of my mother's family, were gathered at the back of one of their cars, and as we drove by them in my newly detailed, two-year-old Lincoln Mark VIII, my mother smiled widely and waved to all of them. I couldn't help notice that none of them waved back. As I pulled into a parking space close by them, they all, except mister high priced lawyer, came over to see the car. I had to explain that the car was in fact my car, and that because my job required a lot of driving, this car got me where I needed to go and back, in the comfort I felt I needed. My mother seemed very proud to be seen getting out of a car owned by me, that was obviously making her brother eat those words said so long ago, words that were still vivid in her mind as well as mine.

Diana, for a very long time, didn't eat red meat. This was something that seemed to be lost on my mother for years. We were invited to my parents' house many, many times over the summers for lunch on Saturday or Sunday, only to find the main course to be some sort of dead animal that Diana wanted no part of. It didn't seem to bother Diana very much. There were always lots of veggies to fill up on. My mother, however, would always, every time, seem to take it very personally that Diana wouldn't eat the meat. We would explain every time that she (my mother) had been told that Diana didn't eat meat. But my mother would always say she didn't know that, and wished that she had been told before going through all the trouble to prepare the meal. Another thing that my mother knew was that I, as well as Diana, did not eat salmon. I grew up with my mother trying, unsuccessfully, to feed me salmon. She had at one point asked Diana if she liked salmon, and was told that she did not.

Having said all of that about the salmon, my mother invited us to have an early dinner one Saturday afternoon. When we got to the house she was out in the back yard, cooking salmon on the grill. I'm not sure if it was me or Diana that asked my mother what she was cooking for us, but clearly, it lit my mother's fuse, and she began to yell at us about not telling her that we didn't like salmon. She went on about how much the fish had cost and what she had done to prepare it. She ended her tantrum by running out of the yard and down the road, screaming at the top of her lungs, and throwing her arms around as if having a very animated conversation with someone. There will be more about my mother's "screaming" abilities later.

Chapter Thirty-Two
The Passing of Dad

If you will remember, I had two children with my first wife. At some point after our divorce she moved to some tiny little speck of dirt somewhere in the mountains, at the very corner of MA, VT, and NY. That made the drive to visit my kids about three to three and a half hours each way and, not to mention it was a very difficult speck of dirt to find. The result of the move was that it cut down my visits to a small handful per year. Then she moved again. This time I had no idea where she went. In the summer of 1998 my mother was able to get a phone number for them. She was told if she gave it to me, the number would be changed, and they would move again. Through the summer, my mother was somehow able to hire my youngest son to come to her house to help with some of the work around the yard. He was at that time nineteen years old. My mother told me when he would be there, so I could come over and visit with him while he worked. Almost every Saturday through the Summer I met with him. We talked and got reacquainted with each other while I helped him do whatever my mother had him doing. I took him out to lunch a couple of times, and over the summer he seemed to get comfortable being with me again. We talked about his older brother a bit, but he didn't seem to want to say much about him. At the end of the summer, I gave my son a business card with a toll-free number on it. I told him that number came directly to my phone, and if I wasn't in the office, it would switch directly to my cell phone. I told him that he or his brother could call that number any time, for any reason, and I would be there for them, whatever they needed. My son took the card, and I have never heard from either one of them since that day.

We had Thanksgiving dinner at my parents' house that year. It was a very quiet, subdued affair with just Diana, Kevin, and me being there. My father was failing fast at that point. I had just picked up a new client about a month earlier. The client was a major developer in central MA. About two weeks after Thanksgiving, I was at one of his houses doing an energy compliance report for the State. I suddenly got a very weird feeling. I can't explain the feeling, but I knew I had to go see my father. He was in a hospital not far from the house where I was working. When I got there, the door to his room was closed. I had to think that was not a good sign. I was right. I went to the front desk to ask about it and was told that he had passed way about thirty minutes ago. My mother was there with him at the time. I was very sorry that I was too late. Even though my parents always had a very difficult relationship, my mother did seem to love the man very much. I called Kevin and gave him the news, and again, Kevin never really got along with my father, but he was sad to see him gone. Kevin came to the hospital as support for my mother more than anything else. When it was time to leave the hospital, I tried to get my mother to ride home with me. She refused saying she just wanted to be alone for a while.

I drove back to my mother's house and began the job of calling family and friends to give them the news. As my mother was coming in the house, I was on the phone with mister big shot lawyer's wife. She asked if my mother was there and at the time of the question, she was not. When I told my aunt that she had wanted to drive herself home, my aunt was in the process of trying to rip me a new ass hole for letting her do that. As she was doing that my mother came in, and I said to my aunt, "My mother's here now. Would you like me to give her the phone so she can explain her reason for not accepting the ride?" My mother, obviously not wanting to talk to anyone, got the idea of the conversation I was having. She took the phone from me and said "I wanted to be alone for a bit. It was not Shawn's fault. And if yelling at him about a ride is the best you can do about my husband dying, then I'm very sorry you feel that way." She then hung up the phone. I called my brother David to give him the news. He didn't seem at all surprised or even all that bothered by the news. I knew he was at work and was not the kind of person to let much emotion show, but I guess I was expecting a little more than I got.

My mother delayed the wake and the funeral, to give David time to make arrangements to be there. As a result of that, the funeral was very close to Christmas. David was just barely on time for the wake. All of my mother's family came to the wake, along with many old friends, and fellow workers. I may not have told you this, but my father had a twin sister. They had not seen each other in many years. I did not recognize her or the two daughters she was pulling along with her. There were some very brief words between my mother and the sister, and then she left. I don't remember seeing her at the funeral. As the wake was winding down, mister lawyer uncle's wife came to me with a small platter of some sort of food. She said she was going to put it on the back of my car, so I could take it to my mother's house. When she asked what car to leave it on I said "It's the Lincoln Mark VIII right outside the door. It's black. You can't miss it." She put the food down on a table and said I could take it with me when I left the wake. Christmas that year was another very quiet, subdued affair.

The following year, 1999 was a very busy year for me. The developer that I picked up last fall was starting a new development that was to have ten very high-end custom houses. The minimum size of each house had to be at least four thousand, five hundred feet. As it turned out, all of the houses were over five thousand feet, with the largest being about six thousand four hundred feet. Each house was to be custom designed for the client and not until the lot was sold. All of the lots sold very quickly, I was very busy indeed. My two designers were working very nicely, and helped the work go along at a good pace. Along with all of the other work coming in, the year was flying by. I picked up another developer from the same town as the first one, and really was starting to overextend myself. I was thinking again that I may have to start turning away work. At some point during the year, I was elected VP of the MA State society of Building Designers. I would serve one term as VP, followed by two terms as President, just to add a little more to my workload. As President, it was my job to schedule and organize four membership meetings each year. The meetings had to be spread out all over New England to accommodate the members belonging to the MA State Society that lived in other states. Each of the meetings had to have some sort of educational seminar that would qualify for two CEU's. Those of us that were nationally certified were required to get eight CEU's per year. Sometimes finding and scheduling those events took more time than one would think necessary.

With my mother now living alone in that large house, with a very large yard needing to be kept up, Diana and I decided to hire someone to help her. My mother loved to work in the yard. She had lots of small flower gardens spread out over the yard, but still lots of grass area to take care of as well. She was apparently not only very picky about how the yard looked when finished, but the process used to get to that point. After going through three or four lawn maintenance companies, all being fired by my mother, it became clear that nobody could do the job as well as she could. We learned not to interfere with the workings of my mother's yard ever again. Even her neighbor would try to help from time to time. He soon learned the same lesson that we had learned. My mother was friendly enough with everyone in the neighborhood, just don't try to help with the yard, and things would be fine.

Chapter Thirty-Three
Your Mother's Been Run Over

One day as both Diana and I were working in my office, I got a phone call from one of my mother's friends. She told me that my mother had just been hit by a car while walking across the street with several other people. The fact was that my mother had just come out of church and was crossing the road, in the crosswalk with five or six other people. A minivan ran into the group, hitting my mother first, and then another person. The police estimated the van to be traveling at about thirty-five miles per hour. The speed limit in the area was thirty miles per hour. My mother had been thrown several feet and had a broken arm, broken leg, several cracked ribs, and internal injuries. She had the imprint of the manufacturer's grill and logo on her right hip. She was taken to a local hospital to be stabilized, and then air lifted to a larger hospital. A few days later, I went to the police department to get a copy of the report, fully intending to go after the driver of the van. I was told by one of the officers that had been at the scene that it wouldn't do any good to go after the driver. He said that according to their investigation, they found no negligence on the part of the driver, and he was not cited for anything. I reminded the officer that all drivers in the state of MA, as well as most states, know that it is against the law to hit a pedestrian with a motor vehicle, while in a cross walk. The officer would only keep repeating his former statement.

After doing some digging, without the help of the police, I was able to find out that the driver of the minivan was a local, very prominent lawyer. He was one of those slimy ones that held no assets under his own name, so on paper he was worthless. Taking him to court would have gotten my mother nothing. He was also the reason no charges were ever filed, even with all of the witnesses to his actions. My mother spent a couple of weeks in the hospital, and then was moved to a rehab facility. We were able to get her into one in the same town she lived in, so many of her friends, along with us, were able to visit her on a regular basis. Diana and I put together a small Thanksgiving meal, and took it over to the rehab facility. Kevin came with us, and that was how we celebrated Thanksgiving in 1999. My mother was home for Christmas and was doing pretty good, considering what she had been through the past few months. She seemed to recover well, but at sixty-nine years old, it left her moving a little slower than she had been. Christmas would again be another somewhat subdued occasion.

Well, there it was, the year 2000! The turn of the century. A new millennium. In the weeks, maybe months leading up to it, there were rumors and forecasts of all sorts of life altering and devastating things that would happen. Computers around the world would crash, stock markets and global economies were going to collapse, causing global chaos, riots, and a general loss of order around the world. Of course none of those things happened. My computer still had all of my client files; my bank still had all of my money, and while there may have been a riot, ongoing war, or general loss of order somewhere in the world, all was well in our little corner. Diana was still working at her quality control job. I was beginning to see almost weekly, less interest in getting up at 4:45 a.m. to be at work for 6:00 am. It was getting much harder for her to force herself out of the house to be to work on time.

I only mention Diana's job in the previous paragraph because it is slightly relevant to this part of the story. In the fall of 1999, the town we lived in announced that they were going to reduce the level of the lake by four feet. The lake was directly across the street from our house, and had several other houses around it that were Summer Cottages converted to year round homes. All of those houses, including ours, had shallow wells. The water level of the lake had a direct impact to the amount of water in your well. The owners of the houses that were going to be affected got together and did a little research. The deepest part of the lake was at the dam, which was just down the street from our house. At the dam, the water was only eight feet deep. As for the rest of the lake, the deepest area was about six and a half feet. So, to lower the lake by four feet, would remove about eighty percent of the lake's water reserve, and more importantly, it would drain every shallow well around the lake. When the town officials were approached with that information, they said we didn't know what we were talking about. Remember that local Engineer that I was very friendly with? Well, he most certainly did know what he was talking about, and he let the town know that he was involved. The town hired their own engineer. I can only imagine his embarrassment, as he stood in front of us, including my engineer, and kept repeating that the water level of the lake had no impact on the height of the ground water around the lake.

The town did lower the level of the lake, and almost all of the wells around the lake dried up. Most of us had to have new wells put in, with no help from the town. The group of us got together and filed suit against the town for some financial assistance with the cost associated with having the wells replaced. As the case was getting close to going to court for a first hearing, it was easy to see the town officials were getting nervous. By that time, we had entered the new millennium. In late January or early February of 2000, a town official reported that there were frozen pipes in the town hall. A plumber was called to fix the problem, which he did, and then left the building. A short time later, the building was on fire. The town hall was an old, historic building built with few fire deterrents. The town had an all-volunteer fire department. Those two things combined, lead to the complete loss of the building, along with all of the records the town would need for their upcoming court case. The plumber was questioned and cleared of any wrongdoing. However, one of the town selectman's cars was seen at the building just after the plumber left and the fire started.

While the State Fire Marshall's office was investigating the fire, they determined it to be arson, and also found that a very valuable antique brass scale had been removed from the building prior to the fire. The selectman was questioned and, while remaining a person of interest, was released. As the investigation went on, however, everything began to come back to him. The selectman in question here lived two houses up from our house. One Friday morning I got up along with Diana, at 4:45 am. so she could go off to that job she was beginning to hate. I happened to look out a window in our bedroom that faced up the road in the direction of the selectman's house. What I saw was approximately thirty to forty state and local police cars lining the road. There were police officers all over the place. Having a dog, it was our normal routine to take the dog out when we got up. I brought the dog out the front door, and before I was able to get off the front porch, I was confronted by a very large state police officer in full swat gear. He ordered me back in the house and to stay there until we were told it was safe to come out. Diana had to call work and try to explain why she was going to be late. Can you imagine trying to explain to your boss that you can't come to work, because you're being held in your house by a State Police Swat Team? Apparently the selectman up the street had a mental breakdown of sorts, and was holding his family hostage at gun point. He later let them go, but he barricaded himself in the bathroom when the police arrived. Somehow while they were trying to talk him out of it, and with all of those police officers around, the man was able to escape. Three days later he turned himself in.

When the story about the fire and the missing scale came out in the paper, an auctioneer from a town about twenty miles away, called the local police and said that he had the scale. He brought the scale to the police and identified not just the man they had in custody, but he also identified a second selectman that had been with the first one when he was approached with the scale. He said the two selectmen had said they wanted the scale appraised, and sold at an upcoming auction. They never said anything about the scale belonging to the town. The second selectman was arrested and, over time, they were each prosecuted for various crimes from theft and conspiracy, to arson and destruction of public documents. While the investigation into all of that was going on, it was also discovered that the town treasurer had been double billing some of the town's homeowners for property taxes, and had embezzled several thousand dollars from the town. She was also arrested and prosecuted. All of them went to jail for a number of years.

My mother called me one day and said she had something important that she wanted to talk to me about. I asked if she meant just me or was Diana to be included in the conversation? After some minor indecision, my mother said it might be a good idea if she came along. When we got to her house, my mother was clearly nervous about whatever she had to say. After a drink or maybe two, and some meaningless small talk, she got down to business. She had been seeing a man. He was apparently an old childhood sweetheart from her school days. She was obviously terrified to tell me, thinking I would be very upset at the news. Quite the opposite, Diana and I couldn't have been happier for her. I know and have heard stories about the children of a widowed parent getting upset when the parent starts seeing someone. I could never understand that logic. We were happy for her, and glad to see her happy and not alone anymore. More about this development to come.

Chapter Thirty-Four
Your Daughter Wants to Be a What?

With our little town turning into the corrupt cesspool that it was, Diana and I began to talk about moving. It made sense for us to start looking somewhere a bit East of where we were. Diana's job was forty minutes northeast of our house, and most of my work was coming out of cities and towns far East of our house. We began talking about the move in the very early spring. As we were thinking about it, both of my central MA developers began to plan new developments. The second developer was going to do a small development of eight houses. All of the houses he built were in the mid-price range, three to six hundred thousand dollars. That doesn't mean the houses were cheap or small. They all still had to be designed with good traffic flow, nice work areas in the kitchen, large family rooms, and four bedrooms including a large master suite. They also had to be designed to have very good curb appeal. My first developer, the high-end guy, was planning a development of fourteen houses all priced in the 1.5 to 2 million dollar range.

I met with both developers to get things started. Fortunately, the timing of the start of each development was going to be offset just enough to give me time to work comfortably on both of them. I could have my two designers work on the smaller houses together to get them out on time, while I worked on the other larger ones. Those were going to go much slower, and would not be needed as fast. When I met with the high-end guy, he told me he wanted me to design a model house for the development, unlike anything that had been built in the area before. I asked him if he had anything in mind as far as the style or type of house he wanted. He said I was free to do whatever I could come up with. I was thinking that was a dangerous thing to say to me. When it came to house designs, I had a very vivid imagination. I told him I would try to keep it in his price range.

The system that I had worked out with my designers was that they could work at home on whatever project I had given them. If they were doing a preliminary plan for a house or addition, when they were finished with it, they would come to the office, and we would go over it. I would download the work into my computer, go through it with the designer and, if needed, I would make suggested changes that may help different aspects of the plan. The designer would take the plan back, along with a new assignment, make the suggested changes, send the plan back to me, and I would present it to the client. If further changes were required before the final plans could be done, I would generally make those changes myself, just to expedite the completion process. All of that would be going on while I was working on my own projects. The one I was working on at that time was the model home for the high-end development. Having been given complete control of the design of the house was something very new and different for me. It showed me that I had earned the man's complete trust. As we were working on the two developments, work was beginning to pour in from individual clients and small builders, from all over central MA.

Still thinking about moving, I had to concentrate on the work at hand. The house I came up with for the high-end development was, to say the least, different than anything in the area. My design was a fifty-six hundred square foot Second Empire design, with a mixed brick and stone front wall. The house had a three-car garage leading to a mudroom and hall into the house. Off the hall were closets, and a laundry room, with a sink, bench, coat hooks, cubbies for small things, a closet, and a window. The first floor had a large kitchen, dining room, family room, and study. The second floor had a large master suite above the family room. There was a double glass wall gas fireplace between the bedroom and the bathroom that, if you laid in bed, you had a view of the whirlpool tub, set on a platform with columns around it. It was a main focal point in the room, and became very popular over the years. At the other end of the house was a mini-suite, a smaller simpler version of the master suite. Between the two suites were four more bedrooms, each with their own small bathroom. The front entry of the house was recessed with double doors, and large columns. The main hall featured an elliptical stairway to the second floor. Beneath the stairway, on the family room side, was a built-in wet bar for entertaining. The bar was curved to match the curve of the stairway. The kitchen featured a gas fireplace with an arched top, to give the appearance of a Dutch oven. It was a house worthy of that builder's talent.

When an individual client or builder called, since I hadn't done any advertising for the last several years, I would ask how they got my name. The answers were always the same, a local building inspector, another builder, or a past client. It gave me a good feeling to know that there was that much trust and satisfaction in the work I was putting out. By the early part of May, Diana and I had looked at several houses, all in a general area about twenty miles East of where we were living. We hadn't found anything that we were interested in yet. One day Diana's daughter came to us and said that she had decided that she wanted to go back to school. She was twenty-nine years old at the time, and divorced now. We knew she was going to need financial assistance. After all, we were paying most of her bills at the time. But I thought that's what student loans were all about. She said she wanted to become a Forensic Psychologist or Psychiatrist. I can't remember which. In any case, it ended up to be neither. Her coming to us when she did completely changed the direction of our house search. Diana asked me if it would be okay with me if we started to look at two family houses. She said she wanted to give her daughter and grandson a safe place to live, rent free, to help her while she was going to school.

So, still being buried with work, Diana and I started the search for a two-family house. We first started looking in the same area we had already been looking, and there was nothing for two family houses to be had. Moving our search to a wider area, we found a very nice 1880's brick Greek Revival, with a nice big yard, a two-car detached garage, and a pool. The house had been a single family house, and technically it still was. The owner of the house had other family members living in a full apartment on the second floor, but they had only one electric service. We bought the house, and closed on the sale August first, 2000. Diana's daughter and grandson moved in the day after we closed. Diana and I would move in one week later. Leaving our little Victorian painted lady was sad and difficult for us. We decided to keep the little cottage and try to rent it through an agency.

When our moving day came, my mother and her new gentleman friend came to help us. We were able to make the move all in one day. As we were moving into the first-floor apartment, with Diana's daughter already living in the second floor apartment, I had an electrician friend install two new electric services to the house. I quickly found out that living in an apartment was nothing like living in our own house. The day we moved in, we also found that Diana's daughter had a new boyfriend, also living in the house. He had a good job, and seemed to be a really nice young man. The deal of course was that they could live there rent free as long as the daughter was in school. All they had to pay was whatever utilities they used. Having the boyfriend up there was never in the mix. After sitting down with the both of them we came up with a deal. After four years, and Diana's daughter was out of school and working, she said she wanted to buy the house from us. So, as I was looking at it, this would be a four, maybe five-year deal at the most. After that Diana and I could go back to our normal lives. There was, however, one little fly buzzing in the back of my head. I never said anything to Diana about it, but in the ten years that I had known her daughter, I had never seen her finish anything she started. I was a bit worried.

Having made the move to the new location, I set up my new office with an entrance from the driveway. The office was much larger than my first one, and being on the front corner of the house, had more windows which made it much brighter. During the move and everything that goes along with it, I was now a bit behind with my work. My two employees were still working out very well, but now with still more work coming in, I needed more help. Along with the two developments going on, and all of the individual projects coming in, Angelo called. You may remember him from my days as a builder, and the mid 90s' design of his house on Cape Cod. He wanted to build some houses on the Cape. I told him that there were any number of highly qualified designers that lived on the Cape, and that I could set him up with one of them. He insisted that if he was going to build houses, I was the one that was going to design them. The good thing about Angelo was that he would only build one house at a time, and not do anything else until that one was sold. The bad thing was we were talking about more very large, multi-million-dollar houses again.

Chapter Thirty-Five
I Turned Myself into a Large Hunk
of Chum!

People began to come to my new office to talk about their plans for their new houses. When we moved in, Diana's grandson was ten years old, and his bedroom was apparently right above my new office. As a ten-year-old, he for some reason had no idea that playing loud music, jumping up and down on the floor, or jumping from his bed to the floor, didn't qualify as being quiet while I had clients in the office. As time was going by, and we were now in the late fall of 2000, I also noticed that Diana's daughter had done nothing about the alleged return to school she had told us about. We had a housewarming party when we moved into the new house. We were never party people before, but now with Halloween coming we were planning to have a large party for that. It was going to be a costume party, and we invited lots of friends and what little family was still in the area for both of us. The weather was still nice that year, so the party was held outside, with just a few lights. I think the darkness helped with the party mood. My mother and her new gentleman friend came. My mother came dressed as little bow peep, and her friend, Elmer, or "Ed" as he preferred to be called, came as Popeye. He made a very good and convincing Popeye, as he looked a bit like him normally. There were maybe about twenty people there, and the party was a great success. Two parties within three months, that's more than we had in the last ten years. What was happening to us?

My two NY Architects were still sending me work. At one point, I got a request from the second Architect for a very complex addition. It was going to mean a trip to the Catskill Mountains and the site of the home needing the addition. As that was going to be an all-day event, Diana came with me. That was going to be the first and only time that we would meet that Architect. Late in the year 2000, I hired another designer. This one was a young man right out of a very good Architectural program at a very well know University. He did not work out. While he was very good with computers, he didn't have any idea how to start an addition project, or what to do with it. After trying to work with him for a couple of weeks, I let him go and hired someone else. That one was working out just fine. Now with myself and three designers, we were putting work out the door very quickly. My little business, the one my mother never really considered a real job, was by that time grossing well into six figures and would do so consistently for several years.

Sometime in the early winter season of 2000, my mother's neighbor bought a new, very large snow blower. When he got it home, he found that he didn't have room to store it in his garage. So in exchange for keeping my mother's driveway and walks clear of snow, my mother let him keep it in her garage. He would, of course, need to have access to her garage if she should happen to not be there, so she gave him a remote garage door opener. The arrangement was working out just fine, for a while. Apparently, at some point, the neighbor was out doing something in his yard. While doing whatever it was, he also had the door opener in one of his pockets. Every time he bent down, or picked something up that hit the remote, my mother garage door would start to go up. He would sometimes hit the remote several times quickly, causing the door to go halfway up, stop, and go back down. It would sometimes do that several times without stopping. At some point my mother got so mad, she went over and demanded the remote back, and told him to get his snow blower out of her garage. As was very common for her, she never did give the poor man an explanation for the outburst. He was obviously confused, and their friendship was never the same after that.

With Christmas approaching, Diana said she wanted to have another party, but not just any party. She wanted to have an open house on Christmas Eve: a party that we would invite the regular group of guests to, but also open the house to anyone in the neighborhood that wanted to come. So, another party it was going to be! Diana spent the last couple of days before Christmas Eve cooking what looked like way too much food. She is Italian, and that's what they do. The house was decorated; the food was cooked, and lots of little Santa bag gifts were bought. Diana had a complete Santa costume, and sometime between 11:00 and midnight, she would make an appearance as Santa Claus. She would go up to her daughter's apartment, get into the costume, and fill a large bag with little gifts, one for every person still at the party. The gifts were wrapped ahead of time, with names on them. A head count would be made before she went to change, and any extra gifts needed would be wrapped by her daughter as she got dressed. These Christmas Eve open houses became a tradition at our house, and happened every year as long as we lived there. It was not unusual for us to see forty or more people come through the house, and by the time Santa made her visit, there often were still twenty or a little more there. Diana made a very good Santa and she loved doing it. As she gave everyone his gift, they had to sit on her lap, and give her a hug and maybe a little kiss. Some of the men would often take this opportunity to steal a longer kiss than was appropriate, but, it was Christmas! Diana was enjoying playing Santa and it was all just good fun.

With the dawn of 2001, and much, much more work coming in, I was again faced with the problem of having too much work. People were again, having to wait too long for their plans. I was considering giving up additions to concentrate on the new houses. With all of the other work I had been doing over the past years, I also had been working with two Community Development Corporations (CDC'S) in the city. Each of them had a certain part of the city where they worked. They each got grant money, State and Federal, to buy and re-hab abandoned or condemned multi-family houses. The idea was to try to redevelop run down areas in the city. I had been doing that work for about the past five

146

years. The work was easy, but very time consuming. I did the work for them at very discounted prices. I sometimes didn't charge them for some services. I felt it was for a good cause, and I could give back a little by doing that. I was also still doing two projects each year where I didn't charge. Those were always for town projects, or people that needed to have work done and couldn't really afford it. The really time consuming part of the CDC work was that each building had to be visited and measured; every interior space, along with the entire exterior of the building. Sometimes I would go into one of the buildings that was abandoned or condemned, only to find them completely furnished, clothes in the closets, dressers with drawers full of clothes, and boxes and cans of food in the kitchen. It was as if people were still living there every day. I was told that the building had been unoccupied for several months. I have also gone into a building to find a dead person in there. Apparently he had died of a drug overdose. There were also buildings so full of trash and human waste, that I would refuse to go in until the building had been completely cleaned out.

In May that year Diana and I took a cruise. The ship left from Boston and went to Bermuda, where it docked and stayed. The Ship left the port in Boston at 4 p.m. on Sunday, and docked in Bermuda at about 7 a.m. Tuesday morning. We would be in Bermuda until 4 p.m. the following Friday afternoon. The ship became our hotel and restaurant the entire time we were there. At that time the ship would dock at the town of St. Georges. After walking around the little town, we decided to take a bus trip to the other end of the Island and the town of Hamilton. If you ever go to Bermuda, you must take a bus ride. There are no amusement rides that can compare to one of these rides. The streets are very narrow, and with the windows open, you will be pulling parts of bushes and trees out of your hair for the rest of the day. The buses go very fast, and the drivers like to play with the tourists that are on scooters when they come up behind one. We had heard of a beach with pink sand called Horseshoe Beach. We made the trip to see the beach and were very disappointed. The color of the sand was only pink when it was wet. The dry areas were almost a normal sand color.

We had signed up to do a snorkeling trip. Neither one of us had ever been, so we thought that would be something we should try while we were there. When the time came, we were taken to a small, maybe thirty-foot boat, to go to our snorkeling destination. There were maybe about ten or twelve people with us. Some of the people said they had done this before, but most said they hadn't. The snorkeling area we went to was off the southern side of the Island. When we got there, everyone got into the water, and then the boat moved to another location where we were supposed to be picked up. The snorkeling was fun. We saw lots of different kinds of fish, and what may have been parts of sunken boats. At one point our guide said that there was an underwater cave that we could go in if we wanted. I was the only one that wanted to see the cave. With that, all of the other people went back to the boat, and the guide and I went into the cave. As I was going in, I quickly noticed that the sides and bottom of the cave were covered with jagged and very sharp rocks. The guide was telling me to be very careful. Too late! As the waves were coming in and going out of the cave, they were pushing me around, and I was being pushed against the rocks. By the time we left the cave I had turned myself into a large hunk of chum! Now bleeding from my legs and arms, as I came out of the cave, I realized that I had about one hundred yards of open ocean to swim across as a bloody mess. I didn't like the idea, and I don't think the guide did either. He told me to go ahead of him, and he would let me know if he thought we were going to be in trouble. As I was getting closer to the boat, I could see people pointing and saying something about the trail of blood I was leaving in the water. We made the swim without any sharks. I sat on the deck making a bloody mess on the boat as the boat hands tried to clean me up and stop the bleeding.

On the way back to Boston, the first night out from Bermuda, we ran into a very violent storm. With gale force winds and very heavy seas, the ship was being tossed around like a toy in a bathtub. Nobody was allowed on any outer deck areas. There were seasick bags taped to the walls of all of the corridors all over the ship. The Broadway style show however, was still going to go on that night. Diana and I went to it, and along with some other people, we made little bets as to how much of our drinks would still be in the cups when they arrived at our seats. Much to our surprise, no drinks were spilled, and the show performers never missed a step through the entire show. We later went up to the observation room and watched as the bow of the ship went completely under water and then came back up again. It continued to do that several times. When Diana and I went back to our state room, we found that the large square picture window in our room was under water, and remained under water for much of the night.

Chapter Thirty-Six
Attempted Bribes, and Mom Shacks Up

When we came back from our trip, I had to get serious about what to do about my business. I was going to have to go back and look at the work done over the past ten years, and compare it to the work being done now. As I did that, I found some interesting things that I didn't expect. I found that in about eighty percent of all of the jobs, additions and new houses, I dealt with the woman of the house. In many cases even if the husband or boyfriend was there, they had very little input as far as the design work went. I also found that over the years, people had tried to bribe me, I was already aware of that part, but what I found was that in almost all cases, it was in connection with additions. The bribes, with the exception of one man, were always made by women, and for one of two reasons. They were always made in an effort to either lower the cost of the plans, or to bump them up in the schedule. Since bribes were offered for lowering the cost of the plans, you may have guessed that money was never offered as the bribe. Before I go any further with this, I just want to say that I never accepted any of the bribes offered.

Some women were much more creative with their bribes than others. There was the simple "You know, we can talk about you doing anything you want to do in my house, and I do mean anything". That was a common one, offered several times. Then there were the more creative ones that would come to the door in semi-shear baby doll style pajamas, or mid-thigh slips, and say "Oh I thought the appointment was later. Well as long as you're here now, maybe we can talk about...." And that one was usually about money. I would always tell them that I would just wait outside until they put on some clothes. When the meeting got started, the conversation would somehow always get back to, for one reason or the other, "You know, you can get a much better look at what you saw before if you..." And it was always money or to move up the plans.

One young woman went so far to get me to bump up their plans in my schedule, that on the day that I went to take pictures of the area of the house being added onto, she did not answer the door when I rang the bell. I went out to the back deck and started to take the pictures, and she came out on the deck through the sliding door. She had a towel wrapped around her and said she heard the bell, but was in the shower. She then began to ask about moving their plans up in the schedule. When I told her that I couldn't do that because it wasn't fair to the people that had already been waiting, she removed the towel. She didn't have anything on under it. Holding the towel out with one hand and striking a pose as if she were doing a magazine layout, she said, "What do you think now?" I said that I didn't think she would be standing there like that if she knew that my wife was sitting in my car just forty feet from us. Lowering the towel, she turned and started to go back in the house. Just inside the door she turned to completely face me and said, "Well that's unfortunate; maybe some other time." My wife, of course was not in the car, but I had to come up with a fast and positive way to shut her down. I actually lost some jobs because I rejected the women's advances. On a couple of occasions I told them that I was not going to be able to do the plans for them. My decision to stop doing additions was easier than I thought it would be. And yes, I know there is that lingering question about the one man. That also was for sex to reduce the price of the plans. I told him I was not going to be able to do their plans for them.

When we moved to the two-family house, you may remember that we kept our little Victorian cottage and rented it. You may also remember that we used an agency to handle the renting of the house. We felt that they would do a better job than we could with background and credit checks of potential renters. Well, don't believe everything you hear or read about rental agencies. We had trouble getting our rent from the agency because they told us that the renter was not paying his rent on time. After several months of that, the renter moved without telling anyone, and left us with lots of trash and junk in the house and yard. The agency said there was nothing they could do about that, but still wanted their fee for the last month the renter was supposed to have been there. I told them there was nothing I could do about that. Sadly we put the house up for sale. The real estate lady that I designed that "Very expensive" Queen Ann handled the sale. She sold the house very quickly, and for much more than we would have thought possible. We used some of the money to pay down some of the mortgage of the two-family house, and put the rest in the bank.

Diana joined one of those all women fitness centers. When she went for her first workout, she came home and said, "I want one!" I told her to go online and find out about it and maybe we could buy a franchise. She found that there was a franchise territory open a couple of towns over from us. The cost of the franchise was less than expected and I told her that I thought we could do it. We bought the franchise, found a space to set up the fitness center in the territory, and started to get things set up. Diana and her daughter were going to have to go to a seminar that all new owners had to attend. It was in Waco, Texas. They were gone for a week, and when they came back, Diana said that was a place she never wanted to go to again. Diana opened her new business in late August, just before the kids went back to school. Within the first couple of weeks, she had signed up almost three hundred members. Very soon after opening, Diana began to see a problem. Diana was still working at her quality control job, and left the fitness center under her daughter's control on the weekends while she was at her regular job.

Diana's daughter was not getting along with some of the other staff members. There was one in particular that seemed to be more of an issue than the others. After talking to Diana, her daughter, and that particular staff member, I ended up firing the staff member. I was trying to ease the tension in the fitness center; I think everyone was feeling it. Things got better and the business began to run along pretty smoothly. About the time the fitness center got going, my mother told me she was going with Ed on a trip to Texas, to see her sister, and then down to Florida to visit some of Ed's relatives. Ed had a very large fifth wheel travel trailer, and they would be staying in that. My mother was gone for almost a month, and when she returned home she asked Diana and me, Kevin and Ed to her house for lunch one Sunday afternoon. She seemed a bit nervous, but told us that she and Ed had bought some land in Florida, and were going to have a house built there. Jokingly, I said, "So-- you're going to shack up with him." My mother blushed and said not to talk about it in that way.

My mother said that she was going to have to sell her house here in MA before the house in Florida was going to be built. She also said that she wanted to make it clear, that if she did that, if anything was to happen to her, the house in Florida would be left in the end to her three sons. Ed said that he would agree to that, as long as he could live there as long as he was able to be on his own. He had no children from his first marriage, and just one brother and an aunt left. None of us had a problem with him staying there as long as he wanted. My mother put her house up for sale, however, there were some things that would have to be done to it. The biggest issue was the septic system. She would need a Title five certificate. (A current state certified septic system compliance report). Knowing that the system was about twenty years old, I held little hope of it passing the test. It did not. The engineer that did the test was going to have to design a new system to be installed. The old system would have to be dug up, and all of the contaminated soil removed. New soil would be brought in, and a complete new system installed. My mother didn't quite understand all of that, but I helped her through as best that I could.

The house was sold almost at the first showing. While that was great news for my mother, it also meant that the septic system was now, a bit of a rush order. Have I told you that my mother panics over the small things? On the day that the Engineer brought over the plans for the new system to my mother, Diana and I were there to help her understand what was going to happen. The buyers of the house unfortunately also decided that they should be there at that particular time. While the Engineer was out in the driveway talking to the buyers, Diana and I were in the house trying to show my mother what the Engineer had planned for the new septic system. I could tell my mother was starting to get overwhelmed a bit. Until now, she hadn't noticed that the buyers were standing in the driveway talking to the Engineer. When she realized they were out there, she began to panic and started yelling about them being at the house. She then, in her classic ear piercing, glass shattering way, she began to scream at the top of her lungs, and ran down the hall to her bedroom. Diana went to try to calm her down, and I went out to talk to the Engineer and the buyers. They had of course, all heard her screams and were a bit concerned.

My mother continued to scream while Diana tried to get her to calm down. The Engineer and buyers were now standing in the driveway, not saying anything, but just staring in the general direction from which the screams were coming. After a couple of minutes of that, the Engineer turned to me and asked me if she was alright, and did I think he was going to have any trouble with her while he was working there. I tried to assure all of them that she was just under some pressure with everything going on at once, and that yes she was fine. There wouldn't be any problem with the work being done. I told the Engineer that I could be there when he was working, if that would make him feel better. He said he thought he would be ok. He did say he wanted to reserve the right to call me if he needed me. I said that would be OK.

Chapter Thirty-Seven
Your Wife's Surgeon Went Nuts

September 11, 2001. We all remember that date, if not the day. On that morning I had an appointment with the head of one of the CDC's that I did work for. When I went into the conference room, he was sitting staring at the television mounted on the wall. He asked if I had heard about what was going on. Saying that I didn't have the radio on, I went around the table to look at the television. He said that a 747 had just flown into the north tower of the World Trade Center, just about five minutes before I got there. As we conducted our business, the second plane hit the south tower. We just sat and looked at each other in disbelief. With the business being completed, I went back home and turned on the television. As Diana and I watched, the towers started to collapse. As I watched them come oddly and questionably, straight down on themselves, many things seemed wrong, terribly, structurally wrong with that. Having some background in structural analysis, I know that it should have been impossible for those buildings to come straight down the way they did, unless the core support columns were cut in sections to allow that to happen. What should have happened was that the buildings should have twisted, and turned, and folded over to one side or another. That's all I'm going to say about the buildings I'm not going to get into any of the conspiracy theories that are out there.

A few days later I tried to reach my second NY Architect and after trying several times, unsuccessfully, called the first one. Through her grief and crying, she told me that her friend and colleague had an office in the south tower. She was apparently working in the office at the time, and that no one from her office made it out of the building. I couldn't believe what she was saying. I felt very sorry for the loss of her friend, and couldn't begin to imagine what those last few moments must have been like for her friend and her employees. A few weeks later my first NY Architect called to tell me she was moving to another state, and she was going to teach at one of the Universities there. She was done with working with the public.

In late September, Diana began to have some very bad stomach issues. After having some tests done, she was told she would have to have her gallbladder removed. Just a couple of days later, she was admitted into a local hospital for the surgery. By that time she was in a lot of pain, so the surgery was scheduled very quickly. Neither Diana nor I had met the surgeon that was to perform the surgery. As Diana was being prepped for the surgery, the surgeon came in and introduced herself very briefly. Diana was then moved into the operating room.

The plan was that the surgery was going to be done laparoscopically. However, when the surgeon tried to get at the gallbladder that way, she was unable to reach it. She was going to have to change the plan, and actually go in and remove it the old fashion way. Apparently, as she began to make the incision required, the assisting surgeon realized that she was doing it in the wrong place. When the assisting surgeon called her attention to the error, she must have begun to get very flustered, and just started to cut across Diana's stomach in a sort of lightning bolt pattern. The assisting surgeon quickly took over, and ordered the surgeon out of the room. The assisting surgeon completed the surgery, and tried to close that horrible gash across Diana's stomach to minimize the scar as best he could. We were told all of that after the surgery, and Diana had been moved from recovery to a room by the nurses' station. We were also told the original surgeon had a breakdown and was removed from the hospital staff. They told us that she would very likely lose her license to practice.

Some years back, I was able to break Diana of her Halloween tradition of going out toilet papering her friends' cars and yards. Having moved to our new location we did however start a new tradition. We were becoming quite the party animals. So, with Halloween upon us once again, and Diana feeling better, not quite fully recovered yet, we were going to have a party. Again it was a costume party, and everyone did their best with their costumes. This year I was dressed as Fred Flintstone. I even made a wristwatch with a sun dial on it to complete my costume. Diana was of course Wilma. The party, as all the others, went very well. We had about twenty people there again, just the right amount I think. Thanksgiving was held at our house that year. Diana and I, Diana's daughter, her son and boyfriend, Kevin and my mother were there. Diana did the cooking, and as usual made too much food. I'm pretty sure it's an Italian thing.

The incident that took place on September 11 caused a ripple effect on the economy. The stock market fell like the towers did. Some of the jobs that I had deposits on were canceled, and the deposits returned. People lost a lot of money when the market fell, and they wanted to wait to see what was going to happen before spending the money on a new house. As a result of the loss of some of the work, I had to let one of my designers go. I was left with three designers plus myself. I still had enough work coming in to keep all of us busy, but the jobs were smaller, and didn't pay quite as much. My business would still gross six figures for the year, but just barely. It took several months before the good work would start to come back to me, well into the next year in fact.

It was Christmas Eve and another reason to party. It was time for another open house, and a visit from Santa. More people were starting to come. Some would stay until the end; some would just stop as they were passing through to some other party. It was always fun, and Diana and I loved to do it, and to have all the people come. It never really mattered how long they stayed, it was just that they came and spent some time with us and the other people there. Christmas morning Diana's daughter, her son and boyfriend would come down and we would open the gifts. A little later Kevin would come over and we would open gifts with him. There was no cooking ever done on Christmas day at our house. We would just eat leftovers from the previous night. I forgot there was always one thing cooked Christmas morning; cinnamon rolls! Those were a must have for me every Christmas morning. Later we would go to my mother's house. That year it was Ed's house, because that was where she was living while they waited for the Florida house to be finished.

At the beginning of 2002, things were starting to change a bit. One of my designers told me she was leaving. She said that because of the slow- down in the housing market, she was concerned that a small company such as mine was not going to be able to keep her busy. She was leaving to go to a larger company that designed and built the small commercial buildings as well as some houses. Telling her that I had been able to keep her busy right along, and saw no reason for that to change didn't seem to matter; she left anyway. Two designers plus myself! Diana's fitness center was losing members as well. The business was still doing ok, but we couldn't see any reason for the loss of membership. Diana called some of the members that left to see if they would tell her why they stopped coming. What she heard from most of the people she called was-- upsetting to say the least. Those that would talk to her about it, told her that they left because of her daughter, and the way she ran the club, and treated the people when she was in charge. She was told that her daughter was rude, using foul language when talking to members, and most of the time just not doing her job. After a short discussion, Diana and I decided that it was time to revisit that "Back to school thing" with her daughter. We had to get her out of the club if it was going to survive. Diana was also going to have to take a leave of absence from her quality control job for a short time to try to get the club back on track.

My high-end developer called sometime around mid-March. He bought a very large tract of land, and was planning a development of approximately forty houses. He said the project would be about a four to five year deal, with all forty houses being different designs and styles. I was going to be busy. The first house plan wouldn't be needed until sometime in May, but there would be plenty of planning to do before then. He again wanted houses that were a little different for the area, but priced in the eight hundred thousand to one million dollar range. Diana made arrangements to take the leave of absence from her job. She was at the fitness center every day now trying to get it back on track, and repair the damage her daughter had done. Diana it would seem, had a good head for business. She was able to repair the damage, and rebuild the membership of the club. We both sat her daughter down and had a talk with her about the damage she caused, and the fact that we bought that house so she could go back to school, and she so far had made no effort to do that. She told us that she had been looking up some different schools, and was planning to go back in September. Meanwhile, she and her son, and boyfriend were living in the house rent free for two years, without her going to school. That was never part of the deal as far as I was concerned. I was a bit unhappy with that turn of events.

Chapter Thirty-Eight
The Big Five-O

As the time was sliding along, Diana's birthday was coming up. It was a big one, the big five-o. That's right! If you will remember you already know that Diana is one year older than I am. And if you or anyone else will ask her, she will gladly tell you that I am her "Boy-toy". With such a landmark birthday, we of course were going to have a huge party to celebrate the event. I rented a large tent, hired a disk jockey, and sent out lots of invites. As for my present to her, I thought it would be fun to fly her best friend, (she hadn't seen her in several years) up from Florida for a few days. Well, her best friend decided that she wasn't going to come up unless I was going to pay for her two daughters to come with her. Some friend! I was trying to think of another equal gift to give her, when one of Diana's longtime friends told me he would pay for the kids, if I paid for Diana's friend. So Diana's friend got to drag her two kids along with her. We bought round trip tickets. The return flight was scheduled for three days after their arrival date. Diana's daughter said they could stay in her apartment with them while they were there.

The tent was delivered and set up the day before the party. When party time arrived, the DJ was there and all set to go. He was, perhaps, in his mid-fifties and had his daughter with him. She was thirteen, and she led people in all kinds of dances, to all different kinds of music during the party. I think she worked harder than her father did. People were starting to stream in. There would be between forty and fifty people at the party. At most of our parties, people would generally bring whatever they wanted to drink with them. There were always a few that would not. I didn't mind. They were, for the most part, very close friends and family. Even though I was not a beer drinker, I always had a few cases on hand just in case they were needed. As for wine, I have been a wine drinker for years. I always kept at least sixty bottles on hand at all times. The party was going along just fine. Some people brought swimsuits, and were in the pool, while others played badminton. Some just mingled and visited as others danced to the music. All seemed to be having a good time. As the cake was brought out, the DJ led us in singing Happy Birthday. Then while the cake was being cut, the DJ, who had no teeth, sang "You're only sixteen" to Diana. Of course he changed sixteen to fifty, but I have to say, for a man with no teeth he did a very good job with the song.

Diana's best friend, that one from Florida, decided to extend her stay for a couple more days. Then she decided to extend her stay for a few more days, and then several more days after that. We couldn't get rid of her or her kids. Keep in mind, we not only have Diana's daughter's family living up there rent free, but now we have three more people up there, all using more water for laundry, showers, and dishes, and whatever else they needed. We were paying the water and city sewer bill for the whole house. Those two bills generally cost about twelve hundred dollars a year. Water was very expensive there. That year the water and sewer bill was about two hundred dollars more than normal. The friend and her kids stayed for about a month before finally leaving. Just before they left, one of the friend's kids decided to use Diana's daughter's microwave as a timer for something. The problem with that was that she turned the microwave on, with nothing in it. It apparently didn't stay on very long before it burnt itself up. I had to go buy a new microwave.

My mother was going on another travel trailer trip with Ed. They were going to try to time it so they would end up in Florida, about the time their house was finished. Before they left, she asked me if I thought it would be possible for Diana and me to go to the house in Florida after they signed all the papers. They were going to have to come back home to get things ready to ship to Florida. She wanted us to be there to take care of the place for a couple of weeks until they could get back down there. I told her that we would be in Florida while she was on her trip with Ed. We had decided to open a fitness center in Florida, and had already been given a territory, just one town from where her new house was. Diana had gotten a new manager for the fitness center here at home, and she was working out just fine, and the members seemed to like her.

With my business being very busy but one of those businesses that I could run from almost anywhere, we headed to Florida. We rented a house and had the real estate agent show us possible locations for our new fitness center. My business was done by the internet and e-mail and that seemed to be working out very well. My two remaining designers were working on house plans based on sketches and drawings that I would send them. They would e-mail me their work and I would review it, and either make changes or send it to the developer for approval. The final drawings were all done by me because I had the plotter with me and was the only one able to print out the full-size drawings. After looking at several locations, we finally decided on a spot for the new fitness center in a large strip mall. Once we had all the paperwork done, we began to renovate the space. One of Diana's old friends came down to help us. He had some knowledge of commercial buildings and also had some pretty good ideas. Shortly after starting the renovation, I hurt my back. I had been having lower back issues for a while. I think the long drive to Florida, along with the construction work just aggravated it enough to cause very strong sciatic pain in my left leg. I went to a doctor in Florida and he was able to get me stable enough to fly home. So I had my plotter shipped back home, and I left Diana and her friend to complete the setup of the space, and to get the club opened.

Diana's friend stayed for about two weeks, and together they got the club ready to open. Over the next couple of weeks Diana interviewed for help, and in particular, a manager to run the club for us. She was able to find all the help she was going to need, and to find a very good and trustworthy manager. With the help in place, she opened her new fitness center on August first. The membership grew very fast, and the club became very busy. After leaving to go back home, I got medical help for my back, and continued to work. About a month after leaving, I was heading back to Florida. Diana, now satisfied that her new club was running well and in good hands with the manager she had picked, was ready to come home. We would again make that long drive, approximately thirteen hundred miles, from the bottom of the country to the top of the country. I was not looking forward to that.

About three or four weeks after returning home, my mother called to tell me that the house in Florida was finished. They would be in Florida for another week or so, but then would be heading home. It was now the middle of September, and as Diana's daughter had told us, she did start back to school. We now were headed back to Florida to my mother's new house. We were only going to have to be there for about a week, maybe a little more. All I brought with me as far as my business went was one lap top computer. That was all I was going to need for a short stay like that. We flew to Florida this time, and rented a car at the airport. My mother had given us directions to her house, and we were able to find it quite easily. We both went over to check on the fitness center, and found it to be running smoothly, and taking in some new members. Before leaving the club, we made arrangements to take the entire staff out to dinner one night that week. Back at my mother's house, between doing some of my own work, and cleaning up the house, we decided to take a dip in the swimming pool. As we were getting out of the pool, I noticed a small snake, curled up at the bottom of the screen enclosure, at the bottom--inside the enclosure. Let me just say at this point, that I am not a snake person, at all. I said to Diana, "How do you feel about snakes?"

Diana doesn't mind snakes as much as I do. First we (she) tried to catch it, but it kept trying to bite her. Then we got a large pot with a metal top and somehow we were able to catch the damn thing as it was in the air on one of its jumping attempts to bite us. With the snake safely in the pot, and the cover on nice and tight, I took it to a vacant lot next to my mother's house, and threw the snake out of the pot. We later learned about something called a pygmy rattlesnake. Apparently they are quite common in Florida, and quite deadly. I looked up images of them on the internet, and found that the snake we were playing with, was in fact one of those. Had I known about them before our little encounter, I wouldn't even have had to think about it. I would have killed it.

My mother and Ed arrived at the house about four days after we did. They had Ed's truck full of stuff, and the trailer was almost as full. As we began to unload all of the boxes and suitcases, I ran into two very heavy boxes. For those of you who have never been to the west coast of Florida, just above the Tampa area, they don't really have rocks. At least not in the New England sense of "Rocks". So my mother, wanting to have some flower garden areas that would remind her of the ones she left behind, brought two large boxes of rocks from New England. When I looked in the boxes and saw the rocks, I looked at Ed and he just shook his head and said, "There's at least one full tank of gas just in those boxes." Given the number of rocks, and how heavy they were, I believe he may have been right. After getting the truck and trailer unloaded, and everything into the house, we stayed for another two days, and then headed back home. October was just a few days away, and for some reason from the first of October to the middle of December was always a very busy time for my business, not that the rest of the year wasn't. We were putting out between seventy and eighty new house plans every year.

When we went to Florida in September, we hired one of the girls that worked at Diana's fitness center near our house to stay at the house and take care of our dog. You may remember him: the one that got shot in the face three times. He was still with us. He was getting pretty old now. He was a stray so we couldn't be sure of his age. Really, all you had to do with him was to put him out on his run in the morning, bring him a little food and some water, and bring him in later in the afternoon. You feed him at dinner time, and spend some time with him and he was a happy dog. Well, for some reason, the girl must have had some sort of full psychotic break one day. Diana couldn't get hold of her, and her daughter's boyfriend and son said that there was a lot of yelling and other noise coming from our apartment. They said they tried to get in but the doors were blocked with stuff inside so they couldn't be opened. Diana called the local police to do a check on the girl, but by the time they got to the house, she was gone. They found her at the fitness center later that day, after it was closed. She had tried to barricade herself inside, but the police were able to get in and remove her. They took her to a hospital for evaluation. She was never mentally able to come back to work for us. We lost touch with her after a short time.

Chapter Thirty-Nine
The Lederhosen

The rest of the year was pretty quiet. No Halloween party this year; because we just had too much going on. Thanksgiving was held at our house with Diana's daughter, her son and boyfriend, Kevin, and Jerry, Diana's friend that helped her get the Florida fitness center set up. Again too much food, but by now, I'm quite sure it's an Italian thing. Christmas Eve came along and another house full of people: lots of food, drink and some fun games played. When people came into the house, a number was taped to their back. When the time came, everyone with the same number got together in a group. Each group was given a well-known Christmas carol and told to take the words out and put their own words back in, using the same tune. They had ten minutes to come up with their new songs. Then each group had to sing their song for the judges: Diana, Kevin, me, and one other picked at random. Some of the songs were pretty good; some were maybe a little off color, but there was alcohol involved. They were all funny and surprisingly creative. Another good game is to pair two people together: one can only use his right hand and the other his left. With that, they have to put together a gift box, and then wrap it. The first pair to finish wins. The gift of course has to look at least somewhat like a gift that you would give to someone. That was that the problem for most of the couples. Most of the finished gifts looked like they had already been attacked by a six-year-old on speed.

Early in 2003, Diana's daughter, going to college in Vermont, had settled into a pattern of staying there for two weeks, and then coming home for a weekend and then going back. When she started going to the school, she was taking the bus from Springfield MA to the city where the college was, and then a taxi to the school. She very quickly decided that she was not a person who rode on public buses. Since she is the world's second worst driver, my mother being the first, there was no possibility of her driving there on her own. She would have her boyfriend drive four hours on Saturday morning to pick her up and bring her home. And then on Sunday morning, drive another four hours to bring her back to the school. Did I mention that was four hours each way? The poor sucker would do that every two weeks. She never really told us what she was studying. We knew it wasn't forensic psychology, or any related subjects, but she said she was doing well and getting good grades. She did in fact make the dean's list at some point.

Diana had quit her job at the factory doing quality control. She was working full time at her fitness center, and it was going very well. My business was starting to go crazy. On top of the development work, I was getting three or four calls each week from individual clients for new houses. I was still getting calls for additions but I was not taking on any more at that time. The CDC work was beginning to take too much time, so I was thinking about letting that go. Another designer decided to quit. He was going to try to start his own business; I wished him luck. He was one that I kept away from the clients because he had no people skills what-so-ever. One designer plus me! I was starting to schedule six months out. Just about every one that called said that they would wait. According to some of the area building inspectors, I was now one of the most asked for designers in the area. There were, however, still some inspectors that had no idea what a Certified Building Designer was. That was going to have to be fixed.

With my two terms as President of the MA State Society of that National Building Designers Organization past me now, I had a little time to give. I got together with three other Certified Designers, and we put together a power point program for presentation at regional building inspector meetings. The idea was to educate as many of the inspectors about the certification process as we could. Each one of us would take a section of the presentation and talk about the program, and then answer any questions that were asked. It was a good program. We were able to reach most of the inspectors in the area with it. When the National board heard about what we were doing they asked for a copy of the power point for other states to use. Knowing that it could only help our cause, we gave them the material and offered any help we could give.

My mother and Ed came back for a visit at Easter that year, so we had a big Easter dinner at our house. Along with the usual family members, a small group of friends were invited and we ended up with twelve or fourteen people. After dinner we were all just sitting around the table letting all that food rest for a bit, and talking about past adventures. My mother began to tell the story of her father taking her to Ireland, Scotland, Germany, and Austria. She was telling everyone about the very nice and expensive Lederhosen she had bought for all of her sons. They were complete with the knee socks with the tassels, and the little felt hats with those funny little brushes in them. She was especially proud of the fact that they were real leather, and had fine embroidery on them. She was telling everyone how upset she got that none of us would wear them when she came home with them. Diana asked how old we were when she did that, and she said she thought I was about fourteen, David about fifteen, and Kevin maybe seventeen or eighteen. Everyone around the table began to roar with laughter. My mother, not knowing why they were laughing, began to laugh a little herself and began asking what was so funny. I don't remember who it was, maybe Diana, but someone took up the chore of explaining to my mother what it might have been like for kids of those ages showing up at school in that area in lederhosen. Once she got the picture, she began to see the humor in it.

My mother often did things that, well, I guess made sense to her at the time she did them, but not to many other people. For instance, take those boxes of rocks she brought from New England. The idea was to make a few little garden areas that would remind her of the ones she left behind. Now you have to understand here that what she left behind was a yard that was littered with large and small flower gardens everywhere. But in New England, a woman in her late sixties or early seventies could take the time to work at them as she felt like it. In Florida, the heat won't let her do that. When she brought all those rocks to Florida we tried to explain that she should only do a small area of flower beds, and see how she was able to handle that before adding to it. That is not how my mother works. Ed said that as soon as they got the house in order, she was out digging up patches of the yard all around the house. She was going to try to put flower gardens all over the yard as she had before. She quickly found that she could not handle the heat the way she thought she would. When she asked Ed to help her with the flower gardens, he told her that he didn't do flower gardens. That quickly became a sore spot between them, and the spot, I think continued to grow.

Life at home was going along. I gave up the very time-consuming CDC work. Diana was doing well with her fitness center. She loved to be with the ladies and made their workout time almost more of a social time than anything else. She had a way of putting people at ease and making them feel very comfortable around her. She was very good at what she was doing. At some point over the summer, my last remaining designer told me that he had been offered a job doing field work for a land surveyor. He always said that would be his first choice of work. I guess I knew it was coming at some time. I thought about hiring another designer, but with just doing the new houses, and a six-month lead time we were doing pretty good with just the two of us. I thought if I put in a few more hours, maybe I could take care of it by myself. As it turned out, working six and a half days a week, I found that I was able to take on a few more houses, and get the lead time down to just over four months. With Diana's daughter having completed one full year of college, she was now allowed to take many of her classes over the internet, and was only required to be at the school one week per month. That was going to save her boyfriend untold hours of drive time, and many gallons of gas. I still wasn't sure what courses she had decided to take, and she wasn't really talking about it. When I asked Diana if she knew, she said she wasn't sure either, but I got the feeling she knew more than I did about it.

We made a couple trips to Florida: one in late spring and the other was in the fall. When we took the trip in the spring, we had a very hard problem to deal with first. That old big guy, the dog that had been with us for so long was not doing well. His hips were giving out, and it was getting hard for him to stand, never mind walk. He was in pain all of the time now; we could see it in his eyes. We knew what we had to do, he was telling us he was ready, but still--it is a very difficult thing to do; I called our Vet and made the arrangements. The Vet would do it after business hours that same day. The big guy was ready. He just got into the car as best he could without having to force him. I think he knew what was going on and was glad it was happening. As we sat on the floor at the Vet's office, we held him, and after one last quick look at Diana, he drifted away. The Vet left us alone with him for a while to say goodbye. Even as I write this now, I am having trouble with it.

We went to Florida to check on the fitness center, so all of the trips were considered business trips. We stayed at my mother's house which saved us quite a bit of money in lodging fees. We always took my mother and Ed out to dinner a couple of times while we were staying with them. The fitness center was doing very well. We had a very good membership base, and the manager was doing a great job running the place. I may not have introduced you to our manager yet. Her name, as it turned out, was also Diana. So, when the two Diana's were at the club, they were called Diana number one, my wife, and Diana number two, the manager. We would sometimes go out to dinner or for drinks with Diana number two and her husband. In some of those cases the two ladies were known as the "Double D's". On one of our visits, we took my mother, Ed, and Diana number two out to dinner and then we went out to a local club for a few drinks. I don't remember where Diana's husband was, but he wasn't with us. As the night at the club progressed, my wife introduced my mother to a drink call a "Slippery nipple". It's a shot of Sambuca, with a little Bailey's floated on top. My mother quickly decided she liked them, very much!

After having several of my mother's new favorite drink, she was ready to start dancing on the tables. My mother was really quite funny when she was drunk. Just seeing my mother drunk was funny in itself. It had been a long time since she had let go and had that much fun. By that time, it was getting late, maybe mid-night or a little after. Some of the people (guys) at the bar were starting to get a bit rowdy and in pretty short order a fight broke out. The fight involved several people, and had spilled out into the parking lot. The police were called and there must have been ten or twelve officers that came to the party. We wanted to leave, as did many of the other people at the club. The problem was that even after the fight had been completely dealt with, the police were not leaving. They were just hanging around the parking lot. Nobody wanted to even look in the direction of their car after having spent the night drinking with all those cops standing there. The police stayed out in the parking lot for quite a while, I assume waiting to see if any of us were going to get into any of the cars. Some of us just hung around in the parking lot talking to each other, and some others stayed in the building, but nobody made a move toward any cars. The police finally left. As they did, we watched to see which direction they went in; we then went in the other direction as we left.

Chapter Forty
Is It Liberal Arts, but with Sex?

When Christmas came around, Diana wanted to do something different that year. All of our businesses had done very well and she wanted to maybe try giving something back. After putting some thought into it, we decided to bring Happy Meals to all of the kids in one of the shelters in the city. I called one that I knew of to let them know of our plans, and to find out how many kids they had there. It was going to be a lot of Happy Meals and we had to order them in advance. With the information we needed, Diana, Diana's daughter and her son, and I picked up the Happy Meals on the afternoon of Christmas Day. We made our way into the city in the pouring rain, and in the early evening hours went to the shelter. Diana was dressed in her Santa costume, and the rest of us were just along as Santa's hired helpers. The gifts having all been made and delivered by that time, all the elves were now sunning themselves somewhere along the Riviera. As we began to pass out the Happy Meals to all of those less fortunate children, two things happened. The first was that the kids quickly realized that Diana was not the real Santa, and was in fact a girl, and then got very upset about that. And the second thing, the one that really pissed us off, was that the adults began asking what we brought for them, and why weren't we giving them anything. By the time we were done in there, we just wanted to take all of the Happy Meals back, and tell everybody to go to hell, and---oh yes, have a very Merry Christmas.

As 2004 came along, I was settling in pretty well working by myself. Some of the days were long, as much as fourteen hours, but most of the work could be done from my house, and I loved what I was doing. Even the really long days didn't seem that long. Back in 2001, I sold our Lincoln Mark VIII LSC and bought a new Acura TL. It was loaded with all the toys, and I ordered it with a navigation system. It was the first car I had that came with one. I found that I used it all the time to fine clients' locations, and just to figure out where I was going. The car was nice; I liked it. Diana was not crazy about it. At some point in the Spring of 2004, I had to go to Fall River MA for a job. Diana came with me, and as we were crossing the bridge into the city, a stone got tossed up from the road and hit my windshield. The stone put a good size pit in the windshield that, by the time we got home later that day, had started to run a crack across the glass. I called my insurance company and they told me where to take the car to have the windshield replaced. I did as I was told, and when I got the car back, with that nice new windshield in it, I noticed an annoying squeak every time I hit a small bump. After checking it out, I found that it was coming from the windshield. I brought the car back to the place that put the new windshield in, and after they played around with it for several hours, they said there was nothing they could do to fix it. And, in fact, they had no idea what was causing the squeak. I took the car to the dealer that I bought it from and had them look at it. They said that there was supposed to be a felt gasket between the glass and the leather dashboard. That gasket was no longer there. Apparently when they took the original windshield out the felt came with it, and got thrown away. The windshield installers would not take responsibility for it, and the dealer said it would take months to get a new gasket. I couldn't stand driving the car, it was making me nuts listening to the squeak all the time. One day coming back from an appointment with a client, I stopped at the local Cadillac store and ordered a new CTS, of course with all of the toys, including the navigation system. The CTS at the time had a base price of about thirty-three thousand dollars. When I was done adding this that and whatever else, the list price on that one was in the mid-forties. I didn't care; I just wanted out of the squeak mobile. That Cadillac became my favorite car; it was comfortable, fast, and lots of fun to drive.

We only made a couple of trips to Florida that year. I had too much work, and Diana was very busy with her fitness center here at home. The trips we made were quick, just a quick little check on the fitness center and back home again. In the early Fall, as Diana's grandson had turned fourteen, we began to notice a disturbing pattern starting to take place in her daughter's apartment. With her daughter only having to be at school one week per month, she was home most of the time now. What we began to see, and I'm not really sure when it started, was that she was allowing her son to have girls stay overnight with him. I had to wonder what the girls were telling their parents about where they were, and with whom they were spending the night. Diana went up to talk to her daughter about it and when she came back down, she said that one of the first things you see when you enter the apartment, is a large jar of condoms sitting on the kitchen table. She said that her daughter told her that she was teaching her son that it was ok to have sex, as long as he was keeping it safe, and not sneaking around to have it. She said she felt it was better for him to know that he could do it in his own house if he wanted. She was also letting her son's friends bring girls over to their apartment to have sex with them. We also learned that her daughter seemed to be quite comfortable walking around the house with just a pair of panties on, in front of her son, and her son's male friends. I brought up the issue of statutory rape and sexual misconduct, but the daughter didn't seem to think any of that would be an issue. We also noticed that besides the boyfriend, Diana's daughter was starting to have sleepovers with girlfriends of her own. I'm not sure what was going on there, but I have some idea.

Both Diana and I were concerned about what was going on up there. But Diana's daughter made it clear that she was going to raise her son to understand that sex was not a dirty thing, something to be hidden or ashamed of. She wanted him to know that the human body, especially the female body was a beautiful thing. She said that she had even given him a copy of the Kama Sutra. She was now in her third year of school. Part of her studies now included some sort of art therapy. As she worked on most of it at home, and then brought it to the school, we got to see some of it. What I saw was a lot of very dark, angry, self-deprecating, paintings. Some of them even showed signs of angry sexual themes, possibly even rape. Much of her paintings focused on vaginas, mostly bloody, or violated in some manner. She had originally said she was going to school to study some form of Forensic Psychology, or at least something related to that field. This art did not, at least to me, indicate the psyche of a person that should be anywhere near anything involving the study of Psychology. When I finally asked exactly what she was studying, we found that she was taking courses in Women's Studies. Now thoroughly befuddled, I asked my wife what Women's Studies was. She said she wasn't sure, but she thought it was the study of women's bodies, and how they worked.

Concerned with what Diana's daughter was doing with her "Going back to school" years, and the fact that we bought that big old two-family house to support her, I took a look at some of the books she was using for her studies. What I found were several books on vaginas, and several more on men that transitioned into women, but without having the bottom surgery to complete the transition. I also found several drawings and sketches of vaginas drawn from many different views. It would seem that she had become somewhat overly interested in the vagina. I had to ask Diana just what a degree in Women's Studies would give her daughter. What exactly do you do with a degree in that field? Can a person make a living off a degree such as that? Those were questions that she could not answer for me. I was beginning to have a bad feeling. Was this just Liberal Arts, but with lots of sex? Now I began to understand her thought process behind her son and her feelings about sex.

Thanksgiving came around again. We had the usual group of family and small circle of friends over for dinner. A couple of years ago we found a restaurant, maybe twenty miles away, that for a very reasonable price would put together an entire Thanksgiving meal for you. They would include turkey, mashed potato, gravy, butternut squash, cranberry sauce, rolls, butter, and a pie. They would put it all together in oven ready disposable pans, and box it up for you. We were able to order the meal to serve twelve to fourteen people. What it came down to, was that we couldn't buy all the stuff to make the dinner, and cook it, for the same price as the restaurant meal. Of course Diana had to add her own little touch to it. A couple of extra pies, some mashed sweet potatoes, maybe some green beans or peas, and maybe even some bacon wrapped shrimp. She is Italian, and it wouldn't be right if there weren't leftovers. It was always great.

Christmas time 2004, and no thoughts of Happy Meals for any ungrateful snot nosed little brats or their parents. Diana had been getting her nails done at a small nail salon owned by a Vietnamese family. It was right down the street from our house, and she had become very friendly with them. She decided that she wanted to have a separate Christmas just for them. So on Christmas Eve Day, they were invited to our house for a small Christmas dinner. When they arrived at the house, as they approached the front door they all fell to the ground. Looking closer I saw that they were on their knees. We had a Buddha on the front steps to our house, and we never gave it a thought. As they entered the front vestibule, again they all dropped to their knees. Damn, we had another Buddha in the vestibule. We had another Buddha in the family room. I very quickly grabbed it and put it in the bedroom. I was afraid these poor people would be crippled by the time they left the house.

After our little Vietnamese Christmas came the usual open house. As people started to come in, the food started to come out. Diana always made two lasagnas for Christmas. One was the traditional with red sauce and meat, the other was made with lasagna noodles, but filled with butternut squash. If you have never tried it, you should look up the recipe and give it a try. It's almost like having dinner and dessert at the same time. Along with the lasagnas there were always meatballs or sausage with onions and peppers, a variety of salads and other goodies brought by many of the guests. On one occasion, I'm not sure if it was that year or not, but I think it was, one of our very close friends and her husband were sitting at the table after the dinner was finished. As they sat there the husband was picking at a basket of greens and grapes in the center of the table. I sat there watching him for a while, and after he had eaten most of the grapes, I said to him, "You know you just ate the centerpiece". He looked at me and without any shame or guilt said, "Oh, well it was pretty good." I said thanks and that I would let Diana know he appreciated it. No matter what happened during the open houses, everyone had a good time.

Chapter Forty-One
Diazepam and Gin

In the early part of 2005, maybe early February, we took another trip to check on the fitness center in Florida. Now, I may not have told you this, but Diana had a fear of height, and an even greater fear of flying. Typically she would sit in her seat and grab my hand, and try to break every bone in it as she squeezed the hell out of it, while she was crying. She would do that as the plane was taking off. On one flight she even took the hand of some strange guy sitting on the other side of her, and squeezed the hell out of it. He was nice enough about it, but I'm not really sure he appreciated her attention. To combat the issue we found that a small amount of valium, along with a gin and tonic would help a great deal. She would still cry and squeeze my hand, but not nearly as bad as if she didn't have her little helper. On the flight we were about to take, she realized she didn't have any valium with her. Fortunately I have one of those brains that can't be shut off, so I occasionally take Diazepam to help me sleep. I gave her one of those. Unfortunately I didn't realize that it was twice as strong as the valium she was taking. So the result of the diazepam and the gin and tonic, was that by the time we were getting on the plane, she could hardly stand on her own. As I was giving the ticket agent the boarding passes and trying to hold Diana up, I was getting some dubious looks from the ticket agent and other passengers. The agent asked me if she was alright, and I told her that she had a fear of flying and that her doctor gave her something for it. I said maybe it was a little too strong, but that she would be just fine.

As I have told you, Diana was always very good at picking birthday and anniversary gifts for me. Even though my birthday is in the Fall, she gave me my present in July in 2005. She didn't really have a choice. What she got me that year was a few lessons driving race cars at a local track in Connecticut. The cars I would be driving were NASCAR Sonoco Series Modified cars. They are basically a tubular steel frame with a very large motor, and a place for the driver. They have very little body work, just a piece of sheet metal for a hood, a roof, and a rear deck. I was told the cars have about 650 horsepower. All I know is that they can go very fast on that track. The track is a 5/8 mile paved oval with 20 degree banked turns. Turns one and two are wider than three and four, and as you come out of turn four, the outside wall comes in a little to make the front stretch just a bit narrower than the turn was. It didn't take long for me to get comfortable with the cars or the track. I found that going into turn one there was a bumpy area that, if you hit it wrong, would get you out of control. Coming out of turn four there was a bump in what I thought was just the inside lane, close to the bottom of the track. I hit that at full power once and the entire car came off the track, while I was in the process of setting up to go down the front stretch. Since the car was turning when I hit the bump, it continued to turn when it came off the ground. I was only in the air for less than a second, and the car only side stepped about two or three feet. When the car hit the ground, I heard the tires screech over the sound of the motor, and felt them grab the track. I was able to keep the car under control, but it scared the shit out of me when that happened.

Before getting into one of these cars, you have to put a fireproof driving suit on and a helmet with a full face guard. At one point as I was following my instructor around the track, I was maybe a little less than two car lengths behind him, going at somewhere in the area of one hundred and twenty miles an hour. I suddenly felt like I got hit in the chest with a small hot stone. When I looked down, I saw a piece of rubber from a tire had come into the car and hit me in the chest. The piece was about three inches long, and maybe a half inch wide, and very hot. It actually melted itself to the fire suit. After my lesson was finished and I drove into the pits, I got out of the car and tried to peel the rubber off the suit. It came off very hard, and left a sort of burnt rubber mark on the suit. My instructor looked at it and said, "You're a real racer now." When I took the suit off, there was a mark on my chest where the rubber had hit me. I had two days of lessons, and when I was done, the instructor told me that he thought I was a natural racer, and that I should have started driving years ago. He said it was like he was racing a professional racer when we were on the track together.

After talking it over with me, Diana decided she wanted to sell her fitness center in MA. It was becoming too much to deal with both locations. Selling it was very easy. The first employee that I had let go just after we opened the club wanted to buy it. She had a partner that was going to help her buy and run the club. We sold it in early September. Shortly after selling it we made another trip to Florida. While we were there, we found several very nice one-acre building lots. The lots were in an area that was dry and flat. All of the lots were selling for five thousand dollars each. We contacted our real estate friend and bought four lots. We did also check on the fitness center. It was still doing very well. We again took all of the staff out to dinner, and Diana spent some time at the club with the ladies. Sometime during our stay, we decided, as usual, to take my mother and Ed out to dinner. We were going to one of our favorite restaurants. Unfortunately it is gone now, but it was a very good, rustic Italian restaurant, a bit pricey, but very much worth it. Now I know I have told you that my mother may have had some little quirks. This particular one, was one that even I had trouble dealing with. As all of us got ready to go to dinner and went out and got into the car, we found ourselves sitting and waiting for my mother. After sitting for several minutes, with my mother nowhere to be found, I went looking for her. I found her out in the back yard, pulling weeds from one of her way too many flower gardens. When I told her that we were all sitting in the car waiting for her, she got mad and said that she had not agreed to go at that particular time, and that the flower garden needed to be weeded.

My mother very often was easily side tracked. She would start doing one thing, and then think of something else that had to be done right then. I know we all have a bit of that in us, but she could really take it to the extreme. We did finally get to dinner that night, but it was a good deal later than we had planned. When we got back from our trip to Florida, I got back to work and Diana enjoyed some of her leisure time by going out shopping with her daughter. At some point in the late Fall that year, Diana and her daughter were out doing some Christmas shopping. I was out at a job site somewhere doing something; I don't remember what. I got a call from Diana and she was very excited. She told me that I had to meet her at a store where she and her daughter were. I told her that I was working and would be along later, but she was very insistent that I go there now. When I got there, what she was so excited about was, that the store she was at sold NASCAR equipment, and there was a race car and trailer in the yard for sale. She wanted me to buy it. The car was a mini-stock. It was a tubular steel frame with a "stock" car body on it. That one was a 1998 Pontiac Sunfire, front wheel drive. The car had been raced the previous year at the track that I took lessons at, in a NASCAR weekly series.

Mini-stocks, all mini-stocks are four-cylinder stock cars, and can be front or rear wheel drive. They have a minimum weight requirement of 2150 lbs. That one weighed about 2300 lbs. It was a tank in race car terms. The store owner called the guy that owned the car and he came right over to meet with us. I had him take the car out of the trailer, and I drove it around the parking lot. I just wanted to make sure everything was working. Everything seemed to work fine and after some minor bullying by my wife and her daughter, I pulled out my check book. Having a check right there, ready to give the guy gave me a little bargaining power, and I was able to get the car and trailer for one thousand dollars less than he was asking. I'm sure that you can probably guess that that of course was just the start of things to come.

In the summer of 2004, just after buying that nice new Cadillac, I also bought a nice new Ford Explorer Sport Track, four-wheel drive truck. I did that so I wouldn't be driving the car in the snow, or onto construction sites. Owning the truck for only about a year, I still owed a large amount of money on it. Now faced with about seven thousand pounds of trailer, car and equipment to pull, that little truck was not going to do it. I was going to need a bigger truck. I could not afford to buy a new truck big enough to pull all that weight, and I was going to have to use the Ford as a trade for whatever I did buy. I was going to lose several thousand dollars on that deal. It was early December and I knew I was going to have to find a truck pretty fast. The car was going to need some work before it was ready to get back on the track again. The store owner was good about letting us leave the trailer and car at the store for a little while, but after a couple of weeks he had someone bring the trailer to my house for me. I checked with the racetrack and found that the first race of the year was the last Thursday of March. That wasn't going to give me much time to get the car ready.

My wife's grandson was, even at fifteen, a very good mechanic. At last I knew he was making his living as a mechanic. He kept telling me how much he wanted to drive the car. I kept telling him, he could drive the car if he helped me work on it. In all of the time I spent working on that car, I never once saw him even poke his head in the garage door to see what I was doing. The body had a lot of damage that I could easily fix myself. I am not a mechanic and need help with lots of little mechanical issues. The biggest issue was that the steering rack was cracked and leaking fluid; that would have to be changed. I ended up having to pay someone to do that. Other things such as changing fluids, giving the motor a tune up, and setting the fuel pump pressure were all things that I could do. Of course all of that work was going on while I was doing my regular day job, and keeping my business going.

Chapter Forty-Two
NASCAR Rookie at Fifty-Two

2006 was going to turn out to be a year that I will remember for the rest of my life. The main event happens in October, but we'll get to that. Late in January, our real estate friend called from Florida. The land we bought less than a year ago for five thousand dollars, was now selling for twenty thousand. She wanted to know if we would like to sell ours. Without even having to think about it, of course we would like to sell ours. And we did. She put the land up for sale, and it sold almost immediately. So for the land that we paid twenty thousand dollars for, we got eighty thousand in return. We would have to reinvest much of the money to avoid the capital gains tax on it.

We found a truck, and traded my Explorer Sport Track. And yes, I lost lots of money on that deal. The truck was a Ford 250 Super Duty. It was a couple of years old and very big. The truck, being big and blue, we named it the "B3", The Big Blue Behemoth. With about one week left before the first race, the car was ready. I had contacted NASCAR and registered the car as number 94, and applied for my driver's license. The car had to be brought to the track the day before the race, and left there overnight. Practice and time trials would be starting first thing in the morning. Now the thing that we all have to remember here is that while it is the last Thursday in March, it is still New England. Thursday morning arrived with sleet and freezing rain. We all had to go to the track anyway, in the event that the rain stopped and they could get the track dry, which is just what happened.

Diana did not come to the track with us. She was home with some very bad back issues. Her daughter, grandson, and Kevin came with me. The first time I took the car out on the track for practice, I couldn't get it to go around a corner. All of the cars entered the track just past turn two, and as I came out of turn four for the first time, the car spun around and backed into the outside concrete wall. Great, rear end damage and I haven't even made it around the track once yet. I brought the car back to my pit, and the guy that I bought the car from was there. He looked the car over, and then he helped me set the car up for the weather and track conditions for that day. Apparently both of those things make a big difference on how the car handles. He showed me how to make all of the adjustments needed, and talked about the different setups for different conditions. I took the car back out on the track, and found it handling much better. After all of the practice runs were done, and the time trials complete, I was going to start my first professional race in eighteenth position. There were thirty-four out of forty-three cars running in that race. That race by the way was called "The Ice Breaker", very appropriate I thought.

Mini-stocks are one of the more interesting race series to watch. Since the cars are reasonably cheap to buy, and there isn't really a lot of prize money involved in the races, some of the driver's aren't too concerned with the body panels of their own cars, never mind other peoples' cars. You learn pretty quickly which drivers to avoid. As the cars lined up to start the race, I was actually pretty calm. With Diana home, her daughter was giving her a play by play report over the cell phone. The race started between turn three and four on that track. Being back in the middle of the pack of cars, I was still in turn three as the leaders were starting the race. The first thing that happened was that the car behind me gave my car a very hard hit on the rear bumper. When I looked up in the mirror to see who was back there, the driver gave me a little wave, as if to say, "Welcome to the races!" Being a fifty-two-year-old rooky driver seemed to be of great interest to some of the other drivers. As the race went on, there were a couple of caution flags for cars that got together on the track, or cars that hit the outside wall and had to be towed from the track. During the race I passed a few cars, or cars passed me, and I ended up finishing twenty-first. I was hoping for a better finish, but it was ok for my first race, and it would turn out to be the worst finish of all of my races.

The next race wasn't going to be until the end of May. Diana got some help for her back, and she was feeling much better. We took advantage of the gap in races and went to Florida to reinvest some of that money we made from the sale of the land. We bought three more lots. I wasn't sure that we should do that. I felt the prices had peeked. Anyway, we did and we paid twenty thousand for one lot, and eighteen for each of two other lots. While we were there, our fitness center manager told us that there had been some interest in buying the business. We talked it over and we felt that if we could get enough for it we would sell it. Diana contacted the woman that was interested and made arrangements to meet with her. The woman had never owned a business, and it was quite obvious that she had no idea how to run a business. We gave her the price, and she said she would have to think about it. My business was still very busy, so we had to get back home. Before we left, we told our manager that the woman might be in to see how things were setup, and how they worked.

Within about a week or so of our getting back home, our club manager called and said that the woman had been coming in almost every day. She would pick a piece of exercise equipment, and sit on it as if it were a park bench. She would stay there for long periods of time, disrupting the ladies' workout routines. When the manager tried to explain that she couldn't do that, she would tell her that she was going to be the new owner of the club, and she could do whatever she wanted. The result of her attitude and actions were quite clear. She did buy the club, but by the time she did, membership had dropped by almost one hundred members. Diana again tried to tell her not to go in there with that kind of attitude. She told her that the women that go there need to be able to think of it as their own personal space. She would not listen. She kept our manager on as her manager, but her personality and attitude drove away most of the members. She ended up closing the club less than one year after buying it.

Diana's daughter was graduating from college in the middle of May. Still not sure what a four-year degree in what a vagina looks like, and men halfway transitioning into women is good for, we went to Vermont for the graduation. After her graduation, the agreement that we had made with her and her boyfriend about the house came up. Her daughter said that she didn't think she was done going to school. She thought now that she wanted to go back and study to become a Chiropractic MD. She was going to have to take a couple of courses at a local college for a year before she would be able to get into the school she wanted to go to. So much for that four or maybe five-year agreement we had. The end of May came around, and it was race time again. I was scheduled to run in nineteen races that year, and my goal for the year was to finish as one of the top fifteen drivers out of the forty-three drivers racing.

Driving the race car was a lot of fun. I loved being on the track with all the other cars, just inches away at over one hundred miles an hour. I was doing pretty well out there. I had top fifteen finishes in the next four races. The next race was not so good. Early in the race, coming down the front stretch at over one hundred miles an hour, I tapped the brakes to set the car up to go into turn one. As I did that, I felt a funny little vibration that I knew was not going to be a good thing. Continuing through turns one and two, I went down the back stretch, and again tapped the brakes to start going into turn three. The second I hit the brakes, I heard a very loud bang, and saw the entire right front wheel assembly flying off the car. The right front corner of the car dropped to the track. When the wheel assembly left the car, it took with it the brake line, (no more brakes), the tie rod end, (no more steering), and broke the axel half on that side, ripping it right out of the transmission, (no more transmission seal). All I could do was sit in the car and watch myself plow into the outside concrete wall at somewhere between ninety and one hundred miles an hour. The right front corner of the car hit the wall very hard, and it spun the car around so violently that it actually bent the rear axle. The car shot across the track and down into the infield. After traveling some thirty or forty yards, it finally came to a stop. The signal to the safety crew and official's, is for the driver to put the window net in the driver's window down. If you can do that, then they figure you're okay. As I sat there not moving, and apparently not responding to the officials, they were concerned that I may have been badly hurt. While I wasn't hurt, I was very dazed and confused, and I don't think I even knew at the time what had happened.

Because of the safety equipment required in those cars, I wasn't even bruised anywhere. Well--my brain may have had a bruise or two, but there were no bruises on my body. And because of the type of frame used on those cars, the damage to the body was minimal, and I had that fixed in a day. The mechanical damage was a different story. Even though we had an almost sixteen-year-old grandson living at the house, who was an excellent mechanic, it would take three weeks and several hundred dollars, paid to other people, to get the car ready for the track again. While we were trying to get the car fixed, my mother's birthday came up. We couldn't go to Florida, and they couldn't come up to us. My mother had always wanted to swim with the dolphins, so Diana got two tickets sent to them for her birthday. They were for the Discovery Cove-Sea World Park in Orlando, Florida. The tickets could be used whenever she wanted to go. She was thrilled. We also had been talking about going back to Bermuda. We were going to take the same cruise we had taken in 2001. My mother said she wanted to come with us when we went. Diana got on the computer, and made arrangements for the four of us to go the second week of September.

With the car ready for the track, the next couple of races went very well. I had my first top ten finish, 6th, and then eleventh. The next race I was starting in the first position. I was very nervous about it. The car starting in the first position is the car responsible for starting the race. And if that's not enough pressure, if you get to turn one, time to shift gears, and you miss your shift, there's going to be a lot of cars piled up on the track behind you, and you will not have made any friends with the other drivers. While the cars were in the pits waiting for our race to come up, the car next to mine was being worked on. They had changed the fuel pump, and were going to check the fuel pressure at the carburetor. The fuel pump is mounted on the frame, beside the fuel cell on those cars. Unfortunately, the fitting at the pump had not been tightened before the car was started. As soon as the car started, 105 octane race fuel began to pump onto the ground under the car. I saw the fuel and began running over to tell them to shut the car off, but just about the time I got to the car, it backfired. The fuel on the ground caught on fire, and within seconds the entire back of the car was on fire. I reached into my car for the fire extinguisher and as I did, my car started to move. The team on the other side of my car was pushing it out of the pit, yelling at me to move it before it blew up. I thought that sounded like a very good idea. The bad part about the idea was that there was no steering wheel on my car, and I was at the side of the car pushing along with the others. Without the steering wheel, I had no control over where the car went. The front wheels turned and the driver's side front wheel caught my left foot, and ran up and over my ankle, and came back down on my foot. I went down and the car rolled over my leg, and came to a stop in the middle of the pit road. Two other pit crew members came with fire extinguishers and put out the fire.

All of that was going on as there was a race being run on the track. The ambulance was called to the pit area, so the race that was being run had to be stopped. Apparently one of the drivers from another car in the pits had been sprayed with powder from a fire extinguisher and was having trouble breathing. He was in the ambulance, while the EMT was working on my foot. While I didn't have any broken bones, the end of my big toe had split open and my toe innards were oozing out. They wanted me to go to the hospital, but if I did that, I wouldn't get any points for the race. I wanted my points. After making sure that both of us were going to survive, the ambulance went back to the track, and the race continued. With my left foot hurting very much now, and swelling to the point that I was unable to put my racing shoe back on, I put a sneaker on, but couldn't lace it up. Needing my left foot for the clutch and brakes, I was now more concerned than ever about starting in first place. I told the drivers of the cars in the next few rows behind me that I was going to stay down at the bottom of the track, and when we passed the flagman, for them to just go around me on the outside. It was very difficult for me to push in the clutch pedal. The race went fine; I finished nineteenth, not great, but still better than my first race.

Chapter Forty-Three
Mom Swims with the Dolphins

Friday morning after the race, we had to drive to Richmond, VA, a twelve-hour drive for us. My foot was very painful, and large, but I was scheduled to race at Richmond International speedway on Saturday. Richmond Speedway was the largest track I ever raced on. It is a 3/4 mile D-shaped oval, and lots of fun to drive on. The race on Saturday was a kind of novelty race, but I didn't want to miss it. I was going to be racing against the best racers in the graduating class of a racing school. The cars we would be driving were retired "NEXTEL" series cars. I was told that when the cars get retired, sometimes the drivers would buy them, and then rent them to driving schools. Getting a chance to race one of those cars would be a very big deal. Diana had a friend that lived about two miles from the track, and she said we could stay with her. We made the drive, and by the time we got there Friday evening, my foot was killing me. I took some pain pills and went to bed. Saturday morning I felt a little better. Diana and I went to the track, and to my surprise there were more people there than I had expected. I was directed to the driver's room, and found that I would be racing against eight other drivers. After getting instructions from the officials, we all went to the pits to be assigned a car. Again, to my surprise, I was given a car owned by Bill Elliot. Anybody that has ever been any kind of race fan will know who he is.

The race was to be a thirty-lap race. When they sent us out on the track to start the race, they had us start in a single file formation. They told us in the driver's room that they were going to do that for safety reasons. I, being the only professional driver, was told I would be starting in last place. As the race started, I was on the outside of two cars in turns three and four, about to pass both. The instructor came on the radio and told me to go back to the end of the line, and stay there until he told me I could pass other cars. I was under the impression this was a race. After going to the back of the line and riding around for, I don't know five or six laps, I was told that I could start to pass other cars. So--I started to pass cars. I'm not sure if the other drivers were sleeping, afraid of speed, or their cars just sucked, but at the end of the thirty-lap race, I finished first, and the second place car was two laps behind me.

At the end of the race, all of the cars went into the pits. The instructor told me to stay in my car, and keep it running. With all of the other cars off the track, he sent me back out, telling me to show him what I could really do out there. With no other cars to get in the way, I was able to just let the car do what those cars do, go very fast and stick to the track. They had a speed gun set up at the end of the front stretch going into turn one. He told me that I was consistently hitting between 139-141 miles per hour on the front stretch. He said that speed like that would put me in the top five, if I were driving in a "NEXTEL" race. My lap times were also consistent with "NEXTEL" lap times. He later told me I should have started racing years ago, and that he thought I could have made it to the top racing series. Oh the things that could have been!

After my Richmond race, I went back to my little mini-stock car. I had a couple more races to run in August. Being the driver, body man, mechanic, set-up guy, tire man, and truck driver, and oh yes, building designer, was getting to be a bit much. It sure would have been good to have some help with the race car. By the beginning of September, I had run twelve of the nineteen races, and was in fifteenth place, out of forty-three drivers. There was a very large gap between me and the next driver back. Our cruise to Bermuda was coming up, and my mother and Ed were flying up a week early, to do some visiting before the trip. They flew into Providence. Diana and I picked them up, and brought them to our house. They had made arrangements to stay with some friends for the week, so I gave them the Cadillac to drive, so they didn't have to rent a car. We still had Diana's car and my truck. My mother was telling all their friends that it was my car, and we ordered it new, and it cost about forty-five thousand dollars. She was also telling them that we owned a race car, although she refused to go to the track when I was supposed to race the week they were there. Since she wouldn't go, I didn't bother to race that week. As it turned out I didn't race again for the rest of the year. Having only run in twelve of the nineteen races, I still finished the year in fifteenth place.

We took the cruise to Bermuda and we all seemed to have a good time. There was something off about my mother, though. She didn't seem to be herself. One night at dinner, she reached across the table, and took my hand. I looked up at her and she had very wet eyes, not really crying but very close to it. In her hand she had a crumpled up napkin that she handed to me. She said, "I know this was supposed to go to Kevin, but I want you to have it." I took the napkin and opened it to find a ring that my father had worn for as long as I could remember. It was a square black onyx ring, with a diamond set in the middle of it. It is a beautiful ring, although I have never worn it. I don't know if Kevin ever asked my mother about the ring, but he never asked me about it. I do know that he knew he was supposed to get the ring after my father died. My mother seemed to look and be tired on the trip. I thought maybe it was just that they had overdone the visiting the week before Ed was also a little tired, so I was sure that was it. They seemed to have a good time anyway.

After the cruise, Ed and my mother stayed two more days, and then we took them back to the airport for the flight to Tampa. Early in October my mother called and said they were going to Orlando to swim with the dolphins, she was very excited about it. I told her to make sure to get lots of pictures and to have a great time. Late in the evening of October twelfth, Ed called me. He sounded very sad and upset. I asked what was wrong, and he said that my mother was in the hospital in Orlando, and that it didn't look good. When I asked what happened he told me I should talk to the doctor at the hospital, and that he was waiting for me to call him. Ed gave me the number to call and we hung up the phones. I knew if a doctor at a hospital was waiting for someone to call him, that can't be a good thing. When I called, I was put right through to the doctor. He told me that when my mother was swimming out with the dolphin trainer to meet their dolphin, she suffered a pulmonary embolism. Her lungs filled with blood, and she couldn't breathe. The medical crew at the park had been called, along with an ambulance. He said that in the very short time it took to get my mother back to shore, she was already blowing bloody foam, and was unresponsive. She was now in the hospital in a coma, being kept alive by machines. He said that he didn't think she could survive on her own. Ed had faxed the hospital a copy of a power of attorney form in which she gave me power to make her decisions for her. I think I was in shock and didn't know what to do.

Chapter Forty-Four
Mom Passes Away

That night was one of the very rare occasions when Diana was out with some of her friends. She got home sometime close to midnight to find me still on the phone with the doctor. I had decided to have him prepare a DNR form and I was telling him to fax it to my office fax number. While I was waiting for the form, I filled Diana in on what had happened. She was as shocked and sad as I was. We both knew my mother was going to die very soon. She got on the computer to book us on the first flight out of Providence in the morning. I called Kevin and David to give them the news. Kevin said that he wanted to go with us in the morning, so Diana added him to the flight. David was not going to be able to get away that quickly. The DNR form came through, and after sitting and staring at it, knowing what it meant to sign it and send it back, I did finally sign it. I was still having some trouble sending the form back, knowing I may never see my mother again. After some very difficult moments for both Diana and me, I did send the form back.

We arrived in Tampa around 8:30 a.m. Diana number two was there to pick us up. She was going to take us to the hospital in Orlando. When we got off the tram in the terminal, I called the hospital to check on my mother. I was told that she had passed away at about 8:00 a.m. She had waited as long as she could for us. I felt very bad that she was alone. Ed was at the house; we were in an airplane, and David was in DC. It was Friday, October 13, 2006. Diana number two took us to the house, where I called to make the arrangements to have my mother's body prepared to be sent back to MA where she had pre-arranged her funeral. We stayed at the house for a couple of days, so I could get a few more things done. While I was trying to get started with settling my mother's things, Ed wanted to talk to me. He told me that he had come to think of me as the son he never had, and that he wanted Diana and me to have the house. I told him that I was glad that he and my mother had gotten together; she seemed to be happy. As for the house, he could stay in it as long as he wanted, and if he would like, Diana and I would move there to be with him. He said he would like that.

When we went back home to get the wake and funeral scheduled, Ed came back with some friends, and stayed with them. I called my mother's family to give them the news. Her sister living somewhere out west came to the funeral, with most of her family. She was very sick and in a wheelchair, but she insisted on being there. My mother had a half-sister living in the UK at the time; she came to the funeral. The only member of my mother's family not to show up was that lawyer brother of hers that told her I would never make anything of myself in life. Apparently he had supersaver tickets to Florida, and couldn't change the flight date, and the money was nonrefundable. Ed had given me a couple of pictures that were taken at the park in Florida. They were of my mother kissing a dolphin. He said she was kissing the dolphin that she was going to swim out to meet, just before she started out with the trainer. She looked incredibly happy in those pictures. It was hard to imagine that they were taken less than five minutes before she stopped breathing.

The wake and funeral went fine. David was at both this time. There were lots of friends that came to the wake, not just my mother's, but mine, Diana's and Kevin's. It rained on the day of the funeral when we were at the cemetery. I thought that was a very good thing for my mother. She always told me that if it rained at a funeral, "Happy is the soul that it rains upon." It made me happy for her. Ed went back to Florida right after the funeral. I got back to work, and Diana started to talk to some real estate people about our house. Diana's daughter and her boyfriend were not in any position to buy it. She was taking a couple of courses at a local college, still planning to go to chiropractic school. Her boyfriend had just started a new business with his brother; it seemed to be going pretty good. I still wasn't one hundred percent sure that I was ready to move to Florida. I knew I could run my business from there, but I still had the feeling that it would remove me from the contact too much.

I had decided to sell the race car. The guy that owned the store where we first saw the car said I could bring it back and put it in his yard again. I did that before all that mess with my mother came up. While we were in Florida in October, the store guy called to say that he had an offer on the car. Someone wanted to buy the car and trailer, and was going to pay fifteen hundred dollars more than I paid for it. I thought that was pretty good. Buy the car, beat it up on the racetrack for one season, and then sell it for more than I paid for it. I told him to sell the car, and keep five hundred dollars for making the deal. We had our normal Thanksgiving and Christmas dinners and open house. It was just a bit sad for me though. In late February 2007 we had to go back to Florida to finish clearing my mother's estate. We would be there for about five weeks, and would stay with Ed during that time.

When we arrived at the house in Florida, I noticed a couple of builders' pamphlets on the table. I asked Ed about them, and he said that he was selling the house and having a new one built. Confused, I asked what happened to change his mind about us living there with him, and then us getting the house. He said, "Your mother really fucked up. If she outlived me she would have gotten the house and about a half million dollars. But since she's dead nobody gets anything." Before I had a chance to respond to that he added, "And I want all of her shit out of the house as soon as possible." So now, not only do I have my mother's estate to deal with, we have this grumpy, pissy, old man that we have to live with for five weeks: AND we have to get all of my mother's stuff out of the house.

My mother had a lot of stuff. We collected as much as we could, and had a couple of yard sales. We sold some of the stuff, not near as much as we had hoped. After being there about a month, and still having too much of her stuff left, we called one of the thrift stores in the area, and donated most of it to them. There were still some things we were keeping to give to David and Kevin. There were certain items that we had talked about. Ed was being a real asshole about everything. He said that we were there just for the money. We told him that all of the money we made from the sale of my mother's stuff was given to the breast cancer foundation. He then accused us of stealing some bonds that he had, and his first wife's wedding ring. We told him we didn't touch anything that belonged to him, and that we didn't want his money. He did find his bonds while we were still there. I don't know if he ever found the ring.

There were still a few things that we were keeping, and they would have to be shipped back to our house, along with Kevin's stuff. We had flown down to Florida, so we would have to ship David's stuff to him, also. Two days before we were going to leave, Ed asked me if I wanted my mother's car. It was registered and insured in Ed's name, but it was her car. The car was a Sebring convertible, and Diana liked it very much. It also made sense to drive it back, and bring David's stuff with us instead of shipping it. Ed said that as soon as we get back home I would have to send the license plate back to him so he could cancel the registration and insurance. I told him I would do that and we packed the car and headed home. We would be stopping at David's house on the way. We also made a few stops at places we wanted to visit. We stopped at a few wineries and picked up some wine for us and some for David. We also stopped and spent a day in Savannah Georgia, and then went to David's house. From his house me made the eight-hour drive back to our house on the third day after leaving Ed's house. When we got home, I called him to tell him I was going to send the license plate back. He said don't bother; he had already canceled it. He said that he went down and canceled everything right after we left his house. So that fucking bastard had us drive thirteen hundred miles across the country in an unregistered and uninsured car that was in his name. If we had gotten stopped, he could have said that we stole the car. I told him what a fucking asshole he turned out to be, and that I never wanted to hear from him again. He died a couple of years later. I hope he had to deal with my mother about the way he treated us.

Chapter Forty-Five
White Water Rafting, 2007

At the beginning of September, living in an old house in New England, as was typical with those houses, we began to have a mouse problem. We decided we needed a cat. We went to a local shelter, and after looking at all of the cats they had, we asked which one had been there the longest. We were shown the cat and decided to take her home. She seemed to settle in pretty good. The day after we got the cat home, Diana, her daughter's boyfriend, and I had reservations to go white water rafting in the mountains of Western MA up near the VT border. The rapids we were supposed to ride were class three. Since none of us had done that before, we thought that would be a good start. When we got to the lodge to check in, they said they could bump us up to class four at no extra charge. We all decided to go along with it; after all how much difference could there be. From the lodge, they took everybody in vans to the starting point on the river. It was a nice calm area where they get everyone into the rafts and give them some instructions on what to do, and what not to do. There were several rafts all leaving from the same spot that day. Our raft had the three of us, plus a mid-twenty something year old couple, and the raft guide.

As we started down the river, we were doing a good job of putting the raft where the guide told us it should be and everybody seemed to be working well together. As we passed through a section of class two rapids, and into a class three, I couldn't help notice a very large change in the size and violence of the waves. They were also moving much faster now. I began to wonder about that decision we all made back at the lodge. Approaching the end of the class three, we could all see the start of the class four rapids. The waves were much larger, and much more violent than the class three. The guide had us pull the raft to the side of the riverbank. From there he pointed out two very large rocks sticking up out of the water at the beginning of the rapids. He told us that we were going to have to get the raft to go between the two rocks if we were going to get into the class four rapids. He gave us a few pointers on how to approach the area, and then off we went. We were doing fine. We had the raft lined up just the way he told us. As we made our way toward the gateway between the two large rocks, the bottom of the raft got caught on something under the water. The raft spun to the right, causing the raft to slam into one of the rocks. On the left side of the raft were the twenty something wife, Diana, and the boyfriend. On the right side were the twenty something husband, and me. The raft guide was in the back, trying to help steer the raft. As it slammed into the rock, the young wife was launched out of the raft, and she slammed into the rock, and then bounced back into the raft. At the same time I saw Diana get launched out of the raft, and go just past the rock, and into the river.

I was trying to keep my eyes on her as she began going down the river. But it was hard to follow her as she was getting slammed into rocks, and pulled under by some of the large waves. She looked like she was in trouble. When a raft gets stuck on a rock like that, the raft will start to climb up the rock. When that starts to happen, everybody in the raft is supposed to get to the high side of the raft to try to push it back down flat on the water. While the guide was yelling, "Everybody get to the high side," I got up and went to the high side, and just kept on going, right into the river. I could see Diana getting slammed around and pulled under the water, and didn't think we were going to get the raft off the rock and down the river in time to save her. So I did what I think any husband that loves his wife would do. I jumped in to try to swim to her to help her. However---keep in mind we were in a class four rapid. When I hit the water, I was immediately sucked to the bottom of the river. The force of the water coming over the rocks and down to the bottom of the river was unexpected and unbelievable. I was being pressed against the bottom by the force of the water, and I could not move. As I was very close to running out of air, I started to sort of crab crawl down the river. After just a few feet, the water that was holding me down, now grabbed me and pushed me up to the surface at the top of a very big wave.

I tried to body surf my way down the river. I found out very quickly that in class four rapids, that does not work. The waves are much too violent, and they come at you from many different directions at the same time. Giving up the idea of surfing, I tried to swim. I am a very good swimmer, but even that doesn't work very well in those rapids. I was getting slammed around and pulled under and pushed back up, but somehow after about maybe three-eighths of a mile, I was able to catch up with Diana. She was facing away from me, and not moving her head or arms. When I got to her, I caught her from behind, and called to her as I grabbed one of the shoulder straps of her life jacket. She didn't answer me, and as I grabbed the shoulder strap, I realized that she felt like a wet rag doll. She was completely unresponsive. I spun her around to try to talk to her, and she was blue. Her face was blue, her lips were blue, and I could see her hand floating in the water and her nails were blue. I looked for a place to get her out of the water, but the area was lined with high rock cliffs. I turned and looked back up the river and saw that the raft was finally off the rock, and was about halfway to us. I started to try to swim up the river to meet the raft. That doesn't work in a class four rapid either. When the raft got to us, I grabbed the side of the raft by the front, and spun Diana around and slammed her into the side near the back of the raft. The boyfriend and the guide pulled her into the raft, and I was helped in by the other young guy. I began trying to clear the water out of my lungs and I looked at Diana. She was just lying on the bottom of the raft, not moving.

Suddenly Diana began to spit up small amounts of water. The guide and boyfriend helped her to lean over the edge of the raft and she put much of the river back to where it came from. A little ways down the river the raft was brought to shore. We sat for a while and Diana's face slowly started to turn back to the right color. It took much longer for her lips and nails to get color back. At some point she looked at me and said that my lips were blue, and my leg was red. I looked at my left leg, and saw that there was a lot of blood running down it. I must have scraped it on some of the rocks as I was going down the river. I never realized it. All of the rafts were loaded onto trailers, and several vans were waiting to take us back to the lodge for a dinner that was part of the package. Diana and I were put into a van by ourselves, with the raft guide and driver. On the way back to the lodge, I was given a calm but stern ass chewing about jumping into the river, and I was told what a stupid thing that was to do. I had to agree with him, but I also explained my reason for doing it. He was twenty years old, not married, and no girlfriend. He didn't get the concept of what I was trying to tell him about husbands and wives.

Diana, the boyfriend, and I sat sort of off by ourselves while we ate our dinners. People kept coming up to us and asking if Diana was ok, and telling me what a brave thing that was I did to save her. Diana said that I was her hero, and some people agreed with her that I was a hero for doing what I did. Apparently there were a lot of people that had already finished their ride, standing along the banks and cliffs of the river watching all of the action. When it was time to go home, I gave the car keys to the boyfriend and asked him if he would mind driving us home. I still had the Cadillac CTS at the time, so he was happy to do the driving. When we got in the car, Diana and I got in the back seat. Before he started the car, the boyfriend turned to Diana and asked her to please not tell her daughter that he didn't jump in to try to save her. He said she would kill him if she found out. Now, the boyfriend was about six feet one or two inches tall, and weighed a little over two hundred pounds. Diana's daughter was about five feet three inches tall, and weighed about one hundred and ten pounds. But he was definitely afraid of her. We have never been white water rafting again. And the cat--well we still have her, and she has never been much of a mouser.

Chapter Forty-Six
Well, It's Later in Life

As long as we're speaking about cats, well sort of, we ended up with two. About a month after we got the first one, a black and white stray started to hang around. One day Diana and her daughter were sitting on the steps by the driveway entry to the office, and the cat was running across the field, so Diana started to yell, "Run Forest, Run". She took the cat in and called him Forest. I don't know how old he was, but he obviously was having a tough life out there on his own. He was missing most of the teeth on one side of his mouth. The only cat food we kept in the house was dry food. At first this was a bit of a problem for him, but he soon began to take a few bits of the dry food, with his paw and put it in the water. After sitting there looking at it for a couple of minutes, he would then pick it up with his paw and eat it. After doing that for a while, he began to get a yellow-brown stain on that paw. We told people that was a nicotine stain; he was trying to quit, but it's not easy. He also loved anything with cheese. He would crawl into a bag of cheese puffs to get one if you let him. He would also try to climb up your pant leg if you were eating cheese and crackers.

Work was very busy that year. I raced only a couple of times, always driving someone else's car. My best finish all year was second place. Diana was getting restless; she needed something to do. She had been a pet groomer many, many, years ago, and saw an ad for a groomer in a shop not too far away. She went to talk to the owner, and got a job washing and taking care of the pets, but not grooming them. She was good with that; it gave her time to be with the pets. Washing and preparing large dogs for grooming is a very hard job, and some days she would come home very tired. The shop was a very busy one, some days grooming between twenty-five and thirty pets. In the fall I was working on plans to build a hybrid, gas/electric race car. I would build the car from scratch, with a NASCAR approved tubular steel frame. I talked to Diana's daughter's boyfriend, and he said I could build it in the shop he and his brother owned. They had the tubing bender and welding equipment that I was going to need.

I was waiting for work to drop off a bit to start working on the car. Work just kept on coming. I had ordered most of the parts I would need to build the car, and had them delivered to the shop where the car was being built. The biggest problem I was going to have, was that the shop was more than an hour's drive from me. That was going to use up a large chunk of time just driving. In the late fall, as I was trying to figure out the logistics of balancing work with building the car, I got a call from a local builder. It was a builder that I didn't know, but he seemed to know me. He said he had done a lot of work off plans that I had prepared. He asked me if I would be interested in bidding on a commercial project in the town where I grew up. After giving me a little information on the project, I told him I would bid on it. A meeting was set up with the building committee for the project, and I went to meet with them.

The meeting was being held in an office building in the center of town. When I walked into the conference room, I saw a large table with about fourteen chairs around it. I wondered if all of the chairs would be filled just for that meeting. I took a seat, and a couple of minutes later a man sat next to me and introduced himself as the builder that I had talked to. As I was talking to him, I noticed that the room was filling up. Even chairs off to the sides of the room were being filled. Still talking to the builder, and waiting for the meeting to start, a woman sat down directly across the table from me. I didn't notice her at first, but then I heard her say, "Hello Shawn, how are you? It's been a long time." I looked at her. She was an attractive woman, maybe eight or ten years older than me. She looked somewhat familiar to me, but I couldn't place her right away. Then it hit me! Now if you think back to the early part of the book, to those wild sex parties that Sarah and I watched, I said that there was a girl that I knew there and would meet later in life. Well-- it's later in life, and there she was sitting directly across from me. The last time I saw her, she was completely naked, and doing lots of things with boys and other girls.

When I recognized her, I said hello, and called her by name. I didn't know if she had seen Sarah and me watching, or, if she was even thinking about that, but the color that her face was turning told me that she may have. After a very awkward few moments, I asked how she had been and said that it had indeed been a very long time. We talked a little about her younger brother. I played baseball with him and we had been friends for several years. Seeing her naked and the sex parties did not come up in the conversation. As we were talking to each other, I began to wonder if she knew what had happened to Sarah or to me after the parties. I wasn't going to ask, so I guess I will never know. The meeting went very well, and I got the job. The job was adding about three thousand square feet to a municipal building in the center of town, and making the building handicapped accessible. I was very familiar with the building, and I knew that it was on the National Register of Historic Buildings. I was going to have to deal with those people through the entire process of the project.

Work began to slow just a bit, so the week between Christmas and New Year's 2008, I started to build the car. I had drawn out how I wanted to put the frame together, so that part went pretty fast. I hadn't done any welding since I was in my late teens or early twenties, so it took a little practice to get those skills back. The idea of the car was that a very small gas motor would power an electric car motor through a computerized system. The computer would control the power going to the electric motor, and would be controlled by the driver with an electric rheostat type pedal on the floor where the gas pedal would be. The computer would also control forward and reverse modes for the car. Once I had the frame, suspension, steering and motors all completed, the wheels were put on and the car was brought to my house. In my garage I built and mounted the body, and had an electrician friend help wire the car. The computer was mounted and connected to the motors and foot pedal and the car was finished. After driving it around the yard a bit, just to test everything, we were going to bring the car to a shop to have it "dyno" tested the next day.

"Dyno" testing the car would tell us lots of things. Most importantly, how fast it would go, and how long it would take to get up to its top speed. It would also tell us how much horsepower the motor was actually able to develop. When Diana and I got to the dyno shop, we rolled the car off the trailer and started it up. There was a fifty-amp breaker that separated the gas motor from the electrical system. I did that so the gas motor could be run to warm up without powering the computer. With me in the car, Diana engaged the breaker---and a power surge or some other wonderful thing fried the hard drive in the computer. With the hard drive fried, the computer wasn't working, which meant the car was not going to work. After trying all sorts of things to try to get around the problem, we put the car back on the trailer and went home.

It was now around the middle of August, and I had not been feeling very well for several months. I went to the doctor in the spring and he gave me some medication. At the beginning of August he doubled the dose. Diana and her daughter were busy getting things ready for the daughter to return to school once again. This time she would be going to a Chiropractic school in the upper Mid-West. She was leaving in early September. With the race car in my garage, I knew that the computer was going to be a weak link in the system. I was going to have to come up with another drive system without a computer. Not feeling very well, I began to rework the drive system in the car. With the motors both out of the car, and working on some other drive system, I was really beginning to feel bad. By the end of September, I knew I was in trouble. I made an appointment to see a specialist. After a quick exam, he said he was pretty sure what the problem was, but I was going to have to come back to his office for another visit. On the second visit, eight biopsies were taken.

All of that was happening as we were in the process of buying the grooming shop Diana had been working at for the past year. The owner told her that she wanted to sell the business and go back to working with horses. She apparently worked on a horse farm prior to owning the grooming shop. We took a look at the books from the shop and they looked pretty good. (We would later find that she kept two sets of books). I thought the price was too high, but Diana wanted the shop, and the owner wasn't budging on the price. So, on October thirty-first, 2008 I had eight biopsies taken. On November first, we bought the grooming business. On November fourth, I was told that I had prostate cancer, and that it was a very aggressive cancer. The doctor said that because it was so aggressive, treating it was not going to be an option for me. I was going to have to have the prostate removed, and as soon as possible. The doctor already lined up had a surgeon for me.

The week that we bought the shop, we found that the two top groomers were stealing client information, and were going to leave to start their own shop. By the reaction of the previous owner I think she knew they were doing that. I promptly relieved the two groomers and had them leave the building. The weekend after that, we had a break-in. Money was taken, and almost all of the client files were copied. The only thing that stopped them from copying all of the files, was that they jammed the copy machine. We found that entry was gained through a window at the rear of one side of the building that had been left unlocked. The police were called. Since the floors got washed at the end of every day, we were able to show them a very clear boot print. A print that one of the other employees recognized as boots worn by one of the fired groomers. I also pointed out a very clear fingerprint at the top of the window used for entry. It was in a spot that a fingerprint was unlikely to be found. The lead detective, a Marty McFly look-a-like did a masterful job of smearing the print to a point of unusable quality. The two groomers were brought in and questioned, but there wasn't enough hard evidence to charge them.

Chapter Forty-Seven
Merry Christmas to Me

When we bought the shop, the original owner agreed to stay on as a groomer for a couple of months. We also now had to hire two new groomers to fill the spots left open. Finding good groomers is not as easy as one might think. To help, I spent some time there washing and prepping the pets for grooming, while Diana did some of the grooming. I brought my laptop and was still able to get some of my own work done while I was working there. In the first week of December, Diana and I met with the surgeon that was going to operate on me. He said that he was going to do the procedure robotically. I would only have five small scars that would look like bullet holes. The operation he said should take about four hours, and the recovery time should be about four to five weeks. He gave me a choice of two dates to pick from for the operation, the day before Christmas, or the day after Christmas. (Merry Christmas to me). I chose the day after so I didn't mess up the open house and Christmas day.

In the very early morning hours, on the day after Christmas, Diana brought me to the hospital for the operation. Diana's daughter had come home from school for Christmas, so she and her boyfriend were also there. When the time came to bring me into the operating room, I was put on the table, with nothing but a Johnny on, and brought into the room. There were five or six surgical nurses all milling about doing one thing or another, and the anesthesiologist. I hadn't been given any drugs yet, just the iv's, but nothing good in them yet. The doctor came in to talk to me for a couple of minutes. He told me he wasn't going to be in the room with me, he would be in the next room playing video games. Funny guy, my prostate was the apparent top level of his video game. After he left the room, one of the nurses came up to the bottom of the table, pulled out some stirrups, raised them in the air, and then gabbed each of my feet and put them in the stirrups. This of course left all of my stuff just hanging out there for everyone in the room to see. While still standing at the end of the table, between my legs, she said, "Didn't you know you were going to be in stirrups today?" Starting to feel just a bit stressed now I just said, "Well, I guess I do now." Seconds later the room began to fade away, and I was much less stressed.

The operation apparently took a little longer than anticipated. When I woke, I was in a regular hospital room. Diana, her daughter and her daughter's boyfriend were there. I don't remember being in very much pain. The worst part was the ride home. Every time the car hit a bump, it felt like everything left inside me was trying to fall down to fill the void left by my prostate. It was not a pleasant feeling. I was sent home with what felt like a garden hose coming out of my penis, with a bag strapped to my leg, and a smaller hose coming out of my stomach, attached to a small plastic bottle. That was a drain to pick up fluids in the area of the operation, and would have to be emptied every day. The amount of fluid removed had to be measured and recorded each time it was emptied. With both of us being self-employed, we had to carry our own health insurance. We had been sold what we thought was reasonably good insurance. Unfortunately we found that it was one of those that had a triple deductible clause in the fine print. That meant that every time you got close to meeting your deductible, it would get doubled. There was no way to ever meet the deductible. In 2018, we finally finished paying for my cancer treatment. Right after having cancer, and finding out how bad the insurance was, we promptly changed to real insurance. It cost us about fifteen hundred dollars a month for the two of us, but it would soon turn out to be worth every penny.

Shortly before Christmas, Diana had hired a new groomer, she seemed to be a good groomer, but was very pregnant and would be needing time off in the very near future. Then the front desk girl left. Diana didn't replace her right away, the groomers would just keep an eye on the desk and fill in as needed. I was doing very well with my recovery. Diana's daughter had gone back to school, and things at the house, at least, seemed to be getting back to normal. Ten days after the surgery I went back to the surgeon and had all of the tubes removed. (I couldn't wait for that). With the tubes out, I felt much better. Within a couple of weeks, I was able to sit in a soft chair, and work on my computer. Things weren't going as well for Diana. The two groomers that took our client info, had opened a shop and began to take some of the clients. The person we bought the shop from was getting ready to leave, and the new groomer was about to have her baby.

When the original owner sold the shop to us, she told us she was going back to work with horses. Diana had been working with her for a year, and they seemed to have become good friends. She had no reason to doubt or question that. A couple of weeks after she left, she was running around town in a mobile grooming van. I can't even put into words how I felt about that. Diana was devastated. By the end of February, 2009, she had less than half the business she did when we bought the place. The new groomer left in early January to have her baby. Diana began to advertise, run specials, and do whatever she could to get customers in the door. Her efforts were starting to pay off, but it still wasn't enough. The groomer that was out having her baby came back in late February, with the kid. She said she had to have the kid with her. All that kid did all day long was scream, yell, and cry. It was causing stress to the animals, and the other workers. After about six weeks of that, Diana finally told her to find something else to do with the kid while she was at work. The groomer told her it wasn't going to be an issue. Her father had given her money to open her own grooming shop. She left in the middle of April.

The groomer with the screaming kid opened her shop right down the street from ours. (Well, maybe about 3/4 of a mile down the street.) She opened at the beginning of May. The building we were in was now costing us more than we could afford. We began to talk about moving the shop to another location. (The rest of this part comes from what Diana has been able to tell me. I do remember some parts, but my memory here has a few holes in it. Pay attention to the very first part of this, it will come around again.) Sometime in the middle of May, Diana and I were sitting in bed reading. It was between ten and eleven at night. I dropped my book, and picked it back up. Without looking at me, Diana asked if I was falling asleep. Apparently my answer was, "I don't understand." A few seconds later, I dropped my book again. Diana looked at me and didn't think I looked quite right. She asked me if I was okay and I said, "I don't understand." Then I started to fall over. She pushed me back up to a sitting position, and left the bedroom headed for my office and the closest phone. She called 911 and told the operator that she thought I was having a stroke. The house we lived in at the time, was less than three tenths of a mile from the police station. A police officer was at the door in about two minutes. When she let him in, she said I was in the bed. The officer looked in the bedroom but didn't see me. Diana looked in and told the officer that I must have fallen out of bed, and that he should look between the bed and the wall. He did, and found me on the floor, half under the bed. He grabbed my shoulders and pulled me out to the living room, where the EMT's would have more room to work on me. By that time my entire right side was paralyzed. When the EMT's arrived, they did some quick little tests and decided that I was having a stroke.

I was taken to a local hospital where a stroke alert team was waiting for me. They did a CAT scan to see if I was bleeding in the brain, and decided that I wasn't and the stroke was being caused by a clot. I was brought back to the same room, and there was a computer monitor set up at the foot of my bed. The head of the neurology department of a large hospital in Western MA was on the computer screen. He was talking to Diana, me, and the attending doctor. After a very short time, he agreed that I was having a stroke, and suggested that I be given TPA to stop the stroke. The upside of TPA is that it will stop the effects of a stroke being caused by a blood clot. The downside is that it can cause you to start bleeding uncontrollably. Diana said that she talked to me about it, and I told her that I would rather take the chance on that, than spend the rest of my life sitting, staring at nothing, and drooling. The TPA was given to me, and I guess it stopped the stroke from doing any more damage than it already had. I was then taken by ambulance to the hospital in Western MA that had been contacted by computer earlier. I was placed in the ICU and hooked up to several machines. One of the machines was to monitor my breathing. The stroke, they had decided, was in an area of the brain that would affect, among other things, my ability to remember to breath on my own. If I stopped breathing, or my respiration rate got too low, an alarm would go off. A nurse would have to come in and shake me, and yell at me and tell me to start breathing again. Diana decided she would sit beside my bed that entire first night, and she would shake and yell at me if needed. Apparently I needed it a lot.

After the first night, I started to get better. By the end of the first week, I had regained the use of my right arm, and some of my right hand. My right leg was still not working. After the first twenty-four hours of giving you TPA, they give you an MRI, to see how much, and exactly where the damage was done. What they expected to find was a large black area on the left side of my brain. What they found, was hundreds of small black dots, all over the left side of my brain. Some doctors began to say that whatever it was, it wasn't a stroke. The head of neurology was saying that it was definitely a stroke. He said that because I was treated so quickly after the onset of the symptoms, that it didn't have time to create the normal large dead area of the brain. He said that the small black dots were the result of the TPA breaking up the clot, and sending what he called "Blood dust" into my brain. The little bits of blood from the clot, shot around my brain until they got stuck in veins too small for them. Those hundreds of tiny blood clots would contribute to the damage of the stoke.

I was sent from the hospital to a rehab hospital that specialized in brain injuries, and stroke victims. I was going to need physical and occupational therapy every day. I was also going to need speech therapy twice every day. I was going to have to learn how to read, spell, count, tell time, and handle money all over again. All that, along with learning to walk and use my hands again. Diana had stayed with me the entire time I was in the hospital, but she would not be allowed to do that at the rehab hospital. She really needed to get back and pay attention to her grooming business anyway. I would be in the rehab hospital for about the next three weeks. When they sent me home, I continued all of the therapy every other day at my house for the next month. So, as I said, most of that is from what Diana was able to tell me. I do remember some things, mostly during my stay at the rehab hospital. I remember things like the first time I was going to get a shower. Two attractive twenty something year old young ladies came and got me from my room, and brought me down the hall to the shower room. You start to think, hmmm--this might be fun, but then when you get to the shower room, you realize that you're the only one that's going to get naked in there.

Some of the other fun things that I can remember are when the occupational therapist and her twenty-year-old intern brought me into the therapy room. They placed me standing on a very thick floor mat and gave me a hula-hoop. I was told to place it around my waist and try to spin it. The fact that I was standing on my own without a walker at the time was challenge enough for me. As I made a gallant effort at that first spin of the hoop, I fell over to the right side, taking a very surprised young intern to the floor with me. Another fun little thing with the occupational therapists was when they were supposed to be training me to approach, and stand at a toilet with a walker. I was going to be shown how to pee without getting it all over the walker or the toilet. What really happened was the intern had me walk up to the toilet with the walker, and then was going to have me pee. I thought that she was going to step back while I peed and then check to see how I did. She stood right there beside me, with one hand on my back as she leaned forward and actually watched the pee come out of me. I didn't get any on the walker or the toilet.

As the end of my stay at the rehab was approaching, Diana was supposed to be shown how to help me get into and out of the tub to take a shower. She made a special trip for that to take place. When she was there waiting with me for the therapist to come, a young man came instead. He said he was a Certified Nurse's Assistant, and that he was sent to give me a shower. We explained that Diana was there to be shown how to help me into and out of the tub by the therapist. He said she could come along to while I took a shower if she wanted. He took me to a room that just had walk in showers, no tubs. We again tried to explain the situation to him but he wasn't going to listen. He said he was just supposed to give me a shower. So, as I took my clothes off, the young man sat on the bench next to me and he and Diana watched, while I took a shower. When I asked him for some shampoo, he got up and took a gallon jug off a shelf, and poured about a quart of it on my head, which was dry at the time. Nobody ever did show Diana how to help me take a shower in the tub, but we figured it out.

Being at the rehab hospital wasn't all that bad. All of the therapists were very good at what they did. The food wasn't even that bad. I was told at some point, maybe two or three days before I was going to go home, that I was going to lose my driver's license, and have to take a test to get it back. I didn't like being told that. I asked if the test could be given before I left the rehab hospital. After some discussion with whoever makes those decisions, I was granted a test. The test was set for the day that I was to get out of the hospital. It consisted of two parts. For the first part, I was shown a series of cards with street signs on them. I had to say what each of them meant. The second part was testing your reaction time to changing traffic lights. What they didn't tell me at the beginning was that you only had a few seconds to identify the signs, and if you got just one wrong, you failed the test. I got them all right, and was allowed to keep my license. I wouldn't be capable of driving for several weeks after getting home, though. One other fun little thing that was to take place just before my being released was the skin-rash inspection. As Diana was sitting in a chair beside my bed, a young nurse came into the room with my discharge papers. She began to go over all the normal stuff they do at that time, and after Diana signed the papers the nurse said she had to check to see if I had any rash or lesions that I did not come in with. That all sounds simple enough, but what she did, was have me pull my pants down so she could inspect my ass, penis and balls, rather closely and thoroughly, I might add, as Diana sat there three feet away from us and watched her do that. By the beginning of August, as I was starting to get well enough to start doing some of my job again, Kevin would drive me to my appointments, until I was capable of driving myself. Diana told everybody not to tell her daughter about the stroke she was in the middle of taking tests and didn't want it to distract her. When her daughter did finally find out, she was furious.

Chapter Forty-Eight
Getting Whacked in the Head Again

While I was in the rehab hospital, Diana had found a new location for her grooming business. She wasn't sure it was going to be the right place for it, but the price was right, and it fit all of her needs. When I went to see it, I thought it was the perfect place for it. It was about one quarter mile down the road from the groomer with the screaming kid. I would have put it right across the street if we could. It's kind of like the drug store and fast food chains. I also found that Diana was beginning to rebuild the business, and had hired a new groomer. He was a young man whose family was from Uruguay. They had been living in this country for about ten years, but they wanted to go back to Uruguay. They did not like living in this country. When she hired him, he made it clear that when he had enough money saved up they would be leaving. When I met him, I instantly liked him. He was a very nice young man. He had a wife and two children, with several relatives also living in the area. When we decided to make the move to the new location, he helped me do the build-out to get the place ready for grooming. With Diana's personality, and business ability, and talent for grooming, she had gotten the business back to a more viable and sustainable one.

Diana's daughter came back home for the summer. She would be there through June and most of August, and then go back to school. She had lived in a dorm on the school campus the first year, and decided that was not for her. She needed better conditions and more privacy. She somehow talked her boyfriend into buying a house on the internet, not far from the school for her to live in. She would move into it when she went back in August. Sometime in June, the new groomer's wife and kids went back to Uruguay. To help him save money so he could get back to them, we let him live at our house for free. He would take care of the yard and sometimes do some of the cooking. Being alone, we told him he could invite some of his other relatives over once in a while for a cook out. When they came they always brought lots of food.

Grilling was the way they normally cooked, so we told him they could use the grill. They never used gas for grilling, they don't use charcoal either. A couple of them would go to the woods out behind our house and forage for sticks, put them in the grill, and cook with them. He was an excellent cook. My only problem with them was that they liked to drink red wine – with orange soda mixed in with it. The first time I saw them do that, it was to one of my favorite wines that I had given them as a gift. As I saw them mix the drink, I just wanted to slap each and every one of them for ruining a very good bottle of wine. Other than that, we loved his family, and got along very well with all of them. It was a pleasure to have been able to help him the way we did. He was able to get back to his wife and kids in August.

About the middle of August, I was feeling good enough to start thinking about getting back to work on the race car. I just had one little problem---I couldn't remember what I was going to do with it. I would go out to the garage and walk around it, look at it, look at the pieces and parts, and hope that something would click. Unfortunately nothing ever clicked. I never wrote down what my ideas were to get around the issue with the computer. Whatever the answer was, it was gone. I had slowly gotten back to doing my real job. All of my clients were very patient with me and hung in there waiting for me to get better. As I was working on trying to get caught up on that, I was still thinking about how to fix the car. When Diana's daughter went back to school at the end of August, Diana flew out there with her to help her get settled in the house her boyfriend bought. She was gone for about ten days, and was a wreck when she got back. Apparently her daughter drove her nuts while she was there. By about the beginning of September, I was starting to drive again. First, just short trips around town with Kevin, and then, when I felt more confident, I started to drive to some of my client meetings. At first Kevin came with me to those, but by the middle of the month I was out on my own. Things were really starting to look better for us, Diana was rebuilding her business, and I was getting back to doing my business. Now if I could just figure out what I was going to do with that car, life would be perfect.

In the third week of September, at sometime between ten and eleven at night, as Diana and I were sitting in bed reading, I dropped my book. Apparently I picked it up, and dropped it again. She asked if I was falling asleep and I said, "I don't understand". Diana said she took one quick look at me and knew it was happening all over again. She said that this time instead of leaving me in bed, she grabbed me and helped me to the first chair she came to in the living room. (The living room was right off the bedroom). By the time she got me to that chair, she said that my entire right side was already paralyzed. I have absolutely no memory of that second stroke, other than the fact that it happened. Anything in here about that one is whatever Diana could tell me about it. She said that when she called 911, the same police officer that came the first time, came this time. The same ambulance EMT crew also came. I had the same attending doctor and stroke support team, and even the same room in the emergency area as the first time. They did their CAT scan, and all of the other little tests, along with the head of neurology at that same large hospital in Western MA The neurologist must have thought that this second stroke was worse than the first. Apparently there wasn't a lot of discussion about the TPA. I guess they gave it to me very quickly after the CAT scan was done. Did I mention that each one of those TPA shots at that time cost about $60,000. It's a very good thing we dumped that crap insurance we had when I had cancer, and got real stuff.

Once I was stable, I was again shipped off by ambulance to that big hospital in Western MA Diana again stayed by my side the entire time I was there. While we were at the hospital, Diana began to get sick, very sick. She had come down with very bad flu like symptoms. The hospital staff at first wanted her to leave the hospital, but then decided she wasn't well enough to be driving. She was so bad that the hospital nurses brought a lounge chair into my room, and told her to sleep in it. They kept me at the hospital one extra day to be sure that she was going to be ok. I apparently refused to go back to the rehab hospital after that stroke, so I had outpatient therapy at my house for the next month. Again my clients were all very supportive and patient with me. I never lost one client due to either of the strokes. Having been treated for the stroke a bit quicker the second time, I guess there was less damage done. I was able to return to work a little quicker than after the first one. I did notice that it was taking me longer to do things on the computer than it used to. I also found that I was having some trouble understanding some things that shouldn't have been giving me any trouble understanding. I was showing some of the effects of getting wacked in the head, twice.

By the beginning of November, I was getting back to work as normal, or as normal as I was going to be now. Diana was doing much better with her grooming business, and was voted the people's choice for groomers in the area. That was a very big deal, and a big boost for her business. She was working very hard at it. I was proud of what she had been able to do. Work for me was very busy, playing catch-up from my time off, along with lots of new work coming in. I started to find myself doing some odd things. Diana also noticed some of them. I would sometimes go out and start my truck in the driveway, go back in the house, get all the stuff for the bank, and walk to the bank. It wasn't far, maybe a half mile, but sometimes I would come out of the bank and get upset that I couldn't find my truck. Sometimes I would just walk back home and find it sitting in the driveway running, and not know why it was running. One time Diana asked me to run to the store for her to pick up something. The store was right next to the bank. I took her car to the store and apparently walked home. Sometime later, Diana asked me where her car was, and I said that I didn't know. After giving it some thought, she asked if I had taken it to the store. Again I said that I didn't know. Getting into my truck and driving to the store, we found her car still sitting in the parking lot where I had apparently left it. At least it wasn't running.

There was one incident that I think was particularly alarming to me. I had set up two appointments outside the office on the same day. I went to the first, and did whatever I was there for. When I got back in the truck and headed to my next appointment, I never made it. About two hours later, I found myself sitting in a parking lot just about a mile and a half from the first appointment location. When I realized that it was two hours later, I called the client I was supposed to see, and said I had run into some issues on the previous appointment and rescheduled for the next day. I then went home feeling very confused. The next day, thinking a bit clearer, I checked the navigation system in the truck to see if I did anything in the lost two hours. What I found scared the shit out of me. It showed that I had driven in a very big circle through five different towns. The breadcrumbs showed that I had driven through several intersections, and on many roads in areas that I know are very high traffic areas. I don't know how I could have done that and not known I was driving. When I told my neurologist about it, he said that it is possible for you to consciously "blackout" while doing something, and your sub-conscious mind can take control of your actions. I don't care how he puts it, that's a very scary thing to have happen.

Chapter Forty-Nine
Percocet and Morphine

As time went on, things seemed to get a little better for me. Early in 2010, I got a call from a man that was well known in the city. He was the owner of two very popular restaurants and very Italian. I only mention the Italian part because what he wanted me to do for him was to take a typical 1960 something ranch house, and turn it into an authentic Tuscan villa. The house came out great, complete with stucco exterior walls and Mediterranean red clay tile roof. The front entry was covered with a porch and four Doric columns supporting a second-floor covered porch with four matching columns. Inside there was, as you might expect, a very large well-equipped kitchen that was open to the family and dining rooms. Down a short hall off the family room, through a double arched door, was the master suite. A guest suite was also located on the first floor. On the second floor was one open room, with a three-quarter bath, and that second-floor porch. At the back of the house, there was a very large deck area. Part of it was covered and part was open. It too had a very well-equipped outdoor kitchen. The owner asked if I would make periodic inspections as the house was being built. That was a service that I did provide for a fee to anyone requesting it. For this client, instead of payment, Diana and I would get free buffet meals at one of his restaurants. That was a very good deal for us.

Diana's daughter's birthday was in the spring. She decided that we should take a trip out and surprise her with a visit for her birthday. Diana apparently knew that her daughter had a boyfriend out there. I don't remember that I was aware of that before going out there. To get to the town that her daughter lived in, we had to fly to Chicago, and then either take a shuttle flight to a small airport local to that town, or drive. Diana as you know does not fly well, so from Chicago, we drove the rest of the way. Diana had apparently made arrangements with the school boyfriend to keep her daughter at home until we got there, without letting her know we were coming. The drive from Chicago was about three hours. We were doing fine until we got into the city where the daughter lived in. Diana couldn't remember how to get to the house. After driving around for a bit, she called the school boyfriend and asked for directions. After giving the directions, he said that her daughter was starting to get upset, and a little testy having to stay at home. He said he was running out of reasons to stay there. Shortly after that conversation, we arrived at the house. I parked the car in a spot that her daughter wasn't going to be able to see, and we went to the front door.

There was a package left by the front door by the post man, so I used it after ringing the bell to tell her it was a special delivery.

When her daughter came to the door, she was completely surprised to see us. I think she was glad to see us, but it was kind of hard to tell. After going in and sitting for a while, the house had very little furniture and places to sit were at a premium. We went out to dinner. We told her we would take her wherever she wanted to go to eat and she chose a Mexican restaurant that she and Diana liked. It was ok, but Mid-Western Mexican food is not the best I've had. After having dinner, we all went to the boyfriend's house, which was in another town. He apparently was not a student at the school she was going to. He worked for the city or county, or some other municipal entity. The two of them seemed to get along pretty good, but there was something that just didn't seem to fit right to me. Something else that seemed a bit off to me was the fact that I didn't see a lot of school stuff at the daughter's house, and she didn't seem to have a lot of studying for someone in medical school. We stayed over the weekend, and then we headed home.

While I was working with my Italian client, I started to have some very serious back issues. Sometime in the early part of the summer, while the house was being built, I went to a back surgeon and was scheduled for lower back surgery. The surgery was just going to be day surgery, and being done at a hospital in the city of Worcester, MA. The night before the surgery, I began to have some very bad pain in my chest and left upper back area. The ambulance was called, and the EMT's thought I might be having a heart attack. So it was off to the little hospital that I was beginning to get to know so well. After tests were done, they decided I was not having a heart attack, but wanted to keep me in the hospital for at least another day. Telling them that I was scheduled for back surgery the following morning in Worcester, they sent me by ambulance to that hospital. Unfortunately, I was left sitting in the ER when I was supposed to be having my surgery. All of Diana and my explaining continued to fall on deaf ears until late in the morning. They finally understood that I was supposed to be in the surgical unit, and eventually sent me there. I had by that time missed my appointed surgery time and was now going to have to wait for an opening later in the day. In the meantime, I was in severe pain. To help with that, they were giving me Percocet and morphine together. They also had a constant iv drip of antibiotics going into me for hours.

With all of the antibiotics being pumped into me, my stomach started to bleed. I wouldn't tell anyone about it because I was afraid they would cancel my surgery. With the mix of pain meds, I was starting to have hallucinations, bad ones. By the time they got around to doing my surgery, I was a mess. All of the pain meds were still being given to me, and then they took me in and gave me anesthesia for the surgery. When I came out of the surgery, I was confused and didn't know where I was or who anybody around me was, including my wife. Everything was one big hallucination. I was afraid of everybody and apparently thought that I was being kidnapped, and was going to be killed. As the drugs began to wear off, I started to come around to being myself again. They ended up keeping me in the hospital overnight, and sending me home the following morning. In a couple of days I was back to work as if nothing had happened.

Chapter Fifty
Uruguay

In the early Fall of that year, my Italian client gave me two tickets to an oldies' show that was being put on in mid-October. It was a very good show with lots of performers for the sixties and very early seventies. It just seems amazing to me that some of the people that were singing in the sixties, could still sing and sound just as good now almost fifty years later. At some point during the show, one of the members of one of those "Wall of sound" all girl groups, produced by Phil Spector was going to perform. A large picture of her was projected on the back drop curtain above the stage. It was a picture of her when she was maybe in her very early twenties; she was very pretty. First, someone brought a very large chair out and set it in the middle of the stage. Then a microphone was setup to accommodate someone sitting in the chair. And then it happened! Two men appeared, helping a very large old woman to the chair on the stage. I wasn't sure she was going to make it all the way to the chair. She sat and looked at the crowd of people. She introduced herself, and then music began to play. The tune was one of those old familiar songs that people of my age would all remember. She began to sing, and---if you closed your eyes, you would think you were listening to her sing back in the sixties. She sounded just like she did back then. The fact that she was very large, I mean VERY large, played slightly into the show. At one point, while she was singing, she reached into the front of the very over stretched jersey she was wearing, and began rooting around her enormous breasts for something. I was sitting there pretty sure that she was going to pull a small car out of there. But she came out with a harmonica and began to play it. Have you ever seen someone with no teeth play the harmonica? That's a bit of a show of its own.

Diana and I were taking the month of November off and going to Uruguay to visit our friends from the grooming shop. We would be flying from Boston to Miami, and then to Montevideo, Uruguay. The flight was a total of fourteen hours, on a 767. Surprising, at least to me, the flight was full. Spending that many hours on a small plane like that, with that many people, was very uncomfortable to say the least. When we arrived in Montevideo, which is the capital city of Uruguay, and the city that our friends lived in, most of the family was there to meet us. Our ex-groomer, his two kids, and his mother-in-law were all there. It was great to see all of them to greet us. Unfortunately, adding the two of us to the group meant that we were not all going to fit in the cab for the ride to their house. I should mention at this point that nobody in their family had a driver's license. So, before leaving the airport, I rented a car. I asked for a full-size car and was given a Nissan something or other, that was just big enough to squeeze all of us into, with one of the children on someone's lap. I was told that was the biggest car they had. After driving in the city for a while, I not only believed them, but I was glad the car was as small as it was. We'll get into the driving habits of the locals later. When I was given the car, I was also told not to leave the radio in the car when it was unattended. This was a new one on me. I had to ask our friend about that, and he just pushed a couple of buttons on the dashboard, and the whole front of the radio fell out of the car. We left it sitting in the house the entire time we were there.

Life in Uruguay is much simpler and laid back than it is here. There are fresh food markets on almost every street corner in the city. The food is much different than it is here. There are no growth hormones used on any of the food, and yet the chickens are the size of small turkeys, and they taste much better than they do here. The beef is everywhere and has a different color, and a much better taste than ours does. While many of the people don't seem to eat much for vegetables they are on every street corner, and are very good. The city of Montevideo is very large. About two thirds of the people living in the country, live in that city. People seem, for the most part, friendly. They speak a blend of Spanish and Italian, that doesn't seem to cross over to most other Spanish speaking counties. While they border Brazil, the Brazilians speak Portuguese, and there is no cross over between the two languages. While we were there, we visited some small Brazilian border towns. Think back to the old west in the late eighteen hundreds here, and you pretty much have a Brazilian border town.

The ride into the city from the airport was several miles. The car we were given didn't have a full tank of gas. They give you the car with whatever gas it has in it. So one of the first things we did was visit a gas station. I don't remember how much gas the tank took to fill it, but I do remember paying just under eleven hundred Uruguayan pesos. We then headed to the market to buy food for dinner that night. Something commonly done there is to buy the food you're only going to eat that day or the next. Here's a fun fact about parking in the city. They have on street parallel parking on most of the main roads. Since the traffic there is horrendous, to help with the parking they have self-designated "Parking Nazis". These are generally old men, with safety vests on, and a stick about two feet long. If you want to park along the street, put your directional on and one of these old guys will find a spot for you, and direct you into it. When you come back out of the store you went to, the same guy will come to your car, and for a few pesos, he will walk out into traffic and stop it so you can get back out of the parking spot.

The city itself was for the most part, pretty clean and more modern than I expected it to be. There were, of course, many reminders that you were in a third world country. Most of the private houses were built of either poured-in-place concrete or concrete blocks. Almost all of the houses had some sort of protective wall around them. The crime rate in the city is very low. That may be in part because every business has armed guards inside all of the time. Not being able to speak the language was a small issue, and didn't really cause too much trouble for us. One day while exploring the center of the city, we found a market call "Inglesa Mercado", or "English Market". We were very happy to find that, so in we went and very quickly found out that not one person in there spoke any English at all. I did learn some of their language by going to the corner market next to the house every day. There was a young man working at that store that did speak enough English so that we would work with each other to teach ourselves each other's language.

Carlos, our groomer friend, and his wife Anna, lived in a house just outside the center of the city. They were close enough to be able to walk to the center. Anna was a nurse, and worked in the medical zone. That was an area that had several hospitals in it. There was an American hospital, a German one, a Spanish one, and a few others. She worked in the American one. On the south side of the city was the American Embassy, and right next to that was a large casino. Across the street was a beautiful white sand beach, with lots of palm trees on it. There were lots of small pub style places to eat with very good food. The old part of the city, the area with the Port Authority Complex, had very beautiful old Spanish style architecture, with more good restaurants. Some of the them were open air places. Again, all of the menus were in their own language, and not many people working in the food industry seemed to be able to speak much in the way of English.

Driving in the city! OK--I said we would get to this, so here we are. There are very few controlled intersections in the city, or anywhere for that matter. But in the city the traffic is very heavy, and they tend to drive a little too fast for the conditions around them. In the main part of the city at almost any time of the day, you can find public buses lined up like trains going down the streets. Sometimes there were as many as eight buses running one after the other. Once they get to the outer sections of the city, they begin to split up and head in different directions. Back to those intersections. Even though there are no signs or lights at many of the intersections in the city, the locals seem to have some kind of system that they all sort of follow. Somehow they all seem to know which side of the intersection can pass without stopping, and which side must stop. My not being a local, and the locals that I had with me not being able to drive, I was at a great loss when it came to handling the intersections properly. You find very quickly that if you are the side that has the pass, and you stop with cars behind you, the locals get very upset. They may in fact even try to push your car through the intersection. There were more than a few near misses at speeds that would have made for some ugly messes in the city. Outside the city things are much more calm. Speeds are still too fast for the conditions, but there is much less traffic. All of this is coming from someone that likes being on a racetrack with lots of cars around going over one hundred miles an hour you say. Well yes, but those guys on the track all know what they are doing, and they belong out there. I'm pretty sure at least half of the drivers I was out there with in Uruguay didn't have any idea what they were doing.

Being away for a month didn't mean that I could just stop working. I brought a laptop with me, and had phone calls sent to my cell phone in Uruguay. Having the calls sent to my phone wasn't cheap. The calls cost about $2.25 per minute.

Most of my clients were made aware that I would be out of the country, and only my most important continuous clients were told that they would still be able to reach me if they had to. While we were there, however, we started to get calls from the company that carried Diana's daughter's school loans. They were not being paid. We explained to them that we were out of the country and couldn't do anything about that until we got back in December, and that the calls they were making to my phone were costing a lot of money. They apparently either didn't care or didn't believe us. After the first few calls didn't seem to help them, they began to call my phone sometimes as much as four of five times a day. Even if I didn't answer the call, if they left a voice message, I was still charged for the call. When we got back home, I tried to file a complaint about that, but I didn't get anywhere. Another problem caller was my oldest brother Kevin. After spending all of his adult life drinking as much whiskey as he could get in, he was starting to have some issues. He had developed Arterial Sclerosis in both legs. He had very poor blood circulation in both feet, and had some trouble walking. He would call me at least once a week while we were gone just to tell me how bad he was doing, and how his feet were turning purple now and were very painful.

About five days before we were scheduled to come home, Kevin called me to say that he was no longer able to walk, and was going into the hospital the following day. He said that the doctor told him he may loss his right foot. He wanted me there with him for all of that. I told him that being in a small third world country, you don't just walk into the airport and hop on a plane. I was going to have to call the airline to make arrangements. The other issue was that when he called with that one, we were up near the Brazil border. When I told Diana what he told me, she got very upset with him. He knew we would be home in five days. He should have been able to handle things on his own until we got back. We called the airline and cut our vacation a few days short so I could be with him. When we got back home, so was he. He never went into the hospital. He said that when I told him we were coming back a few days early, he decided to wait until we got home. I asked him if he was able to do that, why didn't he just wait the extra few days so we could finish our vacation? He never gave me an answer for that. He also seemed to be able to walk as good as he did when we left on vacation. In spite of all of this, going to Uruguay was a great trip, and we hope to get back there again someday.

Chapter Fifty-One
Going to Get Diana's Daughter

Christmas came and we had our usual open house. It seemed more people came that year than most years. I think they just wanted to hear about our trip. We all had fun with the games, food and of course the drinks. After Christmas and New Years, Diana and I had to settle down and pay attention to work once again. In the spring of 2011, I'm not sure of the month, I think it was sometime around May, Diana got a frantic call from her daughter. She was crying and told her mother that she and her school boyfriend had broken up, and she had no place to live. Diana reminded her that she had a house of her own live to in. Well, then some of the truth started to come out. She had apparently moved in with her boyfriend out there, and rented the house to someone. She of course did not tell her boyfriend back here at home any of this, because she was keeping the rent money. Even though she had a car, she needed us to come to the Mid-West to get her, and bring her home. Diana asked about the school and her year-end tests. Her daughter told her that because her hips had gotten so bad, she could not do the type of body manipulation that was required for the tests. She said that they weren't going to allow her to take the tests.

So, an emergency flight from Providence to Chicago cost us over one thousand dollars. Then we had to rent a car at the airport in Chicago, and drive for three hours to meet with the daughter at that little airport near where she lived. Remember, Diana has enough trouble getting on a real airplane, she was not getting on one of those little shuttle planes. We met the daughter at the airport. She had her car packed and ready to go. She also at the time had a full-grown Lab that had to come with us. After turning in the rental car at the airport, we headed back home in the daughter's car: the three of us plus the dog. I remember Diana asking about the school loans when we returned from Uruguay. Her daughter told her that she missed a few payments, but she was now up to date with them again. The drive home was too long to make without stopping one night, more money spent. When we got home, the daughter's boyfriend, the first one was now aware of what was going on with the daughter and the other boyfriend. He had moved out just before we got home. The daughter's son, at that time twenty years old, refused to let his mother live in the apartment with him. It seems he wasn't too happy with her either. We let her live in a small spare bedroom with us on the first floor.

We were, at that time, trying to get the grandson to pay a small rent for the apartment. After all, they had been living up there, rent free for eleven years by that time. I thought it was only fair. We weren't charging the daughter any rent for the small bedroom she was in. She wasn't working; she wasn't doing much of anything as far as I could see. But I was leaving her family matters for Diana to deal with as she saw fit. The grandson, along with his live-in girlfriend, were so upset that we asked for some small amount of rent, that they moved out, and went to her parents' house to live. Doing that meant that a once ten-minute drive for the grandson to get to work, was then going to be about an hour and fifteen minutes. He was working as a mechanic, making between eighteen and twenty dollars an hour at the time. All we asked for was four hundred dollars a month to help with the mortgage, water and sewer bills. Sometimes, when you're just twenty years old, you fail to see the big picture. His car didn't get great gas mileage, not to mention he had to be to work at seven thirty, which meant he had to leave that house by a little past six to be on time. None of it made any sense to me.

With the grandson out of the apartment, we thought we could finally get someone in there that would pay some rent. Diana's daughter wasn't going to, so she wasn't even offered the apartment. When we went up to clean the place up and get it ready to rent, we found that the grandson had punched or kicked several holes in the walls that would need to be repaired. Knowing the kid the way I did, that didn't really surprise me all that much. We made the repairs, cleaned the place up, and rented it very quickly. The new renter was a young single girl that we knew and trusted to take care of the place. She paid her rent on time and never gave us any problems, except one. She found a new boyfriend, and within five or six months, moved out of the apartment to go live with him. That left us with the apartment empty, and winter on its way. In the meantime, the grandson came back to us and asked if we would let him take the apartment if he agreed to pay the rent, and not ruin the place again. We decided to let him take it. I told him that if he didn't pay the rent, I would throw his ass out on the street in a heartbeat. He knew I meant it. I also told him that if I went up there and found one hole in a wall, I would rip his arms off and beat him about the head with them. He knew I meant that too.

While all of that was going on, the daughter was going out with some of her old friends from the area. At some point she had picked up a new boyfriend. She asked Diana if he could move in with her, and after some, unpleasant conversation between Diana and me, the boyfriend moved in. With him in the house now, we needed to get some rent from Diana's daughter and her new boyfriend. He was working and seemed to be somewhat responsible. He agreed on the rent and paid it every month. Diana's daughter had only been to Chiropractic school for three years; it was a five-year program. When Diana asked if she was going back, she told her that they weren't going to let her continue if she couldn't do the manipulation that was required. As we thought back on that, both Diana and I had been to at least two Chiropractors that went to the same school she attended. They didn't do any kind of body manipulation that would require them to have strong hips. We believed that the truth was, she flunked out last year, and didn't want to tell anybody. That still left the question of the school loans, a lot of school loans.

Diana's daughter had a mental health counselor for several years. Sometime during her therapy, the counselor helped her get on disability. She had been collecting it for a few years prior to going back to school. Now living at our house, she was still collecting it, and had no real bills to pay with it. She had a cell phone, but we paid for that. We gave her the car she was driving, and she kept the least amount of insurance coverage she could on it. Her boyfriend did whatever little bit of food shopping they needed to do. And yet she didn't seem to be able to pay those pesky school loans. Diana began getting calls from the loan companies again. Sometimes I'm a slow learner, but this time I realized that if Diana was getting those calls, there was a reason for it. So when I asked her about it, she did finally tell me that she had co-signed for the loans. Trying very hard not to really lose it, I explained that in all of the time I had known her daughter, I had never seen her start and then actually finish anything. Diana had to agree with that, so I asked her why she would put us in that position? She said that she really wanted her daughter to have a chance at doing something, and it seemed like she would follow through with that. Well that wasn't going to happen, and unless her daughter started paying, we were going to get screwed by her own daughter. Diana had a talk with her daughter, and then she helped her get the monthly payments reduced to help her pay them. After that the calls stopped – for a while.

I had given up driving race cars because after having two strokes, I didn't feel like I was capable of making the split-second decisions needed at one hundred forty miles an hour. But I missed racing a lot, so that summer (2011) I started to do some go kart racing. First I tried electric karts and found that about half the time, the kart you got wasn't fully charged. If you got one of those, you would find yourself just putting around the track, while everyone else was racing past you. So, giving up on the electric karts, I started to race gas powered karts. That was so much more fun. I started to run races in Boston at an indoor track that had hills, wide turns, and hairpin turns. There was also a short straight section as you went past the pit area and the finish line. Scoring at that track was done with electronic transponders on the karts. Races were run with between eight and twelve karts, depending on how many drivers there were. I ran six races that year, won a couple and had pretty good showings in most of the races. I was having a great time with it, and found that the reaction time needed was generally much less than what I needed racing cars. I still had the car that I was supposed to be building in the garage. And I still had no idea what I was going to do with the new drive system. In the summer of 2012, I cut the car up, and sold it for scrap, I was more frustrated with my inability to remember things than I was ready to admit, but it was showing to everyone around me.

Chapter Fifty-Two
Go Karts

Over the winter of 2011 and 2012, I began to research go kart racing. What I found was very surprising to me. Apparently it was at that time the fastest growing spectator involved sport in the country. Over thirty million people were driving go karts in this country each year, and the number was growing. New tracks were being built all over the place. I decided that I would really like to get in on that. So I put together a business plan, and designed a track to go with it. I found an eight-acre lot in Arizona that I thought was in a very good location for that type of business. The lot was in between an Army Air base and an Air Force base, and about six miles from the University of Arizona. I began talking to a realtor in Arizona about the property, and I was also trying to find an investment group for the money end of it. All of that was taking a very long time. I was still designing houses as fast as I could to try to keep up with the demand. So the go kart thing had to take a back seat to that anyway. In September Diana and I went to Arizona to take a look at the land. She by the way, was much less enthused about the idea than I was. We flew into Tucson and, as we were getting off the plane, I stopped at the door of the plane, and for a few seconds was unable to move. I was hit at that moment with such a bad feeling about where we were, that I almost couldn't get off the plane.

I have never been able to explain the feeling I got trying to get off the plane, not even to myself. We stayed one night in Tucson, and planned to drive to Yuma the following day. Diana had a friend that lived there and she wanted to see her while we were out there. In the morning, when we left the hotel, we headed for Yuma. We found the main street closed by the police. We pulled into a corner convenience store to pick up a few bottles of water. While I was in there, I asked what was going on. The clerk told me that a short time ago, a police officer shot a man in a wheelchair in the car wash next to the convenience store. That was all the information he had at that point. I don't know, maybe the guy was homeless, and that was his way of washing his chair and taking a shower at the same time. I guess we'll never know.

I'm sure that you've all heard of that dry heat they keep talking about in the Southwest. Well, I can tell you that that's not entirely true. In the Tucson area, if the air temperature is 95 degrees, the humidity may only be 25 or 30 percent, but it still feels hot. When you get into Yuma, the temperature on average is much hotter than it is in Tucson. The lowest temp we had the week we were in Yuma was 108 degrees. The humidity in the Yuma area is about the same as it is in

Florida in the middle of summer. So, at 108 degrees, and 90 percent humidity, it felt more like 115 degrees, and like you were trying to walk under water. It is so hot in Yuma, that all of the exterior door handles on the commercial buildings are wrapped with rope to keep people from getting burned. I found that I was sweating right through my clothes just standing around trying to breath. The bottom line, hear, is that neither one of us found anything pleasant about being in Arizona. We took some time to make a day trip into Mexico that was interesting, but the border towns are nothing but tourist traps. After ten days in Arizona, we came home.

Not long after we got home from Arizona, Diana and I began to talk seriously about moving. The winters were beginning to bother me, and we felt that if we could keep our house rented, we would be ok. I was still going to be able to conduct my business form wherever we ended up. Not long after we started to talk about moving, Diana's daughter broke up with her boyfriend. In November, I scheduled three more go kart races at the track in Boston. When I got there, I found that I would be racing against two members of the Aston Martin factory race team. They said they were there just keeping sharp in the off season. In the first race, I started first, but was quickly passed by one of them. I was able to keep up with him, and not get passed by anyone else, so I finished that race in second place. I don't know where the other team member finished. They did not race in the second race and I won that race. The track lap time record at that time was 18.8 seconds. My fastest lap was 19.1 seconds. Three tenths of a second could have been lost just in how wide I may have taken a corner. In the third race I had the team guys with me again. I started back in the field a little bit, but after a few laps, I had the winner of the first race in my sights. I was able to get around him when he got hung up behind a slower driver. I was in first place with just a few laps left to go. All of the sudden, almost out of nowhere, that same driver shot past me as if he came out of a canon. I got back up behind him, but he was too good at blocking and I was not able to get back around him. On the last lap, not being able to pass him, I just put my front bumper to the back of his kart, and that's how we crossed the finish line.

With Diana's daughter not having the boyfriend anymore, that rent dried up in a hurry. I guess given the choice, I would rather she pay her school loans than give us a little rent. Her ex-boyfriend began to put all kinds of bad and ugly stuff about her on Facebook and some of the other social media sites. He even painted nasty graffiti about her on some rocks at a local public park. Even though there was no proof that he was the one that did it, it was very clear that it came from him. She was very upset about it and even though we told her not to bother going on those sites or to pay any attention to it, she let it get to her. The fact that she was already, well let's just say, on the edge to begin with didn't help matters any. She began to see her mental health therapist on a more regular basis, but I'm not sure the woman was doing anything to help her.

With winter now on us, Diana and I began more serious talks of moving. We decided that we would try Florida. It made sense to us from the point that it was warm, we were familiar with the area we would go to, and we already had friends there. I told my clients that I would be gone for a month, but that I would still be working during that time, and that they would still be receiving whatever work was due from me during that time. Just before New Year's we drove to Florida. We had rented a condo for the month and planned to spend New Year's Eve with Diana number two and her husband. When we got to the condo, we found it to be dirty, smelling like someone had just smoked four packs of cigarettes in the last half hour, and even the bed was dirty. When we complained about it, the owner came to the room and checked it out. He had to agree the room was not fit to rent. We were given a new room, this one with a water view on a canal. This was a much larger suite, and we could sit on the patio outside and watch the shrimp boats come and go. Much to Diana's delight, we could also watch the pelicans, lots of pelicans. Diana loves birds, sometimes the goofier the better, and let's face it, they don't get too much goofier than pelicans.

When we rented the condo we were told we would have free Wi-Fi, which was something I absolutely needed to conduct my business. I found that my free Wi-Fi was about a quarter mile down the road, parked next to another business. It was a bit inconvenient and it just pissed me off. Another funny thing that we found out about Florida, and not just at the condo, but all over the place, is that they use eight-foot sliding glass doors, but unlike most exterior sliders I have seen before, both panels are active. This is not something they tell you because it is common there. Every night when we went to bed we made sure that the panel that always got used was locked. Very much to our dismay, we found out that the other panel was never locked. We found that out one night when we were asleep in the back bedroom, and someone came into the front family room through the unlocked panel, and stole three hundred dollars in cash from us. We have always believed that it was one of the owners, or someone that worked there.

During our one-month trial period in Florida, I found that I would be able to run my business from there without any problems. We spent lots of time with Diana number two; well Diana spent more time with her than I did. Someone still had to work. At the end of the month, I was still on the fence about whether or not I wanted to move there. Diana was putting pressure on me to make a decision. Diana number two wasn't helping; she was putting lots of pressure on me to move there. I wanted to be out of the cold Winters of New England, but I wasn't sure that I was ready to be thirteen hundred miles from my clients. I finally told Diana that if we could find a house that we could rent reasonably, then we could move. We started driving around the area looking at houses for rent. We found a very nice two-bedroom, two-bathroom house that had never been rented. It was nice and clean, and in a good neighborhood, and the rent was less than expected. The house was being handled by an agency, so we met with them. I told them that we were going to have to go back home to get our stuff, and make arrangements to have our furniture shipped down. I wanted to start the rent as of March first. They told us we would have to rent the house as of February first, or they would rent it to the next person that came along. So, we gave them first, last, and a security deposit, all including February, even though we would not be moving in until March.

Chapter Fifty-Three
Who's Flying the Helicopter?

On the way back home, we stopped to visit my brother in Virginia. We stayed at his house with him and his wife (second wife), for a couple of days and then headed home. When we got home and told Diana's daughter that we were moving, she didn't take the news very well. We told her that she could have the whole first floor, and if she needed help paying her utilities bills, then she should get a roommate. The problem with that was that her daughter didn't play well with others for more than a short time. She had been that way as long as I had known her. We took the entire month of February to make the arrangements to move, and to have the furniture that we were taking sent down to the house. I went to see the clients that I needed to see, and Diana made some sort of deal with the girl that had been managing the grooming shop while we were gone. The girl would buy the business, we would hold the papers on it until it was paid for, and she would pay us each month. With everything being taken care of, the last thing I did before we left was to go visit Kevin to say goodbye. That being done, in the last few days of February 2013, we headed off to warmer climates.

I had given up on the go kart project in Arizona, but I hadn't given up on the idea. With that still in the back of my head, the first half of 2013 was far too busy for me to be playing with that idea. Diana two had gotten a job, so she wasn't around too much during the week, but we spent every weekend with her, and sometimes her husband. He didn't seem to be around too much, and we never got to know him like we did Diana. We were going to have to go back up to MA to get Diana's car and our two cats and bring them to Florida. So once we were settled in we, flew back to get the car and cats. The cats had never traveled in the car for more than twenty minutes to go to the Vet's office, so we didn't really know what to expect with them. Surprisingly, they both traveled very well. We stopped at a couple of pet friendly hotels on the way down. We told them that we had one cat with us, and then we snuck the other one in. Almost one month to the day after moving, I got up one morning to find Forest, dead on one of the bathroom floors. I don't know what killed him, but he was very old and frail, and before coming to us, he had a very hard life. We still miss him, he was a cool cat.

Having gotten settled into our new location, I started sending work back to the North Country. I had lots of work to catch up on from the move, and more work always coming in. With the summer on us, and both of us kind of ready for a break, Diana booked my next birthday adventure. She of course wouldn't tell me what it was, but she had an address to put into the navigation system, and all I had to do was follow it. After driving for a while, I found that we were in Clearwater, and turning into the airport there. Once into the airport, we parked at the main terminal and went inside. Diana went up to the counter to talk to the attendant while I waited. After a few minutes, a man came to get us and asked which one of us would be flying the helicopter. I looked at Diana and she told him that I would be the one. Still a little bit in shock, we followed the man to a small building set off to the side of the terminal. Inside was a flight simulator that I was told had the same controls as the helicopter that I would be flying. With the instructor in one seat, me in the other, and Diana standing behind us, the instructor went over all of the controls with me. After that he explained how to raise and lower the helicopter, and what the foot pedals were for. When he was done with all of that, he said, "Okay, so let's go for a ride!"

Okay I thought, let's do that. I started to lift off and to take the helicopter simulator forward out over the end of the runway. At the end of the simulated runway was a residential area. While I think I was trying to turn the helicopter to the right, I almost immediately crashed into someone's simulated house. The instructor reset the simulator and told me to try again. Again I crashed into someone's simulated house. With those two epic failures under my belt, the instructor got up from his seat and said, "Come on, let's go!" I asked where we were going, and he said to the helicopter. I asked if he was going to take me up and give me a ride around, he said, "No, you're going to take you up for a ride around." Shocked and a little scared I asked him if he thought that was a good idea given my performance in the simulator. He told me not to worry about it and that I would be fine.

With the instructor and myself in the helicopter, he again went over all of the controls with me. He asked if I was ready, and I said that I guess I was. He started the engine and then did a quick pre-flight check while it was warming up. With everything checked out, and the engine warm, he said, "Okay, let's go, take her up to one thousand feet and hold her there." As I took the controls and started to move the helicopter, I found that it seemed much easier to fly the real thing than it did the simulator. I was able to bring it up to one thousand feet, and to keep it at that level. He then told me that since we were facing east, he wanted me to turn around and head west until we got to the coastline. I did that with no trouble, and without losing any altitude. Once we got to the coast, he told me to turn north and follow the coast until we got to a bridge that I could see in the distance. Having done that, we turned east and then south east, back to the airport. Once we got to the airport, he had me bring the helicopter down to about three feet above the runway and hold it there. Trying to hover that close to the ground is very difficult because the blades create too much turbulence. It was a very hard thing to try to do. I was a bit shaky on that.

As fall and winter came around, we had Thanksgiving and Christmas dinner at Diana number two's house. We had met some other friends and had them, along with number two and her family over on Christmas Eve. It was nice, but it just wasn't the open house we were used to having on Christmas Eve. I think it made Diana just a little sad. Living in Florida was a whole new life, and we were going to have to get used to the different lifestyle. That was indeed going to take some time. (More I think for Diana than for me.) In the fall of 2013, housing in New England slowed down a bit. With less work coming in, I was able to get back to that go kart thing again. I started to write a new business plan for the idea, and as I did, I began to pitch a new concept to Diana. We could build a park and racetrack based on the prohibition and whiskey runners. She was a little more enthused about this idea than she was the last one.

I spent lots of time doing research on demographics, types of karts, and track layouts. We also decided to have bootleggers running around in the restaurant and in the stands handing people fake moonshine, so when the "Treasury Agents" caught them, they wouldn't have any moonshine on them. The track was designed to be similar to the back-country roads that the whiskey runners typically drove with their moonshine. I found two sites near Daytona that would be perfect for the park. I liked one site better than the other, but they were both good. The site I liked the best had some small hills, a small pond, and it had some areas of open land. I was going to have to create most of that on the other site. When I got all of the numbers put together, and the business plan and track layout completed, we began putting together a mailing list. By this time it was the middle of February, 2014. Our list was a very targeted list. It included most of the big name NASCAR race car drivers. The fact that it was the middle of February was going to be a slight problem. All of the drivers would be in Daytona Beach, getting ready for the Daytona five hundred race. I thought that would mean their business managers would be with them. We sent the packages out anyway, and in about three or four days, I got a call from one of the driver's managers.

After talking to the manager on the phone for a long time about the project, he said that he liked the idea very much and would like to fund the entire amount. He said that he was going to have to wait until the first weekend off for the racers, but he would go over it with the driver while they were on the road. While I was waiting for them to get back to me, I was dealing with the county officials, and trying to get the land ready. The county told me after several conversations that all of the roads leading to the facility were going to have to be full legal county roads. I tried to explain to them the idea of the moonshiners being out on some back dirt roads in the woods. They said, "Nope!" All roads must be full legal county roads. I asked if maybe one or two could remain dirt if we fixed the rest. They said, "Nope!" So the bottom line was that the cost of the project was going to just about double so we could build the county some nice new roads for them.

I couldn't go back to the investor and tell them that the cost just doubled. So I began to look for other sites. Finding a good site to put the park was one thing, but then the area had to have the demographics to support that kind of business. After lots of looking, I found a site near the gulf coast side of Florida. The demographics were actually better than Daytona, and there was an airport not too far away. I went to talk to the owners of the land, and they didn't want to sell it. What they would do, however, was give me a fifty-year lease at a very reasonable price. The price would be fixed and guaranteed for the fifty years. I sent all of the new info to the investor, and as soon as they found that we weren't going to be in Daytona, they backed out, completely.

I thought about looking for new investors, but my real job was getting very busy again. It was time for me to get back to paying more attention to my business. Much of what you read next comes from what Diana has been able to tell me. I have little or no memory of any of it. Sometime in early or mid-May 2014, I got a call from a nurse at that hospital that I was brought to so many times. She told me that Kevin had fallen in his apartment and broken his right leg very badly. He was going to need surgery and to have some pins put in. He was going to be in the hospital for about a week, and then he would have to be sent to a rehab center until the leg was strong enough to walk on. Diana and I decided that we would go up to be with him for a week or two. Since all of my work was coming from that area it wasn't going to interfere with business too much. When we got up there, we found that the issue wasn't just his leg. The owner of the apartment complex that he lived in called me and asked if I would meet him at Kevin's apartment.

Diana and I went to the apartment and met with the owner. He was not happy with the condition of Kevin's apartment. Standing in the kitchen looking around I apparently had to agree with him. The place was a mess. Kevin had become a hoarder. He had stacks of newspapers all over the place, with narrow paths to get from one area to another. There were empty booze bottles everywhere. He had empty cigarette packs stacked in what looked like little buildings forming little cigarette pack towns. There were trash bags full of garbage and trash piled in the living room. He had been smoking so much in there, without doing any cleaning that everything was covered with a heavy film of nicotine. The owner said that he was going to hold me responsible for cleaning the place up. The sad fact was that the place was so bad that all of the carpet, the appliances, heating strips, and even the lights and plumbing fixtures were going to have to be replaced. I told the owner that I would get all of the trash out, along with Kevin's belongings. As far as the smoking damage, he was allowed to smoke in there, so that was up to the owner.

Chapter Fifty-Four
Kevin Comes to Florida

After spending most of the week cleaning out the apartment and sorting out what to keep for Kevin, we went to talk to him at the rehab facility. He was going to be there for a few weeks, but they would not release him on his own. He had lost his apartment, and they were afraid he would hurt himself if he was left alone. He was going to have to come to Florida and live with us. I had to go back to Florida for work, so Diana stayed with her daughter at our house to bring Kevin with her to Florida when he was released. From here it gets a bit strange. At least with the part you just read, I have some small pieces of memory, but not much. With what takes place next, I have absolutely no memory at all. Diana said that she took me to the airport in Providence. I got on a plane and flew to Tampa where Diana number two met me and drove me home. I then spent the next few weeks conducting business, and going about my life while she was still in MA with Kevin. She said that I would call her or she would call me and that I sounded fine on the phone. Diana number two said that she came to the house to have lunch and check up on me a few times a week and that I seemed ok to her.

Around the middle of June, Kevin was released and he stayed with Diana and her daughter at our house in MA for a couple of days and then they flew back to Florida. That was the last time Diana would see her daughter. More about that to come. I apparently drove to the airport in Tampa to pick them up. Diana number two came with me to meet them and to help with Kevin if we needed it. Before going to get them, Diana said that I had moved my office out of the spare bedroom so Kevin could have it. I don't remember flying to Florida, or anything that happened during those three weeks while Diana was in MA with Kevin. None of that time has ever come back to me. When we moved to Florida, Kevin said that he wanted to come to Florida to be close to us. Well, with him in the same house as us, was just a little too close. All he did was bitch and complain. It's too hot; it's too humid; there's nothing to do; I don't want to sit around the house all day. We found a bar that was just a couple of miles from the house, and got the phone number of a taxi service for him. We weren't going out at two in the morning to pick him up at the local bar. After a couple of weeks at the house, going out to eat with us, and going to do some clothes shopping for him he began to go to the local bar.

Apparently when Diana was staying at our house with her daughter, she asked her to pay two hundred dollars per month rent. At the time she wasn't paying anything. She was still collecting disability, and still had no real bills to pay. Her son living on the second floor had been pretty good about paying the four hundred dollars rent each month we asked of him. Diana felt that two hundred dollars from her daughter was a reasonable price to ask for, considering we bought the house for her benefit, and she personally had never paid a dime in rent over the fourteen years that we owned it. The request for the two hundred dollar rent so infuriated the daughter, that as soon as Diana and Kevin left for Florida, she began packing to move. Sometime in July I got a call from the daughter. She was telling me that because we were throwing her out of the house, she was going to have to live in her car and become a prostitute to get enough money to survive. I tried to explain that nobody was throwing her out of the house. If she was leaving that was up to her. As far as becoming a prostitute, I told her that we knew she was still getting disability and there was no reason that she couldn't afford to pay two hundred dollars a month rent. I said that after everything we had done for her and her son, it was time for her to maybe give us a little help. I also reminded her that over the past few years, we had paid about thirty thousand dollars of her school loans to keep them from putting a lean on our house. (We would end up paying another ten thousand before we stopped paying).

That conversation was the last time I have spoken to Diana's daughter. She moved out of the house and sometime in August she called her mother and told her that she was living in her car, and had to give up her dog. We, however, knew that she was living in a house that she was sharing with a young man. When she rented the space in the house, (she was paying five hundred dollars a month, is this making any sense yet?) she told the owner of the house that her mother had died and she had no family. What she didn't know was that the owner of the house had worked with Diana for several years, and they were good friends. He called Diana to tell her that her daughter was living there, how much she was paying, and that apparently she was dead. Diana was very hurt by the fact that, first her daughter wouldn't pay us two hundred dollars rent, but she could afford to pay someone else five hundred, and second that she would tell them that Diana was dead.

Living in the house with that young man, over the course of a few months, the daughter had gotten him to quit his job, and cut off all ties with his family. They changed the locks on all of the doors, and painted all of the windows in the house black. Her daughter told someone that knew the owner that they did that because she heard that her mother had put a contract out on her life. (I thought she said her mother was dead). Anyway, it would seem that the mental health counselor wasn't doing much to help her. The information that Diana was getting at the time suggested that she was still seeing her. Apparently around early or mid-September, both the daughter and the young man disappeared. Diana's daughter called her around the end of September. I have no idea what that call was about or what was said, but that was the last time Diana heard from her daughter. In the meantime, Diana's grandson called sometime in August to tell her that they were moving out of the house. He also told her that he felt that we had done nothing but belittle and bully him all of his life. We had done nothing to help him or his mother, ever, with anything. He seems to have forgotten who

217

paid for his two years in college. He seems to have forgotten who gave his mother the car she was driving, and who put a roof over his head for several years without asking for any rent. He told his grandmother that he hated her and that she was a horrible person, and he never wanted to see her again. That was the last contact she had with him.

Chapter Fifty-Five
Happy Birthday to Me

In late September, Kevin, Diana and I along with Diana number two and her husband, went to watch the cardboard boat races. Yup, it's just what it sounds like. People make full size boats out of cardboard, put them in the water and race around markers forming a little course. The boat that does it the fastest, or doesn't sink is the winner. I remember being surprised by two things. The first surprise was how many people make boats out of cardboard, and then try to paddle around a course in the water. The second surprise was how few of the boats actually sank. Diana said we were there for about three and a half or four hours, and that she thinks I had three glasses of wine during that time. After the races, we went to one of our favorite little pubs for dinner. While having dinner she said that I had one glass of wine. After dinner we all went back to our house for a belated celebration of my birthday. When we got back to our house, Diana said that I opened the door and took a couple of steps into the house, wobbled a little, and then fell to the floor.

An ambulance was called for, and everyone thought that I was having another stroke. The date of that event was five years to the day, of my last stroke. Apparently while I was in the emergency room being checked for a stroke, the attending doctor smelled alcohol on me and saw that my hands were shaking a little. He decided that I was an alcoholic, and had been drinking very heavily that day and was having delirium tremors because I was already going into detox. No matter how many times both Diana's told that idiot that I was not an alcoholic, or even a heavy drinker, and that the tremors he saw were from Parkinson's syndrome, which I had been diagnosed with the previous year, he would not listen. He entered his finding of alcoholic, and detox into my permanent medical record. While he was doing that, a real doctor apparently took over my case, diagnosed me with a possible stroke and I was given the TPA drugs once again.

After being in the hospital for about a week, I was sent to an inpatient acute care rehab facility. I spent the next three or three and a half weeks there. I have very little memory of my time there other than just a few things that stuck in my head. I remember the first time I was able to tie my shoes by myself. That was a big step for me. I remember a doctor, not even one of mine, coming into the central rehab room, and with about fifty people around start talking to me about being an alcoholic and a heavy drinker. Several people heard her ask me about it. I remember telling her that the information she had was wrong, and that I was neither one of those things, and then I left the room without doing my scheduled workout. I made a complaint to the director of the facility about the doctor doing that, first sighting her incorrect information, and then her total disregard for hippa laws or my privacy. The doctor was made to come to my room and apologize to me, which didn't mean anything to me. What did mean something to me was the fact that that information was going to be removed from my record.

It was now the end of October 2014 and I was back home. After not hearing from her daughter for a while, Diana decided we should stop paying for her cell phone. There was another pile of work sitting waiting for me to get back to it. I, however, cannot even remember how to get into my computer programs to do the work. And as I sat there looking at some of the paper copies of the work I was doing, none of it made any sense to me. I couldn't figure out how to do my work anymore! I was left with several cognitive issues, along with a few physical problems. Some of both are still with me today. I was sent to several different neurologists, and after looking at the MRI's of my brain, and talking to me while doing their little neurological tests, most of them said there was nothing wrong with me, and that I hadn't had any strokes. Some of the neurologists even went so far as to tell Diana that I was just nuts (Their words) and should see a psychiatrist. Fortunately for me, they would later be proven wrong. As time went on, my physical and mental abilities improved a bit.

For Christmas 2014 we went to Daytona Beach. We rented an apartment in one of the better hotels on the beach and Kevin and Diana number two and her husband came with us. Diana's niece and her husband were down from MA so they also stayed in the apartment with us. David and his wife were coming down, but they made their own arrangements with the same hotel. They came down the day after the rest of us got there. When they arrived, they were told that check in time was at four pm. and since they were a couple of hours early, the room wasn't ready yet. For some reason, that seemed to really piss off David's wife. We told them that they could put their stuff in our apartment and join us at the pool until their room was ready. David seemed fine with that, but his wife was just going to let her day be ruined, and she was going to try to ruin everybody else's along with her. She was just miserable. I remember making arrangements for all of us to go out to eat. I called David to let him know, and I got his voice mail. I left him a message about it, giving them a couple hours' notice. I never heard back from David about dinner, so we all went without them.

Dinner was at one of the restaurants along the beach, and within walking distance of the hotel. After dinner, we all walked along the beach as we made our way back to the hotel. As we were coming up the steps from the beach to the hotel lobby, we could see David sitting in a chair just looking out at the ocean by himself. I asked how long he had been there, and he had apparently just missed us for dinner, and had been sitting there ever since. I asked where his wife was and he said she didn't want to go to dinner. David came back to the apartment with us. We had some stuff to eat there which we gave him, and then we all sat around having drinks, telling stories, and just having fun until one or one thirty in the morning. David stayed the entire time. I don't think he wanted to back to his room.

I don't remember how long we stayed in Daytona that Christmas, but I remember that David and his wife were going to stay one day after we left. It was a good Christmas. It was good to have a group of people around again, I know Diana was very happy that year. After Christmas we all went back to our lives. I still had no idea what to do with any part of the work I had been doing for the past twenty-three years. We went to a disability lawyer and started the process of filing for disability for me. The speech therapist at the rehab center I was at, was asked if I could be retrained for some other job. She said that because of my particular cognitive issues, she didn't know of any job that I would be able to be retrained to do. In April of 2015, I started to receive disability payments for physical and cognitive disabilities.

As time went by in 2015, Kevin seemed to mellow a bit. He was adjusting to his new life, but would from time to time talk about wanting to move back to MA He was in the habit of going to the same bar every day. Sometimes he would leave the house in the mid-afternoon, and sometimes in the early evening. No matter what time he left the house, he would almost always come back after the bar closed around one a.m. I would sometimes go to dinner with him, just Kevin and me. It was like boys' night out, or something like that. He seemed to like going out with just me, but I wasn't always able to do it. I was having some good days and some bad ones. We were also now in the habit of going out with Diana number two and her husband on Saturday nights. Sometimes Kevin would come with us, but not very often. On those Saturdays that I wasn't having a good day, we wouldn't be able to go out. Diana number two either didn't understand what was going on with me, or she was beginning to think we didn't want to go out with them. In either case, she began taking it a bit personally.

In August Kevin wanted to take a trip back up to MA to see his friends. Diana made all of the flight arrangements and ground transportation for him. Kevin had booked a room in a hotel near his favorite pub so he could just walk to and from the bar. He had lost his driver's license and because he was now living in Florida, he never made any effort to get it back. He couldn't get a Florida license because he lost his license in MA. It was one of those going in circles things. Anyway, he stayed at the hotel for the first couple of nights he was up there, and then one of his friends said he could stay with him for a few nights. His friend was still working and living in another town, so Kevin was going to have to take a taxi to get to the pub and back to his friend's house. I guess that worked for him for a couple of nights, but then he moved back to another hotel next door to the pub. He stayed in MA for a week and came home. He said that he had a very good time up there, and it was good to see all of his friends again. He took lots of pictures and brought some gifts back for some friends back here. But he didn't look good.

Chapter Fifty-Six
Kevin Gets Sick

In the first week of September, Kevin said he was going to the bar and that he had already called the taxi. It was early in the afternoon, but he said that he had some things to give to some people that he would only see at that time of the day. As he normally did, he went out to wait for the taxi in the driveway. About two or three minutes after going outside, my phone rang and it was Kevin. He said, "I think you're going to have to come out to the driveway and pick me up." Not really understanding what he meant by that, I looked out the window and saw him lying on the ground. When I went out there he said that his legs had just given out on him, and he wasn't able to get up by himself. I picked him up and brought him in the house to his bedroom. I put him on the bed and Diana and I started to ask him questions. He looked even worse than he did just a few minutes before when he had gone out to meet the taxi.

There was something obviously not right with Kevin. He was starting to get disoriented and confused. After trying to get a handle on what was going on with him, we decided to call for an ambulance. At the hospital they told us that after checking him out, they found that he was severely dehydrated and malnourished. The doctor told us that when they were talking to him about his condition, he told them that we don't let him get food on his own at the house, and that we would only feed him a little bit of food each day. I was furious with him for doing that, and told him he could have gotten us in a lot of trouble. He didn't seem to care too much about that. The fact was that we did special food shopping just for him, to get stuff that we knew he would eat. We got easy stuff for him, stuff he could just pop in the microwave and eat. The problem was still the one he had most of his adult life; he would rather drink whiskey than eat food.

By the middle of October Kevin had been in and out of the hospital a few times. He was back in, and the doctors were telling us that he would have to go to a rehab facility to help him get some strength back in his legs. He was sent to one that was pretty close to our house so we were able to make frequent visits. He didn't want to be there, so he was always in a bad mood, and somewhat uncooperative with the rehab staff. After being in there for a couple of weeks, they decided that they couldn't do anything more for him and sent him home. What nobody told us when they sent him was that he had something called c-dif. As we found out very quickly, it is a very bad intestinal infection that causes uncontrollable diarrhea and is highly contagious. After being home less than twenty-four hours, Kevin was on his way back to the hospital. This time he ended up with a doctor that had some ideas about his condition.

The doctor ordered a whole battery of tests that had not been done on Kevin up to that point. A couple of days after some of the tests were done I got a phone call from the charge nurse at the hospital. Kevin had gotten some bad news, and he was not taking it well. I went to the hospital to try to calm him down, and was able to at least get him under control. He was told that he had lung cancer, and that it was in a very advanced stage. After keeping him in the hospital for just a couple of days, he was transferred to a long-term nursing home about fifteen miles from our house. Before leaving the hospital I got a chance to talk to the doctor about Kevin's condition. He told me that while he wasn't sure, he thought that by the way Kevin seemed to be, that the cancer may have already spread to his brain. He didn't give Kevin very long to live. At the nursing home, Diana and I made a visit almost every day. Some days he knew who we were, and others he didn't seem to know. Thanksgiving rolled around and we made up a little turkey dinner for Kevin, Diana and me, and brought it to the nursing home to have turkey day dinner with Kevin.

If you will remember back to the introduction to the family, I told you that Kevin had two kids. Over the past ten years or so, he had been in occasional contact with his youngest son and his family. I called him to tell him that his father was dying and that he wasn't going to last much longer. His son and wife came to Florida to see him and he seemed to enjoy that. They came the week before Thanksgiving, and stayed for just a couple of days and went back home, they lived somewhere out West. On November 28th, Kevin's oldest son called me. He said that his brother had called him to tell him about Kevin, and he gave him my phone number. When he called he asked if he could come and see his father. I wasn't sure that would be a good idea. He hadn't seen him, or had any contact with him, in almost thirty years. While I was on the phone with him, Diana asked Kevin if he would like to see his son again and Kevin said yes. I told his son to come to the rest home, and gave him the address. His son and wife live about a five and a half or six hours drive from us. They showed up in the late afternoon. Kevin at that point was not doing well at all so Diana and I gave Kevin and his son some time to spend together.

After Kevin's son and wife had spent some time with Kevin, it looked like Kevin needed to rest a bit. Diana and I went to dinner with Kevin's oldest son and his wife. It had been more than thirty years since the last time I had seen either of Kevin's kids. This one had grown up to be a very nice young man, with a very nice wife. We enjoyed meeting them and spending time with them. As we were just finishing our meals, the rest home called and told me that we should probably consider getting back there. Kevin was not doing well and they didn't expect him to hang on much longer. When we got back to the rest home, Kevin was completely incoherent, but when his son took one of Kevin's hands and I took the other, we just held them and Kevin would not let us go. Approximately eight hours later, Diana and the son's wife had gone back to our house to get something, and were not back yet; Kevin passed away at 1:29, am. November

29, 2015. He was still holding both of our hands as he went. Diana and I have remained good friends with that nephew and his wife, and still keep in touch.

In March of 2016 I had another stroke. This one was not as bad as some of the others I had, but Diana said that it started when we were out. She said that she took me to the closest hospital and when she got me to the emergency entrance, she was told that nobody could help her get me out of the car. Someone brought her a wheelchair to put me in, but they were not allowed to help. Once she was finally able to get me into the emergency room, she said that they did the usual tests and weren't sure that I was having an actual stroke, but decided that I should be treated for it just in case it was. So again I was given TPA and Diana said that I seemed to start getting a little better shortly after that. While at the hospital, the doctors apparently began to debate whether or not I actually had a stroke. At some point a doctor that had nothing to do with my case came into the room and told the other doctors in there that he had been looking at my chart, and I did indeed have a stroke, but it was caused by something called a "Hemiplegic Migraine". Apparently it is a rare and very dangerous type of migraine that can cause stroke like symptoms. If the symptoms are bad enough and left untreated, it is possible for it to turn into a full-blown stroke. That is what the doctor believed happened to me. He said that he thought that was what had happened in the past with at least one other stroke. He said that this type of stroke doesn't look the same as a stroke caused by a blood clot on an MRI. That was why the doctors were having trouble with the diagnosis.

Chapter Fifty-Seven
The End Is Coming

The hospital called Diana after I had been there for three days. They told her that they would need her to pay a five-thousand-dollar deposit. When she asked why they needed that, they told her that it was because they did not take our insurance. She asked why she wasn't told that when they had me in the ER, and had me transferred to a hospital that did take our insurance. The person she was talking to said that she was sure that she must have been told that. Diana said that if that was the case then I would never have been admitted in the first place. She got me discharged that day, and took me home. We later got a bill from the hospital, the total was just under one hundred thousand dollars. They wanted us to send them thirteen thousand, five hundred dollars. Diana called and told them that she would be sending them ten dollars a month. They said they would set up a payment plan, but it would have to be at least fifty dollars a month. She told them that because I was on disability, and she was retired and collecting social security, ten dollars was the best it was going to be.

The hospital later got back to Diana and said that if she paid half of the thirteen thousand five-hundred-dollar bill, they would forgive the rest of it. Diana had some money left in her retirement plan which she had not taken out. She called the company dealing with that and made arrangements for a withdrawal to cover the bill. For some reason it seemed to take a very long time for the money to get to us. Diana called the hospital a few times to tell them that we were still waiting for the money, and they seemed to be ok with it. When she finally got the money, she paid the hospital. After a couple of months or so, the hospital billed us for the rest of the bill. When Diana called to find out what was going on with that, she was told that time had run out on the deal offered by the hospital, and even though she paid half of the bill, she was now going to have to pay the other half. We went to the hospital and explained that we were not told there was a time limit on the offer, and that when the payment was made Diana was told that everything was fine. Even though the hospital couldn't find any evidence that we were told of a time limit, they still wanted the rest of the money. We left the hospital and Diana never paid them another dime. After several months of going back and forth with the hospital, they finally said they made a mistake, and did forgive the rest of the bill.

Kevin wanted to be cremated. He had told me once that he wanted his ashes to be spread in the White Mountains. A few days before he died, I asked him if that was still what he wanted. He said that he changed his mind and that he didn't want to be alone. Unfortunately he was never able to really tell me what he meant by that. So, Diana and I thought the best thing we could do for Kevin, would be to have a bar crawl visiting all of the bars that he liked to go to. We would bring a picture of Kevin, order his favorite drink and set it in the middle of the table with his picture. We would all order some small bit of food and a drink, and we would toast him at each location. Before leaving the bars, everyone would take a sip of Kevin's drink, and then we would leave a little of Kevin at each location. The crawl would end at my mother's grave, where most of the ashes would be placed. We decided to wait to have the crawl in May 2016, when the weather was nice up in MA.

Most of the aunts and uncles that we grew up with on my mother's side came to the crawl, along with some of Kevin's close friends. We had called a limo service that we used a lot when we lived in MA and they gave us a big new van and driver to take us around. At one of the bars, the owner of the limo company was having a birthday party while we were there. He came over and had a toast to Kevin with us, which I thought was very nice of him. It was a sad day for me, but also a good one. If I remember right, I think we went to five of his favorite bars. For those of us that aren't big drinkers, well let's just say it was a good thing we had the van and driver. I felt like we were doing the right thing for Kevin, and that he would be happy with our plan. At the end of the day, I kept a little of the ashes to be put at the bar he spent so much time at in Florida. David and his wife came to MA for a quick visit the night before the bar crawl, but did not stay for the crawl the next day.

After getting out of the rehab facility in October 2014, Diana and I seemed to spend just about every weekend with Diana number two and her husband. Over the next few years we even took several trips to Daytona Beach with them. Sometimes just for one night, and sometimes for several nights. We took small trips to other places with them. But most of the time we just hung around the pool during the day and grilled (burnt) dawgs on a charcoal grill. They're the best thing ever. Sometimes we would go out for dinner. Many times if we went out for dinner, we would end up stopping at a bar for a shot of tequila before the end of the night. There were times when I would not be up to spending time with them due to a migraine, or I was recovering from one. During all of that time we all had been talking about buying a boat together, and just going out in the gulf for a day or a weekend trip. In late April of 2016, Diana and I found a thirty-three-foot sport fisher that was as the man that inspected it for us said, "Sound, but ugly". It needed some work, but it had two very good Cummins 504 v-8 motors in it that had both been rebuilt, and ran good.

We brought Diana number two and her husband up to see the boat, and to ask them if we bought the boat for the four of us, could we count on their help to fix it up. I told them that we were going to convert it into a houseboat that would sleep six, with a large deck above the main cabin. While Diana and I planned to live on it, the boat was for the four of us to enjoy. We had also been talking about taking a trip to the Florida Keys at some point, and with that boat we could do that. Both Diana number two and her husband agreed to help fix it up with us. We thought it would be fun to work on it together. Diana and I bought the boat, and we drove it from Homosassa to a marina closer to where we all lived, and had it dry docked. That would make it much easier for us to work on it. Over the next fourteen months, Diana and I worked on the boat almost every day, without the help of our friends. What we thought was going to be a fun project with our friends, turned out to be back breaking work in the Florida heat with no friends in sight. Diana number two and her husband never even came to look at the boat to see how it was coming along, or what we were doing to it. It was a bit heart breaking.

Because we didn't get the help we thought we were going to get, we ended up having to hire people to do the things that could have been done by our friends. Early in the first summer, Diana had a problem with sun stroke. After that she wasn't able to stay in the sun or the heat for more than an hour or so before she would start to get sick. She wasn't going to be able to help too much more after that. Even though they knew we were working on the boat all of the time, our friends seemed to get very upset with us because we couldn't go out every Saturday and play with them like we used to. We didn't hold the fact that they screwed us with the help on the boat against them, and we remained friends. We still had Thanksgiving and Christmas dinners at their house, and did take some time to take a trip or two to Daytona Beach with them during that time. Over the last maybe four months that I worked on the boat, I began to have episodes of confusion and loss of balance. After falling off the boat three times, the last time from the upper deck, we decided that it was not a good idea for me to keep working on the boat.

After paying people to do things that could have been done by our friends to help us, we had spent way too much money on the boat. My balance got to the point that in late 2017 through the first couple of months in 2018, I required physical therapy, and had to have a custom-made brace fit to my right leg, ankle, and foot. I still wear that brace and walk with the use of a cane. Once in a while I get a bit out of control and tip over, but not as often as I used to. We ended up trying to sell the boat. After a year of that, without any success, we gave the boat to the marina. As for our friends, they were still with us, and after stopping the work on the boat we did start to see more of them again. In February of 2017, the house we were renting was sold out from under us. The owners called me one day to tell us that the house had been sold, and that the rental agency that handled the rental of the house said that we had fifteen days to get out. I called the agency to talk to them about that, and was told that they didn't even know the house was for sale. They got so mad at the owner for going behind their backs, that they not only gave us our last month's rent and security deposit back, but they gave us an extra month back for the inconvenience caused by the homeowners.

Having just fifteen days to find a new place to live, and move to it was pretty much impossible. Diana number two and her husband offered us a room at their house, but I just wasn't comfortable with that. We asked another friend if we could stay at her house for a short time while we looked for a new place. That friend took us in, and we put most of our stuff in storage and moved into her house. Diana two and her husband were nowhere to be found when we needed help to move our stuff. Still we didn't hold that against them and in 2017, went to Daytona Beach twice with them. Just before Christmas, Diana told us that her husband had been diagnosed with cancer, and was very sick. We had Christmas with them at their house. It wasn't much fun, just very sad. In March of 2018 Diana's husband passed away at home with his family and us around him. He wanted to be cremated and to have his ashes put in the ocean at Daytona Beach. So we made one last trip to Daytona Beach and said goodbye to Diana number two's husband. About a month after that, her house got flooded. Diana and I went over to help move all of the stuff out of the house so repairs could be made, and then helped move all of the stuff back in later. Over the rest of 2018, we tried to help Diana number two as much as we could. We even helped repaint the inside of the house after the repairs were done.

As for the young lady that took us in when we needed a place to stay, well two years later we are still living with her. In October of 2017, we went to Disney World (For the first time) with her and her boyfriend. We have also taken a cruise to Key West and Cozumel, Mexico with them. We have become very good friends with her and her boyfriend. She was, in fact, my second mental health counselor. She and Diana became very close friends during that time. Because of their relationship, she felt that it would no longer be ethical for her to treat me, and that was what led to counselor number three.

She is a Licensed Clinical Social Worker, and a Licensed Mental Health Counselor and works at a local hospital Wednesday and Thursday. Tuesday evening and Friday morning she has another local office where she works. Friday afternoon through Monday night or Tuesday morning, she is away, and Diana and I have custody of the house. We pay her some rent, take care of her two dogs and one parrot, and the pool. Our friend taking us in has worked out very well for Diana and me, and I think we are doing okay for two homeless people.

I told you that the end was coming, so here we are, pretty much at the end. Even after all that Diana and I have been through in our lives, prior to being together, and since getting together, we both feel that we have had pretty good lives. The best part, of course, being after getting together. And for me, even after all the shit that Diana's family has put us through, and cost us, I have never let that get in our way. It just hurts me to think about how her daughter and grandson treated her. And after all of the friends that we have had, still have, had and lost for whatever the reason, we still have each other, and that really is all that matters to me.

As for Diana number two, well since the death of her husband, she has made some very big changes in her life and the way she now wants to live. We for some reason are not apparently going to be a part of that new life of hers. She has decided to just throw away a sixteen year friendship without really giving us any kind of reason, and she just walked away and hasn't even looked back.

I know that Diana has some sort of bucket list. I also have one, but mine would be more of a small bowl list. We both have at least one thing in common on those lists, and that's a trip to Italy, hopefully before we get too old to enjoy it. Returning to Uruguay would be something else that would be nice to do before we get too much older. So here we are folks, at the end of sixty-five years of real life history. It will go on, but no one knows how long that would be for anyone.

The End

Epilogue

When I was a child, the house I lived in had a large forest area across the street from it. Not far into the forest were large rock formations with lots of caves in them. One day while crawling around in one of the caves, I suddenly had a strong feeling of being lost, confused, and very much alone. The cave I was in, once familiar, seemed as if it was now a place that I had never been. As I was looking for a way out of the cave, I found an old looking piece of paper. It was very dirty, wrinkled, and worn looking, but it had a drawing on it that looked like some kind of map. With this piece of paper in hand, I was able to find my way out of the cave. When I got it out into the light, and cleaned it up a bit, I found that it was some sort of old treasure map. I sat down and studied the map for a very long time, trying to get my bearings, and figure out where the trail began. After a while, I was able to determine that the trail started at the exact spot that I was sitting. Not really knowing whither the map would take me, or why I should even bother to try to follow it, something was telling me I should, and that I would be glad I did.

As I set out tracing the steps of the map, walking along the trail, I would from time to time realize that I had been walking for a period of some time. While it seemed like nothing more than a very long day, I noticed that I was getting older. I didn't feel as if I had been following the map for years, but suddenly I was in my mid-teens. The path was dark and made me feel troubled. Stopping to look back over my shoulder, I could see a small boy. He seemed lost and abandoned. I could feel his pain and confusion. He seemed to be trying to get to a better place on the trail. Moving on, now there were small but puzzling things getting in my way. I was having to constantly adjust my path to get around them. After following the trail for what seemed to be just another few minutes, I realized that I was already in my mid-twenties. Stopping to rest, I looked back at the path I had just taken, I could only see as far back as the place I had last rested. But I could see things I had passed by and not noticed, or maybe I knew they were there all along, and had just tried to forget.

As I continued to follow the trail set out on the map, it was taking me higher into the hills. The higher I went, the older I seemed to get, and I noticed that clouds were starting to form around me. Somehow, I realized that I was in my forties now. As I turned to look at the trail behind me, I saw some stormy areas that I vaguely remember passing through. When I looked at them they made me feel uncomfortable. There were also some small areas of calm brightness, that made me feel good. Continuing on, I was starting to stumble a little now, and the climb was getting a bit more difficult. I was moving slower, and felt weaker than

I had been. Climbing over a particularly difficult obstacle, stopping to rest again, I saw that I had aged into my sixties. The clouds were getting thicker, the climb a little more difficult, but for some reason, I had to know whither the trail was taking me.

After a few more difficult obstacles, feeling especially tired now, and almost ready to give up my quest, I came to a small grassy clearing. The space seemed warm, soft, and comfortable, and somehow very peaceful. I laid on my back resting and looking up at the clouds still around me. And I began to wonder how I could have aged so much in what felt like such a short time. Then I heard a voice say, "You have found what you have been seeking." I sat up and looked behind me to see an old man sitting on a small flat rock, with the sun shining on him. He said to me, "You have been able to follow the trail to the place whither you have found your treasure." I looked around and didn't see anything that looked like any kind of treasure. Confused, I finally asked him where the treasure was, and how do I get it? With a very kind and gentle look on his face he said, "Your treasure is this, the wisdom to make the right choices, the perseverance and determination to follow those choices, and the knowledge to know when you have achieved your goals." It was then that I realized that the trail I had been following, was the map of my life.